Amanda Gearing is a Walkley Award-winning investigative journalist. She worked for *The Courier-Mail* from 1997–2007, based in Toowoomba, before becoming a freelance print and radio journalist for media outlets including *The Australian* and ABC Radio National. Amanda completed a Master of Arts (Research) in 2012 and a PhD in global investigative journalism in 2016.

AMANDA GEARING

THE TORRENT

A TRUE STORY OF HEROISM AND SURVIVAL

UQP

First published 2012 by University of Queensland Press
PO Box 6042, St Lucia, Queensland 4067 Australia
Updated edition 2017

www.uqp.com.au
uqp@uqp.uq.edu.au

Cover design by Luke Causby/Blue Cork
Cover photograph © Ann-Marie Ryan/Reuters/Picture Media
Author photograph by Jack Lynch MBE
Maps by Gillian Scott
Typeset in Adobe Garamond Pro 11.5/15.5pt by Post Pre-press Group, Brisbane
Printed in Australia by McPherson's Printing Group

National Library of Australia Cataloguing-in-Publication Data
is available from http://catlogue.nla.gov.au

ISBN
978 0 7022 5952 4 (pbk)
978 0 7022 5871 8 (epdf)
978 0 7022 5872 5 (epub)
978 0 7022 5873 2 (kindle)

University of Queensland Press uses papers that are natural, renewable and recyclable products made from wood grown in sustainable forests. The logging and manufacturing processes conform to the environmental regulations of the country of origin.

In memory of those who died:

Donna Rice, 43, and her son Jordan Rice, 13 – Toowoomba
Steve Matthews, 56, and his wife Sandra Matthews, 46 – Spring Bluff
Selwyn Schefe, 52, and his daughter Katie Schefe, six – Murphys Creek
Sylvia Baillie, 72 – Postmans Ridge
Bruce Warhurst, 60 – Postmans Ridge
James Perry, 40 – Toowoomba
Pauline Magner, 65, Dawn Radke, 56, and their granddaughter Jessica Keep, 23 months – Grantham
Christopher Face, 63, Brenda Ross, 56, and her son Joshua Ross, 25 – Grantham
Llync-Chiann Clarke, 31, and her children Garry Jibson, 12, and Jocelyn Jibson, five – Grantham
Jean Gurr, 88 – Grantham
Bruce Marshall, 67 – Grantham
Reinskje 'Regina' van der Werff, 86 – Grantham

And to all the survivors for whom every new day is both a challenge and an opportunity.

Contents

Introduction to the Second Edition

Since reporting on the disaster and writing *The Torrent*, I have kept in touch with many of the flood survivors and followed the subsequent investigations. The flood deaths in the Lockyer Valley were noted at the original Queensland Floods Commission of Inquiry, held in Toowoomba in April 2011, but were not investigated specifically until a coronial inquest was launched in November 2011. The inquest was told that the Queensland Police Service led the search for missing people after the flood, asking 250 Australian Army personnel and 200 police to search 131 kilometres of creeks and rivers from Spring Bluff to Brisbane and hundreds of dams. The entire creek system was searched three times for bodies, but no trace was found of three of the flood victims: James Perry, who died at Carpendale, and Dawn Radke and Christopher Face, who both died at Grantham.

Throughout this time, I maintained contact with the flood survivors via several Facebook pages, one for *The Torrent*, and one to share information about the need for a separate inquiry into the disaster in Grantham. The unprecedented nature of the flood in Grantham led to several hydrology studies being carried out, but more than four years after the disaster questions still remained about the possible effect of the Grantham quarry on the ferocity of the flood and the destruction it caused. A new chapter has been added to this book about the controversy, which did result in the Grantham Inquiry and, consequently, several defamation cases, some of which remain on foot at the time of going to press.

My radio documentary *The day that changed Grantham*, aired on ABC Radio National, won a Walkley Award in 2012, bringing renewed interest in the plight of survivors and the need for improved warning systems. Afterwards, the State Library of Queensland asked for the recordings of my interviews to create an accessible online archive of the event. This rare database captures for posterity the experiences of people during and after a natural disaster.

In 2016, I drove to the Lockyer Valley to interview again the people who had welcomed me so generously into their mud-soaked houses and makeshift accommodation more than five years earlier. Returning to the townships and rural districts was eerie. On the surface, the fabric of the communities was restored and in places improved, compared with pre-flood times. New roads, bridges, houses and shops had been completed. Yet the lives of those people who were most affected by the flood seemed to be forever changed from the trajectory they had been travelling before the disaster.

Many flood survivors were still traumatised from the experience. They spoke candidly with me about the challenges they had faced rebuilding their lives. Grief, stress, ongoing financial difficulties, and a lost sense of safety had all left their mark. Health problems had also impeded recovery, with several people injured in the flood requiring operations and many contracting itchy, painful skin rashes. Some flood survivors were diagnosed with stress-related illnesses, cardiac problems or cancers. In the six years since the flood, some of the people who were most severely affected by the disaster have died of chronic conditions or cancers.

My awareness and understanding of the experience of trauma and recovery have developed significantly in the years following the flood. Just as there were wide variations in the degree of trauma to which people were exposed during the disaster, I found there were wide variations in the degree to which they have recovered. My increased knowledge in this area meant that my follow-up interviews with the flood survivors could better explore their experience of trauma and their journeys towards recovery. I have outlined some of my findings in the appendix 'Why report on trauma?' My recordings of the second round of interviews will be added to the State Library of Queensland's flood archive.

Despite the overwhelming tragedy of the flood disaster in 2011, I was inspired by the courage of civilians to rescue others in danger even at the risk of their own lives. I was similarly inspired in 2016 by the extraordinary courage many people have shown in rebuilding their lives. I am humbled and grateful that so many of the survivors were willing to speak about their struggles and vulnerabilities. Their collective wisdom will hopefully provide information that shapes public policy regarding post-disaster support for people bereaved or rendered homeless, injured or traumatised by the fury of a severe weather event. The accounts here will also hopefully provide validation for readers who have or will endure a similar event, giving them the necessary support and encouragement to make their own journeys of recovery.

Amanda Gearing
December 2016

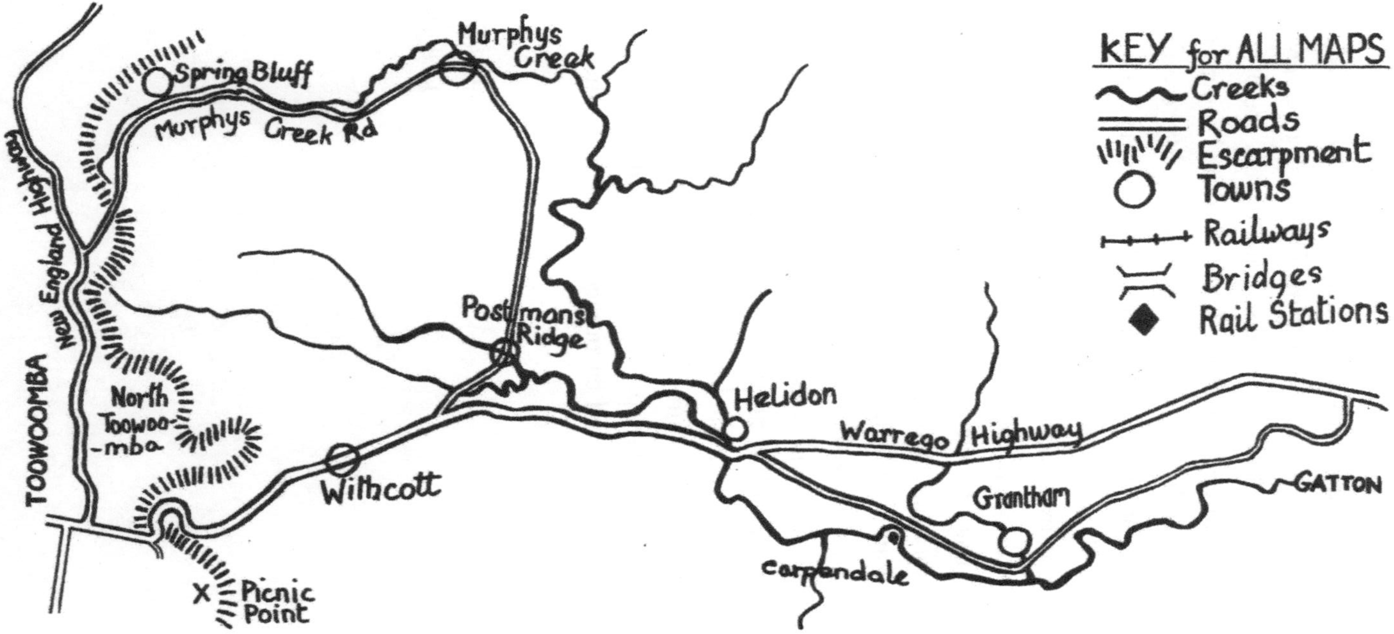
KEY for ALL MAPS
Creeks
Roads
Escarpment
Towns
Railways
Bridges
Rail Stations
Murphys Creek
Spring Bluff
Murphys Creek Rd
New England Highway
TOOWOOMBA
North Toowoo-mba
Postmans Ridge
Withcott
Picnic Point
Helidon
Warrego Highway
Grantham
Carpendale
GATTON

Preface to the First Edition

~

At my home on the Toowoomba escarpment, days of steady rain became intense heavy rain – by far the heaviest I had seen since moving to the city in 1986. The huge La Niña system in the Pacific Ocean that I had watched build up over the previous six months was now delivering torrential rainfall. I used my camera to take video footage of the road covered in rushing water and pooling before it tumbled over the edge of the escarpment. I posted the video to Facebook at 12.49 pm. I also phoned my brother-in-law in Jindalee in Brisbane and wrote a list of things for him to pack – photos, documents and clothes – and told him to be ready to get out of his house because Brisbane could be flooding in a couple of days.

Within about half an hour my friend Monica, who lives beside the creek at Murphys Creek, phoned to say the water was almost up to her house and that she had to get to higher ground. She was panicking and couldn't remember what to take. I read her the list I had already made. Monica asked me to phone her husband Ian, and let him know she was safe.

Monica and her teenage daughter Sophie packed three suitcases. They waded through floodwater, carrying a suitcase each on their heads, to get to higher ground – a picnic table across the road. Sophie returned to the house to bring the third suitcase across.

I posted to Facebook at 1.15 pm that the town of Murphys Creek was flooded and residents were evacuating. Our local ABC radio station was taken off networked programs and went to live broadcast of the disaster, taking phone calls from people reporting on flooded roads, landslides and raging creeks. At 1.30 pm I posted on Facebook what I'd heard on the radio, that a landslide at Mount Kynoch had cut the highway north of Toowoomba.

Minutes later, at 1.37 pm, Monica's husband Ian was driving home to Murphys Creek when he stopped at a flooded causeway. Two women in a car went past him and into the water, where their car stalled. They phoned triple zero and were told to climb onto the roof of the car. That call was the first to alert emergency services that there was flash flooding anywhere in Toowoomba or the Lockyer Valley. The fire brigade dispatched two vehicles but neither could get to the scene.

Ian drove to a nearby house and phoned triple zero but by then the phone lines were jammed. Unable to contact emergency services, Ian raced with a mate to rescue the women.

Within a few minutes of the flash flooding at Murphys Creek, severe flash flooding was also striking Toowoomba city streets, and the local ABC was taking talkback calls from people reporting flooded streets and pedestrians and motorists being swept away. A woman and child in a car had been swept down East Creek and were feared drowned. The Brisbane chief-of-staff at *The Australian* phoned me and asked me to report for the newspaper. I called a local photographer and went to East Creek, where a car was being dragged out of the water. There were no bodies inside. By then the mobile phone network was so overloaded it had melted down. I headed to the Toowoomba CBD, where I knew from previous storms the flooding would be worst – in Dent Street, outside Grand Central Shopping Centre. Once there, I spoke to people who had seen the height of the flood. I took eyewitness accounts and phoned them through to colleagues at the newspaper. Once home, I used my landline to try to confirm the number of people killed. Police could not confirm the number of dead or missing.

I had not been able to contact Ian to let him know Monica and Sophie had escaped from their house. I tried his mobile again and finally got through. He told me he had rescued two women whose car had been caught in the torrent, and that his friends Steve and Sandy Matthews had been swept from their house.

Families of missing people in the Lockyer Valley were posting photos of their relatives to Facebook in the hope they would be found somehow and recognised.

For the next three weeks I reported on the disaster and realised more with each passing day that there would be long-term impacts for the families and friends of those who had died, or those who had narrowly escaped perilous situations. I also realised that the many children involved would one day want to know – 'What happened?' As I spoke to more and more survivors I discovered that many people needed to find out what had happened around them to understand why the disaster unfolded as it did, with little or no warning to most people.

More than 100 people have taken part in my research for this book in the hope that improvements can be made to warning systems and disaster responses, and so that life and property may be protected in the future. I am privileged to have been told these stories.

Amanda Gearing
October 2011

From drought to flood

'Love, how are we going to pay the rent this week?'

'The front steps are gone!' Marie yelled. Her husband Peter hurried up the hall just in time to see the front staircase of their highset house floating down the main street. Muddy, churning water raged past, three metres deep and rising fast. Within seconds, jets of water began spurting up through knot-holes in the floor and between the floorboards. Logs crashed against the timber walls. The house was shaking. They needed help and they needed it fast.

Peter phoned the State Emergency Service (SES). He waited for several rings. Someone picked up the phone and the line went dead. Peter did not have time to phone again. He unplugged the computer and lifted it higher, along with his DVD collection. Marie grabbed their photo albums and put them up in the wardrobe in the bedroom. Outside, the murky torrent was almost level with the windowsills. Marie remembered the guinea pigs, and waded to the bathroom. Downstairs, the car was swept from the garage and thrown into a tree. Something hit the back verandah hard and shook the house. The back steps and verandah smashed off.

Peter phoned the local bishop, told him they were flooded and asked him to pray for them. He assured Peter he would. The phone went dead. As Marie entered the bathroom, a tree smashed through the wall. She fell over in the water and came up spluttering. She was panicking. 'Help! Help! Help! Somebody help!' she screamed. The guinea pig cage had fallen over and the animals had swum for their lives. One reached the bathroom basin and clung desperately to the taps. Marie picked up the shocked, soaked animal. Peter hurried to help Marie from the bathroom.

Suddenly the house bounced up like a cork. It floated a metre higher in the water and was swept away. It hit a large tree and the kitchen smashed off, setting the house spinning as it moved along. Peter and Marie needed to get to the centre of the house.

They headed for the dining room. Their blue cattle dog Chloe was standing on a floating couch. Chloe sprang on to Peter's shoulder and held on tightly as they waded into the dining room. Peter and Marie stood in the water either side of the solid timber table, holding the dog and the guinea pig on the table. Marie was still crying for help.

Peter remembered he needed his medications for the deep vein thrombosis in his legs, and insulin for his newly diagnosed diabetes. He waded to the bedroom and saw rushing water outside the house, halfway up the windows. Water was swirling almost waist-deep inside. They were fighting a losing battle.

Peter still had his mobile phone, so he dialled triple zero and asked for the police. They asked him what he could see. He told them, 'There's all sorts of stuff floating down the street. There's bird aviaries, shipping containers, sheds, cars and wheels.' Peter looked out the side window and saw powerlines in the water. He told the operator, 'And you can add live wires to that.' Peter gave their address at 11 Anzac Avenue, Grantham, adding: 'But don't look for us here because the water is taking us wherever it's going to take us.' Peter knew there was not much the police or anyone else could do. The water was running too fast for anybody to get close enough to help them. The operator told them, 'Try and hang on.' As the phone line cut for the last time, hanging on was all they could do now.

The house moved out of the yard. There were no more trees, just a large, flat farm paddock. The house sped up and soon it was travelling at what felt like 60 to 70 kilometres an hour. The trees and flood debris, which had been slamming into the house, were now travelling alongside it. The water was still roaring. Marie was frantic. Peter took out his hearing aids and put them in his pocket so they wouldn't get wet. He wasn't thinking very clearly. He needed to be able to hold on to Marie to calm her, but he couldn't hold the animals and comfort her at the same time. He pulled out a drawer, tipped the paperwork into the water and put the guinea pig in. The drawer drifted away with the wet, shivering guinea pig aboard. Chloe the dog climbed back onto Peter's shoulder.

As the house sped across the paddock it missed other houses, went between power poles along a road, under the powerlines, crossed over a road and continued, at the mercy of the current, into the next paddock.

Peter and Marie Van Straten had been retired for two years and had always wanted to live in the country. They found a highset Queenslander for rent, on acreage in the small rural town of Grantham, and moved in seven months before the flood. The new house in the country provided them with a spacious home with prolific fruit trees in the backyard and space for their guinea pigs and chickens. The cheaper rent stretched their pension further, and they were accepted warmly into the community. As winter passed and spring and summer rain arrived, the wide, flat farm paddocks became green, and vegetable crops grew fast. As the rain continued, water began to lie in the paddocks and the drains beside the roads. The water level in Sandy Creek near their house rose and fell, but stayed within its banks. On Boxing Day the creek brimmed over the banks, sending muddy water flowing across the main road of the town, Anzac Avenue, before subsiding again into the creek.

In the following weeks the water rose twice more. It ran under the house a few centimetres deep and left a thin layer of slippery mud.

Marie was helping in the clean-up when she slipped and broke her arm. On 10 January 2011, Peter and Marie woke to find a pile of logs and debris blocking the gate; the water had come up again during the night and receded. Peter called the council to have the debris removed, and Marie checked the weather bureau's website and saw that the creek levels in local Ma Ma Creek, Tenthill Creek and Sandy Creek were all falling. The only creek that was rising was Lockyer Creek, but it was miles away in Helidon – she felt sorry for the people of Helidon who were about to be flooded.

After cruising for 1.7 kilometres, Peter and Marie's house suddenly came to rest in a vast farm paddock. A protruding bore pipe had stopped a car that had been swept away, which in turn had stopped the house. The current began to rush through it, carrying their furniture and goods away. They saw a dozen cars float past. Peter was grateful none of them smashed into the wreckage of the house. 'They were going at a pretty fast clip. If any of them had hit us we would have been finished – it would have demolished what was left of the house.' The water was waist-deep but flowing fast. Peter could see out where exterior walls of the house had been torn away by the force of the water. Four or five waves were heading towards them. As each one hit, the house moved and the water level rose again. Soon it was up to Peter's neck.

Marie could not touch the floor. She couldn't swim. They needed some flotation. Peter saw the fridge floating on its back in what was left of the kitchen. Marie hung on to him and he waded towards it. One side of the kitchen ceiling had fallen down on an angle when the exterior wall of the kitchen had smashed off. Now the fallen ceiling was trapping the fridge and holding it inside the house, on the last remaining quarter of the kitchen floor. The top of the fridge touched the fallen ceiling, and the bottom was held in by a fallen beam. Peter lifted the fridge door open to give them something to hold onto. As he worked his way around the fridge, the current pushed him against the collapsed ceiling and swept Marie on top of him. Peter struggled to keep Marie's head above water. He managed to get to his feet and stood on one leg. He lifted his other knee for her to sit on.

They discussed options. Marie suggested trying to grab something that was floating past and getting to a boat she could see, but the current was too dangerous. Peter tried to push open the manhole in the ceiling, hoping they could climb out of the water into the roof cavity. He pushed hard on the manhole cover but it was jammed. Debris was still rushing through the house. Something in the water smashed into Peter and the two collapsed as his leg was knocked out from under him. They felt themselves floating away and grabbed for each other. Peter finally got his feet on the floor and his head above water. He held on to Marie, whose shorts had been swept off by the current. They were together, but their future was precarious.

With time to contemplate their situation, Marie looked at the plaster on her broken arm. She remembered the staff at Toowoomba Base Hospital who had told her only four days before to be careful not to get the plaster wet. She laughed as she thought how angry they would be that it was drenched. Peter's mind suddenly turned to the household bills. 'Love, how are we going to pay the rent this week?' he asked Marie. Marie's wet plaster and paying rent on a house that was falling apart around them helped distract them from their fears.

After being in the water for an hour they heard rescue helicopters overhead. The thump, thump of the rotors became louder and then faded away, as the helicopters picked up survivors from rooftops and dropped them to higher ground, returning for more, over and over again. The helicopters worked for an hour but they didn't come to Peter and Marie. The couple realised they would need to signal for help.

Peter had been standing on one leg, with Marie on his knee, for about two hours. Marie, a nurse, could see that Peter was becoming hypothermic. He was shivering and had turned a nasty shade of grey. The sun was going down. They had to try to get out of the water and get medical attention as soon as possible. Marie was also beginning to feel hypothermic – her toes were numb, her hands were shaking and she was losing the ability to control the movements of her limbs. She didn't think she could last much longer.

For Peter to signal for help to the helicopters, he had to move towards the edge of the house wreckage. But he couldn't do this unless Marie could hold on to something herself to keep her head above water. She climbed onto the beam that was trapping the fridge, until she was lying on it with her arms and legs dangling either side. From there she could hold onto the fridge with her unbroken arm. Now, Peter needed to climb out of the kitchen and find a way to get the helicopter's attention. He pulled away a piece of timber that had him trapped. It hit Marie on the head as he pulled it out, but luckily she was okay. More pieces of wood were trapping him in and he couldn't pull them free. He would have to dive underwater and swim under the fallen timbers. He took a deep breath and went for it. He could feel his body being sucked out of the house by the current and he thought, 'I've done something wrong here.' He raised one hand above the water, hoping Marie could reach him. She realised he was in trouble and grabbed for his hand with her broken arm. Their hands found each other and she pulled him towards her. Sharp pain shot up her arm: she had re-broken her wrist.

Peter got his head back above the water and grabbed the timber beam that Marie was on to get his balance. Now he could move closer to the edge of the house wreckage. He reached up and grabbed onto a timber picture rail, and let the pressure of the current hold him up against the wall. From here he waved his arms, hoping the helicopter rescue crews would see him.

A helicopter that had been plying across the town flew low over the house. Peter and Marie waved desperately. Marie was at breaking point. She began to cry. 'Please see us, please see us.' The helicopter flew low over the house: it had seen them! The helicopter ascended again and flew away. The sound of the rotors faded, as the familiar roar of the water filled their ears once again. Maybe the crew hadn't seen them after all.

From June 2010, a La Niña climate pattern had been deepening in the central Pacific Ocean. Cool surface water was streaming across the equator. The pattern continued intensifying, becoming one of the strongest La Niña systems on record. Sea surface temperatures in the Australian region during 2010 were +0.54 °C above the 1961 to 1990 average, the warmest on record for the Australian region. Record high monthly sea surface temperatures were set during 2010 in March, April, June, September, October, November and December. From August, heavy rainfall became increasingly widespread across Queensland. Many areas of the state received double their long-term average rain, and during September many locations received more than four times the normal monthly rainfall.

The Bureau of Meteorology conducted briefings and exercises with local councils to prepare for the coming extreme wet season. In October, the Bureau briefed the premier and cabinet. In early November, Emergency Management Queensland's (EMQ) Toowoomba office coordinated an exercise for five disaster management groups in the Lockyer Valley and Darling Downs to practise their emergency response to a major flood and storm event, simulating a tropical cyclone crossing the coast and causing widespread flooding. For two days during Exercise Orko, evacuation plans were rehearsed, call centres were given practice dealing with large numbers of emergency calls, public information and warning systems were refined, and ideas for improvements were noted.

Monsoon rains began from the end of November, causing major flooding across the southern half of the state. Over Christmas an intense rain band flooded the coastal cities of Bundaberg and Rockhampton, as well as many inland towns. Queensland Premier Anna Bligh launched a public appeal to help victims of the floods.

By early January the situation was becoming so serious that the regional director of the Bureau of Meteorology personally briefed the State Disaster Management Group and the premier and her cabinet. At the briefings he predicted several hundred millimetres of rain over the following four to eight days. Widespread flooding continued.

For the first time in the state's history, entire populations of small towns beside major rivers were evacuated by helicopter, as floodwaters engulfed them.

The intense monsoon was then enhanced by the arrival of a periodic pressure wave, the Madden Julian Oscillation, on 9 January. At 5 am the next morning, the Bureau of Meteorology issued a severe weather warning for heavy rainfall leading to localised flash flooding. Unfortunately, residents of the Lockyer Valley are not generally aware that they belong to the Bureau's south-east coast district, so they didn't realise that flash flood warnings in that area posed a threat to them. From 1 am on 10 January, a group of thunderstorms started to cross the coast. Between 9 am and 9.30 am, two intense thunderstorms in the band of storms crossed the coast. A flood warning was issued at 10.28 am for Lockyer Creek and rivers in the Brisbane Valley. One of the storms moving south-west converged with another moving west and formed a single storm at about 11 am. It passed over Somerset and Wivenhoe dams, the main water supply dams of the state capital, Brisbane. A severe weather warning was issued at 11 am for heavy rainfall leading to localised flash flooding. The combined storm measured about 40 kilometres across. It continued moving south-west at 30 kilometres per hour, intensifying as it went, until it was producing rainfall of 100 millimetres per hour as it passed across the Upper Brisbane River Valley towards Toowoomba.

As the storm cell approached Toowoomba, it was forced upwards over the Great Dividing Range, then slowed down and continued to intensify. The situation was becoming more dangerous. At 1 pm the Bureau phoned the State Disaster Coordination Centre, reporting exceptionally heavy rainfall of 75 millimetres in one hour, west of Wivenhoe Dam. They were expecting flash flooding in Toowoomba in the next hour or two. The Bureau also reported that a volunteer 'storm spotter' at Cressbrook Dam had reported several landslides caused by the heavy rain. By early afternoon the Bureau realised the conditions could result in the most severe flooding in the Brisbane Valley since the record flood of 1974. With the city of Ipswich and the state capital under threat, their priority was flood forecasting, warning and monitoring of the lower Brisbane River to estimate potential flooding levels and to liaise with the major dam operators and the city councils of Brisbane and Ipswich.

Medical sonographer Neil Pennell, a keen weather watcher who lives at Kalbar, 60 kilometres south-west of Brisbane, was checking the Bureau's radar. The centre of the storm was showing as yellow to orange, indicating a very heavy rain rate of at least 50 millimetres per hour. He knew that anyone outdoors looking at the sky would not see the storm coming because it was embedded in a broad area of light rain. There would be nothing to prompt people to go indoors and look at the radar. That storm, falling on an already-sodden catchment, was going to be a disaster. People who lived near creeks needed to get to the nearest hill. He looked at the home page of the Bureau's website. There were no warnings. At 1.10 pm he asked meteorologist Anthony Cornelius via an online weather forum: 'Anthony, do you think BOM [the Bureau of Meteorology] is on the case with that [storm] cell. If not you probably know who should be told about it. Those rain rates between Esk, Crows Nest and Toowoomba are truly frightening. I fear that there could be a dangerous flash flood very soon particularly in Grantham. Am I overreacting?'

Another weather forum member, Adam, posted at 1.41 pm: 'It has absolutely bucketed down in the last 30 minutes in Toowoomba. I wouldn't be surprised if we got 50 mm. Keep a close eye on the Lockyer Creek at Helidon and now Cressbrook Creek. There will be a wall of water coming down it.'

Neil Pennell was becoming very anxious. He looked at the home page of the Bureau's website again. There were still no specific warnings. He posted again to the forum at 1.42 pm: 'Dave, I live in an area that is equally not used to being so saturated and equally not used to falls of that nature. I just know that 56 mm in an hour right now here would produce a flood of frightening proportions and one likely to put lives at risk. Falls higher than this in the immediate area are likely. I repeat my question . . . Does someone in Esk,

Grantham, Toogoolawah need to know what's possible. Who do we tell?'

The Bureau's computer system registered river rises at Helidon, but only a few readings were available because the computer system had automatically marked most of the readings as being incorrect. Shortly after 4 pm the Bureau's Flood Warning Centre saw the readings. It seemed the gauge must be faulty, because there were significant jumps in the water level readings as well as missing values. The Bureau had no network of flood warning rainfall gauges above the Helidon gauge to be able to work out whether the suspect readings at Helidon could be true. Televisions in the Flood Warning Centre showed news footage from Toowoomba of a red-brown churning torrent sweeping cars down creeks like toys. By 4.50 pm the Flood Warning Centre staff realised the water level rises in Lockyer Creek were most likely to be accurate. The centre directed radio and television broadcasters to use the Standard Emergency Warning Signal (SEWS) and issued an extraordinary flash flood warning for Lockyer Creek at 5 pm. The warning was repeated at 8.37 pm: 'Very heavy rainfalls have been recorded in the Toowoomba area and caused extreme flash flooding. This rainfall is also causing extreme rises in the upper Lockyer Creek at Helidon with very fast and dangerous rises possible downstream at Gatton in the next few hours. Rises will extend downstream of Gatton during tonight.'

The warnings came too late for Peter and Marie. Their hope of rescue had faded away.

They looked at each other. 'I love you so much,' Marie told Peter. 'I love you, too,' he said. 'I'm so glad we've had our life together.' Peter wrapped his arms around Marie, hugged her and kissed her. The sun had set. Peter didn't think anyone would be able to find them once it was dark. Waves of floodwater were still hitting the house. Marie knew they would not be able to survive in the water until morning. She gave up hope, and started sobbing once again.

Spring Bluff

'If anyone could survive, they would.'

Spring Bluff is named for the natural springs emerging from the steep, rocky side of Mount Kynoch, which form the headwaters of Murphys Creek. The water flows down the mountain into rocky pools and then through a thick eucalypt forest teeming with birds and rare wildlife, such as the small mountain platypus. Winding steeply up the mountain is a train track built during the 1860s to link the Darling Downs' pioneers with the colony at Moreton Bay. More than 1,500 workers blasted tunnels through basalt and sandstone ridges, built timber and iron bridges across ravines, and laid track from the foothills of the range, and emerged 612 metres above sea level to the north of Toowoomba. The railway's completion meant that bullock drays were replaced by faster steam trains that took passengers, timber, wool, grain and other farm produce to Brisbane and returned with supplies for the fast-growing pioneering township of Toowoomba.

Workers building the railway line discovered fresh water springs flowing from the rocks. Main Range became a station where steam trains stopped to refill their water tanks halfway up the long, slow climb. The secluded station here, renamed Spring Bluff, is built in a sunny clearing surrounded by mountains. A road winds down Mount Kynoch to the township of Murphys Creek, following the valley just above the creek level. The railway line, built high above the creek, follows the ridges to maintain an even gradient through the steep terrain. The line still works to capacity, carrying up to ten trains a day loaded with coal from the Darling Downs to the Port of Brisbane. Each train carries 2,000 tonnes of coal worth $800,000 and returns empty to collect another load.

Spring Bluff station is a tourist destination, best known for its spring garden display. This tradition began in 1914 with a competition to beautify railway stations, which Spring Bluff won for several years running. Station managers have maintained the gardening tradition. The current gardener, Craig Ritchie, presents an autumn display and the main spring display during Toowoomba's annual Carnival of Flowers.

Over the past 20 years the district has become increasingly popular. Houses with tranquil acreage and spectacular views are now dotted through the mountains. In 2004, on the turnoff leading to Spring Bluff railway station, Steve and Sandra Matthews bought a house on ten acres of steeply rising land beside the trickling mountain creek. Steve, an electrical contractor, owned his own business and employed their son Sam, 20, as his apprentice. Sam and his sister Victoria, 15, both lived with their parents. Their elder daughter Sarah Norman, her husband Jethro and their children lived in a cottage across the creek on the same property. Steve, a keen weightlifter, won a gold medal in his age division at the World Masters Games in 2009. A devout Christian and pastor, he had told his wife he thought God's plan was that he would not grow old. As his belief became stronger, he and Sandy confided in their family and closest friends that they believed they would not live to be old people and that they would die together. By the end of 2010, Steve believed he should not make plans for 2011.

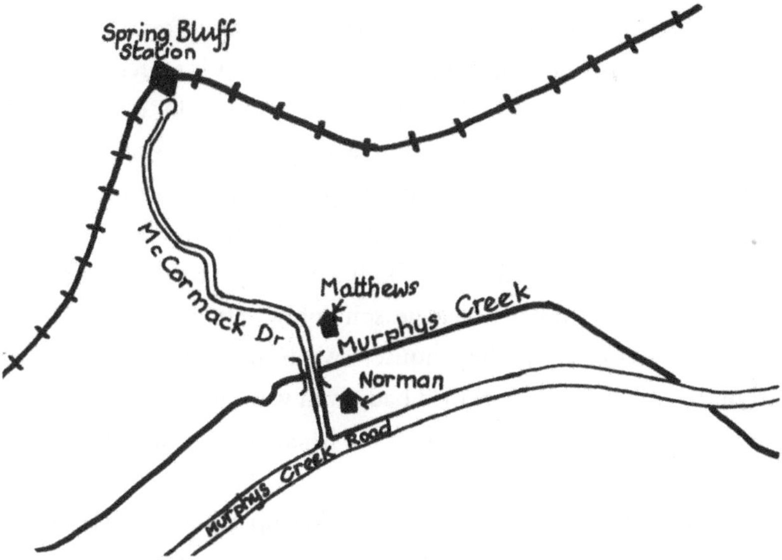

Craig Ritchie keeps rainfall records in his diary. During December 2010, Spring Bluff received 436 millimetres of rain, more than three times the average rainfall for December. In January there was brief respite, but from 5 January it rained every day, a total of 139 millimetres. As the wet weather continued, Queensland Rail became concerned about the safety of its track down the mountain. A team of assessors was sent to survey rain damage.

They were on the line on the morning of 10 January when the steady rain suddenly became a deluge around midday. Rocks began falling down the mountain, so they sheltered in a tunnel. Craig Ritchie recorded rainfall of 110 millimetres that day. 'The ground was already saturated. All that 110 millimetres was run-off,' he said. Steve and Sandy Matthews saw the water level in Murphys Creek rising quickly. Steve and Sam began clearing furniture from the verandah, while Sandy and Victoria retreated inside and turned off the power and lifted electrical goods up higher.

Two kilometres uphill from his house on Murphys Creek Road, landscape worker Michael Hare saw that the rising creek was beginning to erode his driveway. He was shovelling dirt to divert the creek from the driveway when suddenly the creek rose. Within minutes the usually sober stream became a mad, drunken torrent, uprooting trees and carving away the creek bed and banks as it roared down the mountain. Michael was cut off from his house so he ran downhill towards the Matthews' house where Kirsop Bridge crosses the creek, hoping to pass over and climb back up the mountain to his house. As he headed down the road towards the bridge, he had to dodge mudslides and trees falling from both sides of the road cutting.

Craig Ritchie and his teenage son John went to see the spring about 50 metres from their house. 'We heard a noise, we looked around, and all of our backyard had given way and spread across the rail lines. We ran back and had a look. There was a gouge five metres wide by three metres deep through our yard,' Craig said.

By the time Michael Hare reached Kirsop Bridge, it was barely visible above the rising water. He saw four people in raincoats with umbrellas on the opposite side of the creek: they did not risk crossing over. Michael decided it was too dangerous to cross the bridge. He saw the Matthews family go into their house.

Across the creek, Sarah Norman was at home with her two young children when her brother Sam phoned to ask if she was alright and to let her know the water was up to the back deck of their house. Sarah heard her mother Sandy in the background shouting that water was coming into the house. Sam told Sarah he had to go. Sarah heard metal twisting and breaking and she looked across the creek just in time to see a shed on her parents' property breaking up and washing down the creek. Huge eucalypts began to fall and sink into the now raging and churning creek.

Michael tried to walk back up Murphys Creek Road but it was now submerged under several feet of floodwater. He was amazed to see polystyrene boxes of plants from his garden floating down the creek and hitting the bridge. The rising creek now reached the gutters on the Matthews' roof. Powerlines began to fall. A Queensland Rail stream gauge at Spring Bluff recorded that the level peaked at 1.40 pm at 4.96 metres. The small catchment was generating 360 cubic metres of water per second.

The enormous force of the creek water burst open the front door latch, and water poured into the Matthews' house. The front windows smashed. The immense power of the water now struck the piano, lifting it up off the floor and carrying it from the house. The water hurtling through the house became so strong that Victoria and her mother could only attempt escape by climbing onto the kitchen benches. Once there, they could feel the force of the water moving the built-in kitchen benches. Above them, shelves tilted, tipping jars and bottles down on them and smashing on the bench.

Watching from the outside in horror, Michael saw Steve emerge from the house and climb on the fallen trees that were now piled up almost to the gutters. 'I communicated with him a couple of times. He looked exhausted. He was asking for help.' Michael asked people stranded on the road to try to contact emergency services to get help for the man. There was no reception on either of the two main mobile phone networks. A council driver, who had captured video footage of Steve standing on the trees, had an ultra-high-frequency (UHF) two-way radio. Michael asked the driver to radio for help for the man. When Michael returned to see if the council worker had made contact, Michael overheard him telling his wife he'd be late home for dinner. 'I wanted to punch him in the head,' Michael said.

Water roared down the five gullies near Spring Bluff, over the railway line and down the mountain. The flow from one of the gullies ripped the bitumen car park off the side of the mountain, joining up with the other four water courses and then plunging about 100 metres down to Murphys Creek, to the small creek flat where the Matthews' house was already inundated. Michael Hare saw the deluge, which carried rocks and trees, flowing down McCormack Drive from Spring Bluff. 'I turned to see what was happening and the man [standing on the trees] was gone,' he said.

From her home across the creek, Sarah saw that her parents' house was almost completely submerged. Her panic rose: where were they? She rushed indoors to phone the police and ran outside again. She couldn't see anyone, so she ran up Murphys Creek Road where she found two men. One told her he had seen someone come out of the house, looking exhausted, signalling for them to phone for help.

Further down the mountain, the rainfall was also very heavy. A rain gauge at Holmes siding recorded 93 millimetres between 1 pm and 2 pm. The rain gauge is not connected electronically with the Bureau of Meteorology, so the extreme rainfall was not registered immediately by meteorologists on duty. The Matthews' neighbour to the east, Ean Stewart, was on his way home across the valley. He was in convoy with a mate, Andrew, who was driving Ean's four-wheel drive. As they began climbing Murphys Creek Road, they came to where floodwater had filled a dam, overflowed the dam wall, and flooded three or four feet deep, moving at 60 to 70 kilometres per hour across the road. Here it poured into Murphys Creek, which was now like ocean surf.

The floodwater surged a foot higher. Ean knew the empty truck he was driving might be swept off the road because the back wheels would not have enough traction. He stopped and tried to phone his family while he waited for the flow to subside, but there was no mobile reception. The road was blocked by fallen trees, so Andrew and Ean walked two kilometres up the road to Ean's driveway. 'It was biblical. Trees were falling like dominos. It was like a dam release. Powerlines were twanging between power poles like a rubber band between two matchsticks,' Ean said.

Once back inside his house, Steve Matthews asked his son Sam to go down the hall to the laundry and open the manhole into the ceiling. Victoria went with him, wading through rushing waist-deep water. She held on to the walls to avoid being sucked out of the house. 'I got on the laundry bench and Sam pushed me up the manhole,' she said. 'I was panicking and praying my parents would be okay. I didn't want Sam to go because I was worried he would not get back to me and then I would be alone.' Once in the ceiling, Victoria could feel the house shaking and moving as trees slammed into it. She could not hear what was happening to her parents and brother over the roar of the water. Outside, the creek had grown into a 100-metre-wide roaring torrent. It smashed the back wall from the house and swept Steve and Sandy Matthews away.

Peering desperately down the manhole, Victoria watched as the washing machine flew out the back door. After a few minutes, Sam returned to the laundry and climbed up the manhole. 'He told me it would be okay,' Victoria said. She was wet and very cold. Sam reached down the manhole to a shelf that was still above water. He took some towels from it and wrapped her up to keep her warm. The brother and sister then held onto each other for an hour as the creek raged beneath them, sweeping away almost everything in the house. 'We weren't talking. We did not give up on Mum and Dad. Dad is a weightlifter and very fit and strong. Mum is also a strong swimmer. If anyone could survive, they would,' Victoria said.

After an hour, the rain began to ease. Craig Ritchie and his son ran to look at the creek. With surprise, they saw it wasn't flowing there at all. Boulders swept down by the creek had sealed the creek's normal course, so the water flowed across some grass and down two sets of steps. They went further round the corner and saw a big slip underneath the rail line. 'It was ten metres deep by 50 metres wide,' he said. The railway survey team walked over the wash-out to get back to the station. It was about 1 pm when they phoned Brisbane to say, 'Stop all trains!'

Michael Hare was very worried about his family. As soon as the water on the road had receded enough, he walked towards his home. He tried to cross the creek by clambering up driveways. The concrete and rock culverts that crossed the creek had all been swept away. He could see his property from the road – the front of his land had slipped into the creek. He needed to get his family out of the house in case it slid down the hill.

Inside the ceiling of the Matthews' house, Sam and Victoria could hear the torrent subsiding. Debris blocked their exit from the manhole. Sam punched a hole in the ceiling above the kitchen where his mother and father had been trapped. There was no-one there and nothing left in the kitchen; even the benches had been ripped out of the house. Sam punched another hole above the living room and climbed over debris until he reached the front door.

Across the swollen creek, Sarah saw Sam holding on to a post near the front door. She ran back up to the road and told two men who were stranded there that her brother was signalling to her but she couldn't understand him. Neither man followed her back to help her work out what he was trying to communicate. This time Sam wrote with his finger in the air MUM and DAD and waved his hand in a sweep towards the creek. Were they gone? Sam then wrote a V in the air and pointed inside the roof of the house. Victoria was there, he seemed to be saying. Could she be alive? Sarah ran back up to the road and told the two men her mother and father had been washed away. There was nothing they could do. Sarah ran inside her house and phoned the police again.

Sam turned and went back inside the flooded house and helped Victoria down from the ceiling into the living room. They climbed over debris to what had been the front yard. In barely an hour the torrent had risen, destroyed their family and their home, and disappeared, leaving mud and destruction in its wake. Sam crossed McCormack Drive to Sharyn Powlesland's house. No-one was at home. He broke in through a window and found some dry towels to keep Victoria warm. There was no sign of any water damage in the house, even though it was only a few metres higher than the Matthews' place. It seemed incongruous that safety and devastation should exist so closely to each other. Victoria used the phone to contact her sister. Their parents were gone. Sarah tried to comfort her distraught sister even as she realised the horror of their loss. Sarah assured Victoria that police and some friends were already on the way to help.

The railway workers went with Craig and his son down McCormack Drive towards Murphys Creek Road to let his wife know it was safe to come back home. When they reached the bridge they found one end of it had collapsed. Fallen trees were piled up to the gutter against the Matthews' house. Craig saw Sam and asked if everyone was okay. Sam told him their mother and father had been washed away. Craig offered to help search for them. 'They'll just be around the corner. They'll be okay,' Craig assured them. Craig took Victoria up to the station master's house, which had escaped damage, so she could have a warm shower and get into dry clothes. The railway workers used an extension ladder to climb across the break in Kirsop Bridge. Sharyn Powlesland, returning from Toowoomba, saw the railway workers climbing across the broken bridge. She was shocked by the devastation. Sam apologised to her for having to break into her house; Sharyn told him not to worry about her window.

As Michael Hare continued walking up the road, someone in a car stopped and told him Steve and Sandy had been swept from their house. Michael redoubled his efforts to get home to check if his family was alright. He continued up the mountain looking for a way across the creek. At last he found a property where he could cross the creek and climb up to the railway line. His plan was to follow the line to the back boundary of his property, but as he followed the gravel track he noticed that much of the access road had slid down the mountain, knocking over scrub and trees. Boulders were still tumbling down and large eucalypts now lay across the railway line. Michael waited whenever he came to sections of the track where rocks were still falling, hoping they would not trigger bigger falls. Some of the rocks were the size of wheelie bins, crashing and bouncing down the mountain. At times, he had to climb over fallen trees that were trapped in mudslides and still sliding down the mountain. He stopped and watched, assessing the danger before climbing over the moving trees. In some places the foundation of the railway lines was gone, and the tracks were left in mid-air. Michael chose what looked to be the safest of the tracks and walked across.

Sam found a snatch strap, and used it to help the railway workers across the bridge. Without telling Sarah, Sam then headed down the creek to begin searching for his parents. He reached Ean Stewart and Andrew, who by then had gone home for chainsaws to clear the road so they could retrieve their vehicles. Ean commented on the young man's selflessness: 'Sam said to me that I should go and check on my wife and my kids, which was pretty amazing for a young man to say to me. He said he'd seen my wife and she was okay. I said I should help him search for his parents and he said, "No, go and check on your family first." We realised emergency services would need to come through so we cleared the fallen trees off the road.'

After a couple of hours of negotiating mudslides and fallen trees, Michael Hare reached the back boundary of his property where he discovered a landslide. He considered avoiding it by going through a railway tunnel to the other side of his back boundary, hoping the land would be more stable there, but when he looked through the tunnel he saw that uprooted trees had slid down the mountain and were blocking the other end. He decided to try to cross the landslide, and plunged downhill through the sodden bush. Water was still running very fast nearly a foot deep down the mountain. He was totally exhausted and worried that the force of the water could knock him over.

Two police officers were speaking to Sarah Norman when her husband Jethro returned from the search. Friends of the family had found the body of Steve Matthews and, a bit further down the creek, his wife Sandy. Childhood sweethearts, together in life, were now joined in death. Sarah calmly told Victoria the news that their parents had been found dead. The two held each other as they cried together. Sam came indoors and Sarah met his eyes and told him as well. Devastated, the children decided they wanted to identify their parents' bodies. Sam left first with his mates, and Sharyn drove the girls to the scene.

It was almost sunset when Michael Hare was finally able to make out his house through the trees. It was still standing. Relieved, he pressed on, stopping to wash thick mud off his body with the water still flowing down the mountain. He called out to his family that he was back and fell, completely fatigued, onto the verandah. His wife and children had been indoors cooking and didn't know there had been any danger. As soon as Michael closed his eyes he was haunted by a vision of the man standing on the fallen trees beside the house, exhausted and desperately signalling for help. Michael knew he had to move his family to a safer place. He could not rest yet. He got up and asked his family to pack a few things so they could leave the house. The relentless rain continued. As the night closed in, the Hare family walked through the sodden bush to take shelter with their neighbours.

A few days later, Sarah, Sam and Victoria returned to the house to see if anything could be salvaged from what had been their home. Victoria opened her mother's wardrobe. On the top shelf, beyond the waterline, was a box. Inside were photos of the children. They were dry. Unbeknown to the children, their mother had carefully saved copies of her most precious baby photos and the box had miraculously escaped the torrent.

Murphys Creek

'Everything under the water went quiet. I saw colours.
It was very calm. Very quiet. The panic stopped.'

At the foot of Mount Kynoch, the landscape flattens out. The creek widens and meanders through sandstone outcrops, weaving along a wide, sandy floodway where long-forgotten floods have deposited smooth river stones, coarse gravel and sand.

Eucalypts and scrub grow thickly on either side of the main channel. Once at the bottom of the mountain, the creek flows south down a valley between the range and the rugged White Mountain State Forest. Near a curve of the creek is the small rural village of Murphys Creek, with its primary school, tavern, small shop, railway station and a few dozen houses on small town blocks. The population is 300 and comprises working and retired professionals, business and trades people, most of whom live on rural residential properties ranging from secluded bush properties to large town allotments. Drought had prevailed for almost 20 years and the creek the township is named after had dwindled to a series of waterholes. As the drought persisted, awareness of the potential danger of a flood had subsided. Local authorities had no restrictions on where houses could be built, and owners had built within 50 metres of the main creek channel and within the floodway.

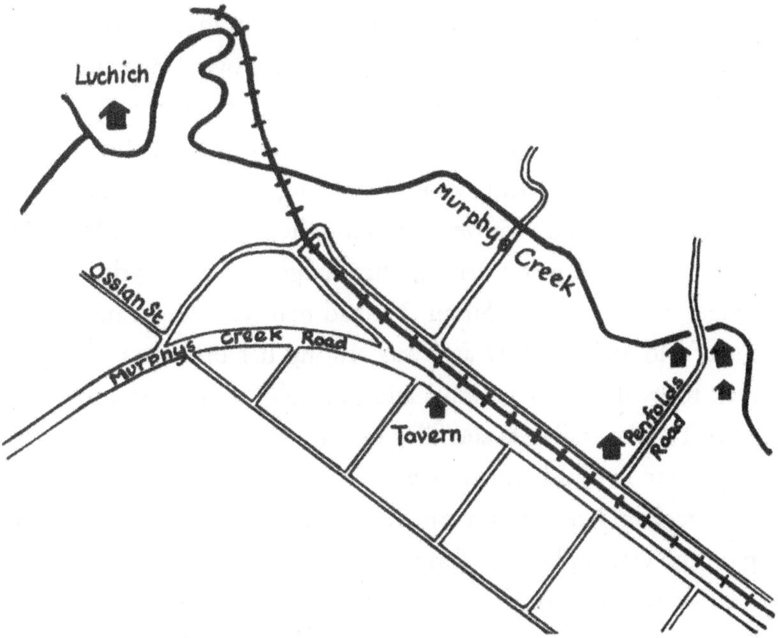

Many Murphys Creek residents commute to work in Toowoomba, Gatton or Brisbane. Local residents Angie Pohl, 54, and Thelma Hughes, 69, are friends and business partners who clean houses together in Toowoomba. On 10 January they left home early and cleaned all morning as steady rain fell outside. Murphys Creek couple Wade Foster and his wife Shauna had also left home that morning to drive 130 kilometres to Brisbane so that Shauna could have a planning appointment in preparation for five weeks of radiation treatment for cancer to commence the following week. Their children, 12-year-old twins Jessica and Joshua, and Sharlee, six, were staying in Brisbane with relatives during the school holidays.

In the village, people were returning to work after the Christmas holidays. Construction worker John Taylor and his sister Susan Mouflih were both due to return to work in Toowoomba that day, but stayed at home out of concern that the creek bordering two sides of their five-acre property had risen the night before – if they left town and it rose again they might be cut off from home. They went out in the rain several times to check the creek level and monitored storm cells on the Bureau of Meteorology's website radar. At about 11 am they saw a storm cell hovering over Wivenhoe Dam, 30 kilometres to the east. The rain started falling heavily. 'It was beautiful to see the amount of water getting around, but all of a sudden you started getting a bit of a feeling it was not normal – this had never happened. We were checking the Bureau site and weather channel. There were no warnings this was going to be anything above average,' Susan recalled. Susan, 34, had married Moroccan national Youssef Mouflih in 2009 and was visiting her brother at Murphys Creek to work on a visa application to help her husband make his first visit to Australia. As she filled out the paperwork on 10 January, she spoke to her husband on Skype and showed him the rain and the rising creek on her webcam. She returned indoors to continue working on the visa application forms.

In Toowoomba, Angie and Thelma became increasingly worried when the steady rain became a torrential downpour at about lunchtime. They left work early to be home before the local creeks rose and cut off the roads. There was one more causeway near Minora Road that they had to cross to return to town. Water flowed rapidly across it. Just ahead of them, another car had stopped just before the causeway and pulled over. Angie was reluctant to continue but when an oncoming four-wheel drive safely crossed, she ventured into the water. Without warning the floodwater surged down the creek. Her engine stalled.

In nearby Watts Road, Selwyn and Catherine Schefe lived with their daughter Katie, six. Katie's puppy Trixie often accompanied the little girl as she roamed their mountainside property. The house was built on a grassy creek flat and their only road access from the property was via a causeway across the creek. On 10 January Selwyn, Catherine and Katie were all at home. They heard that an eight-metre-high 'wall of water' was hurtling down the creek. Quickly they packed their car with a few essentials so they could leave and not be isolated by the swollen creek. By then the water was up to the back step of the house. They scrambled into the back of the ute, but were all swept from the vehicle by the powerful torrent. Catherine, a strong swimmer, managed to snatch breaths as she tumbled in the churning water for just over a kilometre. She could only wonder what had happened to her husband and her daughter. As the creek continued to rise it destroyed their house, leaving only the concrete slab and foundations.

At 1 pm John Taylor went indoors and told his sister Susan to come and see what was happening outside. She went out with him, taking her video camera in one hand and an umbrella in the other, and filmed the rising creek. She watched in astonishment as their mostly dry creek bed of the past nine years filled to 15 metres deep, tearing trees from the banks and carrying them along with it.

Suddenly the creek lifted over the banks and roared down the centre of their block of land. At the same time, water flowing along the higher side of the railway line began cascading over the line and pouring down Penfolds Road towards the creek. With water heading at them from two directions, they urgently needed to find a way of escape.

John ran to the ute and drove through overland flow up his driveway to the road, leaving the engine running in case they needed to abandon the property. Susan went quickly to the shed and began loading emergency supplies into John's boat – fuel, torches and a generator. In two minutes she was chest-deep in water. The water flowed into the house. A tree slammed through the side window and the wall closest to the creek. Furniture toppled over. Three of the four dining chairs fell. The fourth chair, with the visa paperwork on it, was pushed against the back door but stayed upright. Their dog and cat scrambled to safety on a bed. As the water rose, the mattress started to float.

Outside, John saw the water hit the shed and ran to his sister. He yelled, 'We've got to get out!' They got out the back door of the shed and saw an area of calmer water they could wade through to get out to the road. They had gone only ten metres from the shed when an eight-foot-deep wave of bubbly red water hit them. 'I didn't comprehend the force and the sound. It was like the ocean. It wasn't flat.

It was just bubbles. It took me. I was doing forward somersaults. I was tossing and turning in the water, trying to get my raincoat off, trying to get my gumboots off, trying to get my head above water,' Susan said. John was screaming to her to grab onto the above-ground pool next door. Susan was swept right past it. 'I remember fighting to try to grab the pool but I had no chance,' she said. Susan knew she was being dragged towards barbed-wire fences and the main force of the flood. There was nothing to hold onto. 'I held my breath, went underwater and grabbed into the dirt,' she said.

Murphys Creek resident, teacher Ian Hoddinott, was almost home from Gatton when he saw Angie's car go into the flooded causeway near Minora Road. He quickly got out of his car, took off his shoes, and ran towards the water, intending to help the women back to safety. He was a strong swimmer and a fit hockey player. Suddenly the water was flowing up to the bonnet of Angie's car. Ian realised it was too dangerous to go in, even for him. Inside the car, Angie phoned triple zero. She got through immediately. Her call at 1.37 pm was the first emergency call from the disaster zone. The operator told the women to climb on to the car roof. Two Queensland Fire and Rescue units were dispatched to the scene, but neither could get to them because of landslides. Angie and Thelma wound down the car windows, stood on the window ledges and held onto the handles inside the ceiling of the car. The car lifted off the road, floated off the causeway and hit a small tree, pushed it over and floated down the middle of the gully. Angie shouted to Ian: 'See you later, we're gone.'

Uphill of the township, recently retired couple Lynette Campbell and her husband Kerry had just finished their lunch, put on yellow raincoats and gone together to check the level of the creek. The couple had bought a ten-acre block on Murphys Creek Road 30 years earlier and built their house just 50 metres from the creek. After a long career in the most elite regiment in the Australian Armed Forces, the Special Air Service, Kerry loved the peaceful seclusion of their bush block. At the time they built their house there were no regulations about how far houses should be built from the creek, or even any guidance from local authorities. Kerry and Lynette saw the creek was full and flowing fast but the water was still within the creek channel. They turned and walked back towards their house. Lynette climbed the few steps to her back door, and as she opened it, water swirled around her feet and into the house. She turned to look for her husband. He had vanished. Within moments, a metre of water had swirled through the house. Lynette could not risk going outside. She phoned triple zero but the lines were overloaded. 'I panicked at first but I thought he might be in the shed where it wasn't so deep, hanging on to something,' she said.

But Kerry had been swept about 300 metres down the creek. A wave of floodwater took him under and when he surfaced he managed to grab a tree before another larger wave came. This one swept him off the tree. The water carried him towards a paddock, off to the side of the main flow. He grabbed for another tree and held on. His wife Lynette looked out the windows and, peering down the gully through the bush, she saw something yellow that appeared to be wrapped around a tree. It was not moving. Lynette kept watching. Eventually it moved. There must be someone there and they were okay. She hoped it was Kerry.

Across the road from John Taylor's house, Nelly Gitsham, 23, a slightly built horse-breaker, was outside her home in Penfolds Road with her sister Tamara when they noticed the creek rising very fast and suddenly breaking its banks. They ran indoors to alert their mother and get Tamara's daughter Alani to safety. Nelly told her mother to get out of the house: 'Grab your bag. Get in the car. Drive it up the road with Alani.' Nelly watched long enough to see them drive through a foot of water and get to safety, then she and Tamara frantically tried to gather their pets.

Two of the dogs chased Nelly's cat into the flood and the women saw the cat drown. The dogs were also caught by the current and swept away. Tamara screamed for her dog to come back. Nelly grabbed her sister to stop her running into the water after her dog. There was nothing they could do. Nelly then saw a horse trapped chest-deep in very fast-flowing water beside the creek. She ran to the shed and grabbed a halter. The horse, Henry, could hear a mare that had been swept away across the creek. Taking the halter, Nelly ran down the paddock, shook his food bucket and called him. The water was up to her chest. 'The closest I got was a metre away. I chased him for half an hour. I lost my footing a few times and went under but I came up. If I had stayed any longer I wouldn't be here to tell the tale. In the end I had to leave him because my sister was getting into deeper water trying to help me. I didn't want to risk her life for the horse – not when she has a six-year-old daughter.' The sisters held onto each other with a monkey-grip, each holding around the other's wrist, so that even if one let go the other could hold on. The sisters both used their free hand to hold the top wire of the fence and began to slowly walk against the current back along the fence towards the gate. When they reached the gate, Nelly saw she had left the gate open and now she couldn't reach across to where the fence continued.

At the Minora Road causeway, Angie felt the car tipping towards her. She decided her only hope was to abandon the car and try to swim to safety. She held her handbag over her head and jumped in. 'I went under. I was being tossed around and I was trying to get air. I thought I was going to drown. Everything under the water went quiet. I saw colours. It was very calm. Very quiet. The panic stopped,' she said. When Thelma saw Angie go underwater she desperately watched for her friend to surface again but did not see her. She was praying, 'Save me and save Angie.' Thelma realised that if the car sank it could suck her under, so she pushed off from the car and swam as best she could. 'The torrent took me. I went up the middle of the river. The surging went over my head. I came up again. I prayed, "Lord save me," and I went under again.'

Fortunately Ian knew the Eddison family, who lived in the closest street to the causeway. He got in his car and quickly drove to the house and phoned triple zero. 'I waited on the line while the operator tried to get a line. I said, "Come on, two ladies are drowning here." I got through and told them we were at the first gully out of Murphys

Creek.' Ian did not expect his friend Matthew Eddison to run to the rescue of the women with him, because he knew Matthew had had chronic fatigue syndrome for several years. Instead, Ian asked Matthew to draw a map of the gully. Matthew picked up a pen to draw a map but the pen didn't write. He threw it down and grabbed another one. It didn't write either. The gully, which had now become a torrent, would be carrying the women towards a dam. They had to hurry. 'I'll show you,' Matthew said. Knowing the ground was very muddy, the men quickly put on rock fishing boots with metal spikes on the soles and ran out the door.

Thelma had been swept 250 metres down the creek and was still struggling in the water. 'I swam with all my might and was somehow carried to the bank. It was a miracle. I grabbed a trunk of a small tree. It broke,' Thelma remembered. 'Another surge came over my head. I grabbed another tree with two hands and it held. I got my head and chest out of the water. My feet were going like a spinning wheel trying to get up the bank.'

Angie had been swept 550 metres down the creek. 'I hit a tree under the water. I tried to grab it but it was too big and I had to let go,' she said. 'I thought, "Find the next tree." I went about another 20 metres down the creek and found a little tree and hung on.' The tree was about 15 centimetres in diameter. Angie put the handles of her handbag over her head so she could use both hands to hold on. She clung on for 20 minutes and the water got higher and higher.

> Surges came on top of the flood about every 20 seconds. Each surge pushed me down again and I had to pull myself up above the water and hold on higher up the tree. There were big logs going past. All the big ones missed me. I hid behind the tree but the water was swirling around the tree and the current was getting stronger by the minute. My strength was going but I knew someone had seen me go in and would be trying to find me. Each time I had to climb higher I had less strength. I had my back to the bank and I was yelling, 'Help!'

About a kilometre up the creek the rushing, churning water was roaring down the floodway, carrying Catherine Schefe along with it. Suddenly, she was in among trees. She grabbed on. Despite having broken some ribs, she managed to keep her head above water. She had lost her glasses but could see one house through the trees and yelled for help. There was no response. She rested for a while and tried again. Again there was no response.

The house belonged to Rick Luchich, a former outback stockman who now turned his hand to practical jobs, working as a fencer, painter or meatworker. He had not gone to work that day because two causeways on his property had gone underwater, and he was at home with his children who were on school holidays. Rick and the children watched in astonishment as the creek rose quickly from its bank, and cars, parts of buildings and shipping containers rushed past in the flow.

An hour after the deluge subsided, Rick heard what he thought was a child far away calling out: 'Help!' He could not see anyone. The calling stopped.

As Susan dug her fingers into the ground as hard as she could to stop herself being swept into barbed-wire fences, the water gushed over her head. She was exhausted. Suddenly, she felt a hand grab her from above. It was her brother John. The current was so strong Susan could not stand up. John dragged her to an area of calmer, shallower water behind their neighbour's house. Once there, they both heard someone in the house screaming. Their neighbours Colin and Sue Patterson and their children had visitors staying with them. John helped take the younger children to safety as Sue Patterson rushed to take documents and photo albums upstairs. Her visitor, Matt, was yelling to her, 'We have to get out!' Sue ran downstairs and saw their three cars bobbing down the creek. 'It was like watching a cartoon. I found it very difficult to connect with the fact it was a serious situation,' she said. The water was up to the windowsills of the house. They knew they had to go. Sue and her teenage daughter Sarah, and

Sarah's friend Jacinta, held hands and stepped into the water. At first the house protected them but as they moved into the full force of the current, they had to dig their toes into the ground to hang on.

Susan recovered her breath and tried to walk herself to safety. She was suddenly hit by another surge and was swept off her feet again. This time she managed to grab a small tree. Her brother John saw her and powered towards her through chest-high water, shouting for her to stand up. 'I couldn't stand on my legs. My thighs and knees were so sore from fighting the current that I couldn't stand,' she said. John grabbed her and dragged her about 100 metres towards Penfolds Road.

As he did this, John saw Nelly struggling to get her sister across the gate opening of the horse paddock. He ran to them and pulled Tamara to safety, and then Nelly. The mare that Henry the horse had been trying to reach had swum across the creek by then. John cut a gap in the fence of the paddock and Henry came to shallower water and walked through the gap towards the mare. Both horses were safely out of the flood.

At the causeway near Minora Road, Matthew Eddison saw Thelma on the creek bank. He rushed to help her, but Thelma shouted at him urgently, 'Go and get Angie!' Matthew and Ian ran further down the gully that was thickly choked with lantana, pushing through the prickly undergrowth, looking and listening for cries for help, and shouting that they were coming. They heard nothing in reply but pressed on anyway.

Angie was becoming weaker and knew she could not hold on much longer. The men ran further down the gully. Again they stopped and pushed through the lantana towards the water, where they called and listened. They heard only the roar of the water. They ran on again, stopped and pushed through the lantana, ran further, pushed through to the creek, repeating the process several times and calling out as they ran. They had run more than 500 metres but they kept going. Again they pushed through the scrub towards the creek, shouting as they went, 'Hello! We're coming!' Matthew parted the scrub. He saw a head. They had found her. 'Water was splashing over her head,' he said.

Angie heard his voice and turned. 'Suddenly a person's face appeared. His face will be etched in my mind forever.' Matthew ran straight into the swift current up to his neck. Angie yelled to Matthew, 'Get out of the water and get a rope!' Matthew told Angie to let go of the tree and go to him, but she didn't let go.

On the bank, Ian hunted around for a piece of rope or fencing wire or a long branch – anything they could use to safely get her from the torrent. Matthew went into the water a second time, but again Angie was too scared to let go of the tree.

Angie still had her handbag around her neck. Matthew asked her to pass it to him but she wouldn't. The torrent was still rising and covering Angie's head with each new surge. Finding no rope or wire anywhere, Ian decided to try making a human chain to reach her. He held the base of a lantana bush and went out in the water. Another surge came and they waited for it to pass. Matthew grabbed Ian's hand and went towards Angie but he could not quite reach her hand. She stayed anchored to the tree.

Ian found a longer, thicker lantana branch. Now he could get far enough out into the water that it was up to his chest. Ian held Matthew with a monkey grip. At last Matthew could reach Angie's hand. They all waited for another surge to go past and then finally, Angie reached out for Matthew's hand and let go of the tree. Using the lantana bush to anchor himself, Ian pulled Matthew and Angie towards the bank. The two men helped her out of the water and up on to the bank, where she recovered her breath.

The men walked with Angie half a kilometre back upstream to where Thelma was waiting anxiously. As Thelma saw them coming through the bush, she shouted in relief, 'You're alive! You're alive!'

In her tree beside the creek, Catherine Schefe had been holding on for more than two hours. The rushing water had receded into the channel of the creek. No-one could hear her screams. She needed to get to help. She made her way slowly down the tree but she was too weak to walk in the deep mud. She tried calling out again. This time Rick Luchich heard her. He went outside again to look around. 'I saw somebody sitting down in the mud. She told me her name was Catherine. She was very calm, considering what she'd been through. She had lost her glasses. She couldn't see me but she could hear my voice,' Rick said. 'I was talking to her to calm myself down. I probably blabbered like a drunk. I wanted to get her out but the water was still roaring down. There was no way I could help her,' he said.

Rick was amazed she had survived. 'Anyone in the water that day had very limited chances of survival. I think God was with her because I don't like anyone's chances of repeating that again. If it had been me I'd be dead. I swim like a brick. I take my hat off to the lady. She's very courageous.'

Rick took his mobile phone and ran up the hill at the back of his property trying to get reception. Someone answered but the line was bad and the operator hung up. Rick then phoned a friend, Col Crawford. Col was also isolated by floodwater but he knew a concreting contractor, Jeff Neumann, who lived halfway between Murphys Creek and Postmans Ridge and owned a truck. Jeff answered his mobile phone. Col told him, 'Rick just tried to phone triple zero. There's a woman in the creek. Rick's keeping an eye on her.'

Jeff told him, 'Well, you're lucky. I'm with some fire and rescue blokes now.' Jeff handed over the phone to the incident controller, who sent the crew to Ossian Street to search for Catherine. The crew, Nathan Chadwick and Phil Paff, didn't know the area, so Jeff offered to go with them in the fire truck.

Once there, Jeff Neumann and the Queensland Fire and Rescue Service (QFRS) crew found a woman who had fled the rising water by climbing an electricity transmission tower. She was now safe. The crew was about to leave when Jeff realised he had not yet seen Rick Luchich. The fire crew activated the fire truck siren briefly and then turned it off. They listened. They heard Rick yelling, 'Over here, over here!' They ran towards Rick's voice and as they got closer, Nathan heard Catherine. 'We heard a faint sound like a bird. It was a female voice in obvious distress. We grabbed some ropes and raced out across the paddock – it was like walking through the tidal zone of a mangrove swamp. We got to the edge of the mud and looked out through the trees at the raging torrent, and there was a woman in a back eddy hanging onto a tree.'

The water was still rushing around her. It was almost 4 pm when Jeff and the crew carefully lifted Catherine from the mud and helped her walk to the truck. Catherine told the rescuers she didn't know what happened to her husband and daughter who had been in the back of the ute. She couldn't remember being tumbled in the water. 'All I can remember is this wall of water coming, being hit by it and getting swept. Then I grabbed this tree,' she told them.

Jeff and Nathan walked up the creek to search for Selwyn and Katie, while Phil took Catherine to the tavern in Murphys Creek, which had become a make-shift evacuation centre even though it had also been flooded. Tavern manager Sue Haughey wrapped Catherine in blankets.

As Jeff and Nathan searched upstream along the creek for any sign of Selwyn and Katie, they saw how the torrent had uprooted hundreds of trees from beside the creek, and swiped houses off concrete slabs and others off their stumps. Some houses were still standing but everything inside had been washed down the creek. They checked these houses for any other survivors. Once they climbed the creek to the Schefe's place, Jeff realised that Catherine's husband and daughter could not be further upstream. He and Nathan walked to Murphys Creek Road and caught a lift back to the tavern.

Sue Patterson and the people with her walked up the road to the Murphys Creek shop and climbed on to the roof. From there they saw their neighbour John's large steel shed sheer off at the ground and float away. John and his sister Susan decided to try to drive to higher ground, but there was too much water flowing over the railway crossing. They went to the nearby sportsground where the highest end was just above the waterline. Overhead a news helicopter crew was filming the disaster. Within hours, the vision of Murphys Creek roaring down the range and engulfing houses, including John's distinctive deep red corrugated iron-clad house, was beamed around the world. Susan's husband Youssef in Morocco saw it. He was horrified. The house he had seen a few hours before while Skyping with Susan was the centre of a disaster of global significance. He thought his wife must be dead. Once the water had receded far enough, John and Susan waded from Penfolds Road back to the house and saw their dog barking at the front window. He was still floating on the mattress. The cat, wet and covered in mud, was also on the mattress, huddled between the pillows at the head of the bed. In the kitchen, Susan's visa paperwork had stayed dry.

By that evening 22 people in Murphys Creek had been reported missing, many of them presumed dead. Seventy survivors had gathered at the tavern. They bedded down on the floor for the night as best they could. Late that night, a warning was given that another 400 millimetres of rain was forecast for during the night. Everyone at the tavern might need to be evacuated. Fortunately the forecast rain did not arrive.

Next day Wade and Shauna Foster, who had gone to Brisbane for Shauna's medical treatment, finally returned to Murphys Creek and found what was left of their house. Two bedrooms had been broken off and swept away. Shauna's medical appointment had saved their lives. 'If we had been here we wouldn't be alive. We couldn't have worked it out at the time but the kitchen bench would have been the best place to get to. An empty glass vase on the bench didn't move,' Shauna said.

The final death toll in Murphys Creek was two. The body of little Katie Schefe was found three kilometres downstream from her home. The body of her father, Selwyn Schefe, was carried down Murphys Creek and Lockyer Creek, past Helidon and Grantham to near the town of Lowood.

Toowoomba

'We're nearly drowning. Hurry up. Please.'

Severe flooding was a natural disaster never expected to affect Toowoomba, a city positioned 700 metres above sea level on the crest of the Great Dividing Range and home to 130,000 people. The eastern edge of the city forms the watershed between the Lockyer Valley and the Murray-Darling Basin. Rain that falls on the escarpment flows east across the coastal plain to the ocean.

But rain that falls in the city runs from the ridges around the edge of the city towards the lowest point in the centre. Early settlers in the mid-1800s discovered two permanent natural springs emerging from the red volcanic soil, which formed the headwaters of the two small spring-fed creeks: East Creek and West Creek. Pioneers established businesses near the creeks because of the easy access to water. Once the creeks converge they form Gowrie Creek which flows northwest, through the fertile undulating farming and grazing country of the Darling Downs, and down the Condamine River system and into the Murray-Darling Basin.

As the CBD developed, the small creeks were gradually diverted into 'pipes' running under roads and buildings. Heavy rain sometimes caused flash flooding in West Creek, which spilled into Dent

Street near the large Grand Central Shopping Centre. Heavy rainfall could also cause East Creek to rise suddenly and cut off main roads running from east to west across the city.

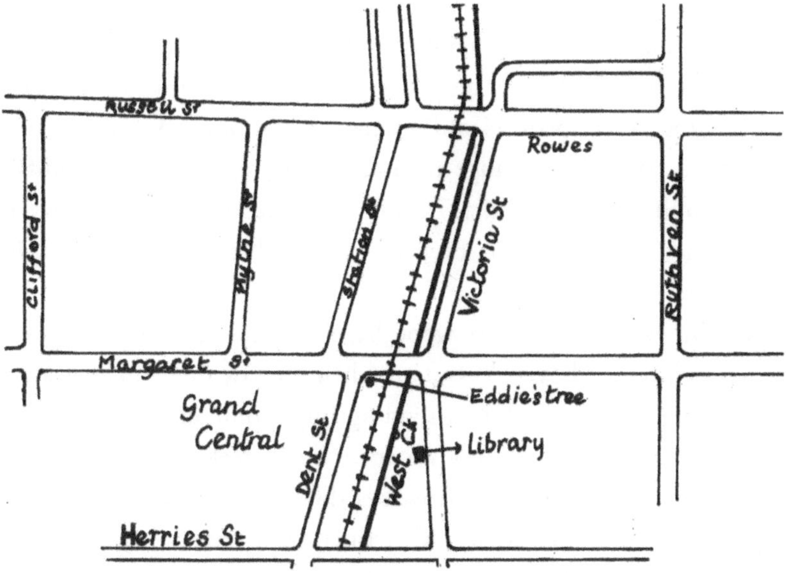

After almost a decade of drought during the 2000s, welcome spring rains fell in 2010. During summer the rain continued, yet there was no fear of flooding. With low risk of fires, local firefighters prepared their vehicles for swift water rescues by equipping them with ropes, an inflatable boat and lifejackets in case they needed to rescue anyone caught in floodwaters. By 10 January, the ground was sodden.

Steady rain that morning gave way to a very intense thunderstorm, which fell from 12.50 pm for an hour. Senior Queensland Fire and Rescue staff in Toowoomba joined a teleconference with the state disaster coordination centre, but were given no warning of possible dangerous weather conditions. The city's firefighters, based at the Kitchener Street fire station and the Anzac Avenue fire station, each had their usual complement of staff – a total of ten firefighters, including two specialist swift water rescuers. After the teleconference ended, staff returned to their normal duties. The Bureau's weather radar showed storm cells joining to form an ominous weather system that was now over the city. However, the Bureau could not measure creek rises because it did not receive live data from creek gauges in the city, and the rain gauges that do relay data to the Bureau are west and north of the city, not at the headwaters of the creeks. The Toowoomba Regional Council has a rain gauge network in the city but the information is not relayed in real time to the Bureau. The city gauges recorded up to 94 millimetres in one hour. A Toowoomba Regional Council rain gauge at Mount Lofty registered daily rainfall of 138 millimetres, of which 74 millimetres fell in the hour between 1 pm and 2 pm, a rainfall intensity estimated to occur only once in 100 years.

On the eastern side of Toowoomba, elderly resident Denise Reeves was watching the heavy downpour when she saw three mains waste-water drains suddenly burst, sending huge fountains gushing four metres into the air at the headwaters of East Creek. The water began to flow several metres deep, towards the centre of the city. Denise knew the water could be deadly by the time it travelled two kilometres to where East Creek crosses major roads: James, Herries, Hume and Ruthven Streets, before joining up with Gowrie Creek in the centre of town. She ran to the phone and tried desperately to reach Toowoomba City Council. The phone rang out. She dialled again and again but the line rang out. She tried a final time. Again the phone rang out. In desperation, she dialled the local newspaper. No-one answered. Critical minutes had passed.

In the Fire Communications Centre in Toowoomba, the first triple zero call was received at 1.37 pm. Two women in a car were on a flooded causeway at Murphys Creek. Two firefighting crews were dispatched and senior firefighter John Ryan was on one of the fire trucks heading north from the city. The red fire engine travelled along the main road, the streets on either side of it carrying huge volumes of water up to a metre deep, and flowing fast across each intersection. The truck drove through two intersections but the third was too deep.

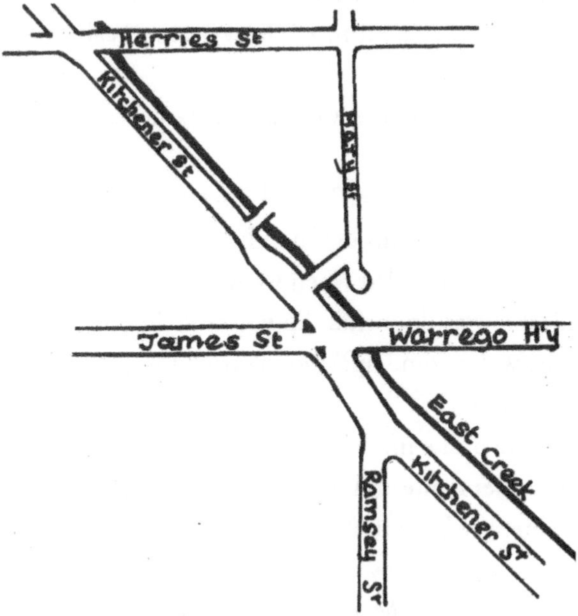

Toowoomba mother Donna Rice was driving with her two younger sons, Jordan, 13, and Blake, ten, both on school holidays, to collect her older son from his house to take him to sign some legal documents. Donna turned from Margaret Street into Kitchener Street and proceeded towards the intersection with James Street. The rain was torrential and water was rushing along the gutters. Water started flowing along the road. The traffic lights ahead turned red and Donna stopped. Suddenly the water got deeper. Her car stalled. She was about 500 metres from the Kitchener Street fire station. The water was rising so fast she could hardly believe it possible. She phoned triple zero. The phone rang out. She tried to dial again but dropped the phone in panic as the water continued to rise. She tried over and over again but kept dropping the phone because her hands were shaking uncontrollably. She tried again. It was 1.49 pm. The triple zero lines were overloaded. She waited for 28 rings. More than a minute and a half passed. Finally her call was answered.

'I'm stranded in Kitchener Street,' she said.

The operator, Senior Constable Jason Wheeler, had just ridden to work on his motorbike through heavy rain. 'Yeah, water over the road?' he asked her.

'Yeah. I'm trapped and the water is just about ready to come up the door,' Donna told him.

'Yep, you're stuck, are ya? Why'd you drive through it if you're stuck? Why'd you drive through floodwaters?'

'Because it wasn't flooded when we were coming across.'

The constable was doubtful. 'So you're saying in the space of one second all the water come up?' Donna tried to explain how suddenly the water had risen.

The constable broke in. 'Yeah, well, what's ya name?'

Donna gave her name and spelled it out. She gave her location but didn't know her pre-paid mobile phone number.

At the same time, Toowoomba businessman Chris Skehan was driving and turned from Margaret Street into Kitchener Street. Three cars were stopped at the red lights. One, a four-wheel drive, looked like it would be able to get through. Chris took off his boots and socks and went to another of the cars where an elderly woman had frozen in panic. Water was halfway up her car door. He told her to put the car in reverse. She backed out of the water, did a U-turn and drove away. Chris turned to the next car. Water was splashing over the bonnet.

Another man, Warren McErlean, arrived at the intersection and helped push a green car from the water. Then he noticed the white Mercedes Benz with a woman and two children inside. He tried to walk towards the car but the current was too strong. Warren yelled to bystanders for some rope, and someone threw three pieces of old tie-down ropes. They didn't look like they'd hold but they were all he had. Warren tied the pieces together, tied one end around himself, anchored the other end to a traffic light post, and waded towards the car. When he was five metres from the car the current suddenly swept his feet out from under him. He lost his footing and went under. Unable to stand up or pull himself along the rope against the current, he swallowed a lot of water and thought he was going to drown.

The water was getting dangerously high. Chris Skehan ran to move his ute further from the rising water when he saw Warren lose his footing and ran back to help pull him out of the water. Chris and another man hauled the rope until Warren was safely back. Water was flowing fast around the post but there was a circular guardrail around it, which they stood inside and clung on to. Chris saw a child in the Mercedes and a woman on the phone.

Inside the car, Donna was still talking to Constable Wheeler. He told her it would be a while before he could get police to her. Donna needed to get out of the water, and asked if he could phone for a tow truck. Constable Wheeler told her, 'You can ring a tow truck – we've got a million phone calls coming through at the moment.' Donna told him she had no credit on her phone. The police officer asked what make of car she was driving.

'A Mercedes Benz.'

'Well you shouldn't have driven through it in the first place. Alright?'

'Yeah, I know . . .' Donna was still talking when the police officer butted in and dismissed her. 'It doesn't matter. It was a flooded road. Bye.'

Donna's voice was flat with resignation. 'Bye.'

Chris asked Warren to give him the rope so he could try to get to the Mercedes to rescue the woman and her two sons. Chris tied the rope around himself and walked into the water. Once at the car, he undid the rope from his waist and tied it around the hinge of the rear driver's side door. Jordan told his brother to go first. Donna told Chris, 'Take Blake first.'

Chris put Blake on his back and sidestepped with his stomach towards the rope, so the force of the current would hold him against the rope and prevent them both being swept away. The current was growing stronger and Chris was panting with exhaustion. Warren could see him struggling to stand up so he went to meet him and grabbed Blake, held the boy tightly against his chest and headed for the post. As he tried to lift Blake to safety, Warren felt a sudden intense pain in his shoulder and felt the boy being dragged under the water. Warren held Blake as tightly as he could and reassured him, 'We'll be alright. Help is coming.' A heavily built man in a black T-shirt appeared and he and Chris grabbed Warren and Blake and pushed them towards the guardrail. They all grabbed on.

A kilometre to the west in Toowoomba CBD, a group of teenagers and young singles had met to see a movie together that day. Among them was Eddie Spark, 22, who had a day off work. He had moved with his family from Perth three years before and lived at Crows Nest, 45 kilometres north of Toowoomba. Eddie had parked at Grand Central and walked across the Margaret Street intersection, where West Creek is piped under the road, to meet his friends. Water from West Creek was overflowing and running fast across the road.

Eddie waded in knee-deep water and urged his friends to hurry back to Grand Central in case the water rose any higher. They set off across the intersection. The water rose to their waists. They were almost across when they realised the current was too strong to risk going further. They clung to pipe railings at a bus stop on the corner of Dent Street. One of Eddie's friends saw what he thought was a person trapped in a car further along Dent Street, and Eddie went with him, against the current, to rescue the person.

As the fire truck with John Ryan on board turned back towards the CBD, calls for help started pouring in to triple zero. Cars and pedestrians were being washed away off the city streets. Water smashed shop windows in, trapping shoppers and staff and sweeping stock, shop fittings and furniture down the raging creek. The fire crew managed to get the fire truck across West Creek and along Margaret Street to Grand Central Shopping Centre. They saw a disoriented elderly man walking into the floodwater. John shouted for him to turn back but he kept going so John sprang from the truck, grabbed him and guided him back to higher ground. 'The water was dangerous and getting more dangerous by the minute. We were all astounded by what we were seeing,' he said.

While he was guiding the elderly man to safety, John noticed the group of teenagers stranded at the bus stop on Dent Street holding desperately on to a railing. He saw Eddie and his friend heading through the floodwater towards a car. They signalled to him. John took a tool for breaking glass and waited momentarily while a colleague, Shane Ott, tied a safety rope to the back of John's harness. Shane held the anchor rope while John moved towards the car. Once he was closer, he saw that there was no-one inside. What Eddie and his friend had thought was a person in the front seat was only a headrest.

Eddie's friend returned to the bus stop but Eddie thought it was too risky to get back. He clung to a tree. Bystanders saw them and phoned triple zero while Eddie started wondering if he would escape with his life. 'The water was getting higher, over my head. I started to climb higher in the tree but I couldn't get a good enough grip so I had to get up, get a breath, and go back down in the water,' he recalled. Although he had been a wrestler and boxer, he did not think he could hold on against the current.

About 300 metres south of where Eddie clung to the tree, Kathryn Reardon-Smith and her adult daughter Hannah drove along Herries Street, which crosses West Creek, and turned right into Dent Street. As they rounded the corner a surge of floodwater lifted their four-wheel drive from the road and floated them along. The car turned sideways and the current pinned them to a telegraph pole outside Treg Smith's car repair business. Kathryn and Hannah quickly clambered on top of the car. Treg saw them and grabbed a towing strap from his car. A shopper at Grand Central, Jim Gray, had seen the women in distress and also ran to help. Treg offered Jim the strap, and Jim tied it to himself and waded into the current while Treg anchored the other end. Treg shouted at the women to stay on the car, assuring them the water would not reach as high as the roof and that they'd be safe.

At the intersection of James and Kitchener Streets, Jordan Rice phoned triple zero at 1.56 pm, seven minutes after his mother's call.

The phone lines were still overloaded; it rang ten times before a fire communications operator answered and asked him urgently, 'Fire and Rescue, what's the location of your emergency? Queensland Fire and Rescue, what's the location of your emergency?'

Jordan did not know the name of the intersection and asked his mother, 'Where are we?'

The operator heard screaming in the car and spoke sternly to Jordan. 'Would you calm down and tell me where you are?'

Jordan told her, 'We're stranded! Hurry up.'

The operator needed more information. 'Where are you? If you can't tell me, I can't help you.'

'Kitchener and James.'

The operator could hear Donna screaming for help. 'And what's the problem there? Are you in a vehicle? Tell the woman beside you to stop yelling.'

'We're stranded. Kitchener and James.'

'Kitchener and James Street. Okay. Are you in a vehicle or what are you in? What are you in, a vehicle?'

'A Mercedes. We're nearly drowning. Hurry up. Please.'

Jordan then shouted to his mother, 'Get on the roof!'

The operator told him, 'Alright, I'll send a crew straight away to you.' Then Donna screamed to Jordan, 'Get on the fucking roof!' The operator heard a rush of water. The phone call cut out. Three fire trucks were dispatched to the scene.

Chris Skehan stepped sideways, holding on to the rope as he waded towards Donna and Jordan, keeping his stomach towards the rope and with the current striking his back. The torrent of water was even stronger than before. Chris's legs were swept from under him and he pulled on the rope to get his head above water again and stand up. He continued on. Again his feet were swept from under him, and again he pulled on the rope to get his head above water and stand up. Jordan was on the roof of the car. Jordan yelled, 'Take me!' Chris told him he could not carry him as he was barely able to stand up and get across himself. Chris desperately thought how they could do it. Donna said she wanted to try getting across using the rope. Chris told her he didn't think she'd make it because even he had had trouble crossing. The car started to move.

At the post, Warren McErlean could see the rope become very tight and yelled to Chris, 'You're not going to make it back. It's going to break.' The rope in Chris's hand tightened and broke, and Warren jumped sideways as the rope snapped. At the car, Chris, Donna and Jordan all clung to the vehicle as it drifted towards a signpost. Chris yelled, 'Grab the post!' Jordan reached across the car roof and Chris reached across the bonnet of the car, both trying to grab the post. The car knocked the post over before any of them could grab it. Donna grabbed Jordan as they both fell in the water and were carried away.

Chris tried to stand up. He felt grass under his feet and staggered towards a street light post. He clung to it with his chest towards the post and the current directly hitting into his back. The water was still rising and flowing with more and more force. Chris saw Donna and Jordan stand up and also stagger towards the next street light post. They held on to either side of it, but Donna lost her grip and was swept downstream towards a tree with low branches. She disappeared out of Chris's sight. Jordan then lost his grip on the light post and was also swept downstream. Warren stepped over the guard-rail around the light post to try to help them. He fell in the water but managed to grab what was left of the broken rope. Just then the crowd of bystanders yelled, 'Car! Car!' A floating car was hurtling towards him, between him and the post, and threatening to break the rope. Warren pushed the rope down his body to try to quickly get free so he could move to avoid the car, but the rope lodged around his legs. He quickly undid his jeans, threw his legs in the air, and the car almost immediately swiped away the rope and his jeans. The man in the black T-shirt grabbed Warren. He was naked and shaking with fear, but alive.

Shortly after 2 pm truck driver Greg Twidale, from John Kelly & Sons Transport, arrived at the intersection of James and Kitchener Streets, travelling west. An eastbound sedan had stopped in the intersection with the water level up to the top of its tyres. Greg used his UHF radio to ask if anyone was in the car. Then he saw a woman in the driver's seat waving out the window and signalling for help. The water was still rising. Other truck drivers at the intersection were talking on their UHF radios and agreed someone needed to help. Greg drove his semi-trailer forward into the water, using his truck to shield her car from the current. The woman climbed out of her window and sat on the roof of her car with her feet on the windowsill. The rain was still falling heavily.

Once Greg was close enough, he shouted to the woman not to panic. He had a ten-metre strap for securing loads and threw one end of it towards her, but it only went about halfway. He tried again, and again. On his fourth try the end of the strap landed on her lap. She wrapped it around her body and fastened the hook. Greg's end was only just long enough to reach to the truck but there was not enough to tie it to the truck. If the car moved, Greg feared he might not be able to hold her. He extended his seatbelt and tied the end of the strap to the seatbelt, so that if the car moved the woman would be secured to the truck. Greg stayed with his vehicle in the floodwaters for an hour until rescuers arrived.

Along East Creek the torrent carried dozens of cars that were parked beside the creek. It carried them past the fire station, across Margaret Street, and down East Creek beside Chalk Drive, before smashing them against the large drains under Ruthven Street. The creek was soon choked with cars, and floodwater spilled across Ruthven Street. A family in a four-wheel drive was lifted off the road and swept onto the loading dock of a flour mill in Ruthven Street. They grabbed their baby and scrambled from the car onto the roof. Even on the roof, the water was higher than their knees; they needed to get higher. A wooden pallet floated close to the car. They pulled it onto the car roof and stood on it as they phoned for help.

In Dent Street, Kathryn and Hannah watched the floodwater continue to rise. Cars were being swept rapidly towards them, sometimes crashing into each other as they rushed down the torrent. A swift water rescue crew arrived just as a car smashed onto the bonnet of their four-wheel drive. Kathryn jumped into the water and hung on to the rope the rescuers had thrown for them to tie around the telegraph pole. A van careened towards the telegraph pole, but just in time a bow wave from a building diverted the vehicle and it missed her. Swift water rescuer Peter McCarron and his colleague John Burrows knew they had to rescue the women quickly.

John attached a safety rope to Peter's back and Peter took hold of the rope that had already been tied to the telegraph pole and ventured in. The current pushed him so fast across the rope that it burnt his hands, despite the coldness of the water. Hannah was still standing up on the car. Peter concentrated on the older woman first because she was in the water. He looked down into her face and she looked up and seemed to apologise for her predicament. 'Oh, I'm so sorry,' Kathryn told him. Peter assured her, 'Don't worry about that now; we've got to do something about this.'

Just then a surge of water dislodged both cars and the vehicles started moving. Hannah jumped in the water and grabbed hold of the rope that was tied around the power pole. Now all three were in the water. As the cars were washed away, the bow wave that the cars had been making, and which had dissipated the full force of the water, was gone. Kathryn was leaning over the rope with the current holding her on. Hannah was behind the pole so she was protected. But the full force of the water now hit Peter, and he was instantly wrenched from the rope. 'I couldn't believe I'd been swept away. I'd gone out there to rescue these ladies and I'd been swept away.'

John Burrows grabbed his Firecom radio and yelled, 'Red! Red! Red!', a code for everyone to clear the airwaves. Moments later Hannah was also swept off the telegraph pole. Her mother clung on as long as she could but she too was soon thrown into the churning water. John reported on the emergency radio that Peter McCarron and two women had been washed away. He called for rescue trucks to go downstream to try to find them.

The van that had almost hit Kathryn floated backwards down the flooded road, towards the line of small trees where Eddie Spark was desperately clinging on. The van slowed slightly after hitting one tree and then it knocked over a second tree. Crowds of people in the shopping centre watched in horror, screaming when they saw the van heading for Eddie's tree. 'People started yelling. I wondered why everyone was yelling out. I looked around behind my tree and saw a van just after it knocked over the tree in front of my tree. I thought my tree was going to go over when the van hit it. I thought I was gone.' Eddie said a quick prayer and held on as tightly as he could. 'I closed my eyes. I didn't want to see what was going to happen.' The van hit but the tree stayed upright. 'I felt the tree shake. Once it stopped shaking I opened my eyes and the van was round the side of me and went down the road. The suction of the van was so strong it nearly pulled me from the tree.'

At the intersection of James and Kitchener Streets, Greg Twidale saw one swift water rescue technician at the scene and used his UHF radio to ask him to help rescue the woman who was trapped on her car in the water, still holding desperately onto the snatch strap that Greg had thrown to her. Greg urged the rescuer, 'If you don't hurry up and get her, I'm going in.' The rescuer told him not to go in. Undeterred, Greg took a couple of steps into the water but the current was too strong. He realised he would be swept away if he went any further. At the same intersection, Chris Skehan, who had tried to rescue Donna and Jordan Rice, was still holding on to the light pole. The water rose until it was splashing around his shoulders. Finally, it began to recede.

Outside Grand Central, Peter McCarron surfaced. 'I looked over and saw a calmer area of water and started swimming for that. I got in there.' Peter recognised a young woman with long black hair – it was Hannah Reardon-Smith. 'I turned around and I saw her come floating down towards me and I thought I'd get her to swim towards me. I yelled out, "Swim to me! Swim to me!" She started swimming and she got to me and I grabbed her by the right arm.' Then a car floating down the road hit them both, knocking Hannah from Peter's grasp. 'She went around the front of the car and I ended up going over the bonnet of it. I went under the water,' he said.

At Grand Central, firefighters in the water were also trying to throw a rope to Eddie, who was still clinging to a tree. Over and over again the rope fell short. To gain extra height they took a ladder from the fire truck and stood it in the water. They tried again. This time Eddie caught the rope.

A second swift water rescuer, Dave Crighton, arrived on the scene. He had been trying to get across West Creek, working his way progressively south until he reached the Margaret Street crossing, not knowing he was desperately needed. Eddie tied the rope around himself with one hand while still clinging to the tree with the other hand. 'When the rescue team pulled the rope tight I realised I should have tied the rope around the tree, so I took it back off me and tied it on the tree. They yelled, "We're coming across," and Dave Crighton started coming. When he was halfway across he disappeared under the water. He lost his footing.'

Dave couldn't get his feet back down to the ground, so he pulled himself along the rope with his hands towards Eddie, rolling on to his back and lifting his head to create a small pocket of air to breathe. Other firefighters in the rescue team threaded the rope through the buckles on the front of a lifejacket and pushed it into the current so that the power of the water would push the jacket across to the tree. Dave unclipped the lifejacket from the rope and put it on Eddie. Then he clipped himself to the tree and got the firefighters to move downstream which would create a new 'ferry angle' that would help the current push them both across the street and out of the water. Dave clipped the tag line on his back on to the rope, held Eddie and let go of the tree.

When Peter McCarron surfaced near Grand Central he couldn't see Hannah. 'I thought, "Oh God, she's gone under. She's been drowned," and it was pretty devastating. I looked around and I couldn't see her mother any more. I thought they were both drowned. The water was moving me around a lot, like I was in a washing machine. I had to get out. It was too dangerous.' Peter looked across and saw the Grand Central car park and swam hard towards it. 'I grabbed some bushes there and got my breath and then grabbed the railing and climbed over. I was trying to see the mother and daughter.' He couldn't see either of them. Peter ran up a side street back to the rescue truck to raise the alarm.

After being hit by the car in the water and knocked from Peter McCarron's grip, Hannah managed to raise her head above water. As she was swept along, she grabbed a tall hedge beside the high-rise car park that Peter McCarron had left moments before. On the ground level of the car park, tow truck driver Jason Iacono, his brother Wayne, and his mate Steve Seefeld, were standing against steel railings at the front of the car park, surveying the flooding. Wayne suddenly noticed something and looked down. 'A hand came up and grabbed one of the bars near my feet. Then I saw a head. We leaned over and grabbed her and pulled her over the railing.'

Hannah was exhausted and breathless. She couldn't speak but raised one hand and pointed out to the water. As soon as she had enough breath to speak, she told them, 'My mum! My mum!' Wayne asked her, 'Where's your mother?'

She pointed and said, 'In the water.'

At that moment her mother was carried past and Hannah cried out, 'There she goes!' Jason plunged into the water and yelled to the rescuers at the corner of Margaret Street who were trying to rescue Eddie. They couldn't hear him over the roar of the water. Jason and Steve had no ropes but they headed into the torrent anyway. Kathryn had grabbed a signpost and was holding on to it. 'We walked out and grabbed her. When we got to her she was panicking about her daughter because she didn't know where she was. Once we told her that we already had her to safety, she calmed down. We took her to her daughter,' Jason said.

When Peter McCarron returned to the fire truck, his colleagues were amazed to see him alive. Peter wanted to know what had happened to the woman he had been trying to save when he had been swept away himself. John told him she had let go and was 'bobbing around like a dead fish in the water'. He didn't know if she was going to survive. John called in to the Firecom to tell them that Peter had been found, but that the two women, Kathryn and Hannah Reardon-Smith, were still missing. Peter searched downstream but found no trace of either of the women.

Meanwhile at Eddie's tree, Dave Crighton held Eddie and let go of the tree. The carabiner attaching them to the rope opened, and they shot off down the current. John Ryan had a split second to react as they were swept along. He lunged over the bonnet of a car and tried to grab hold of the two men as they were pushed along the side of it. All three hit the car at once. John grabbed them. The rope attached to his back went taut as his rescue team anchored him. He held both men and helped them to their feet. Dave reached around his back to see what had happened. Only the cord attachment with the carabiner appeared above the surface. Dave shook his head in disbelief, wondering how the fitting in his hand had come undone from the rescue rope.

Dave and John supported Eddie as he staggered unsteadily from the water. The crowd cheered and a very cold, exhausted Eddie waved to them. John gave him his fire jacket. The crew was soon called to another rescue, so John retrieved his fire jacket but gave Eddie his own T-shirt to keep him warm until an ambulance could collect him.

At the intersection of James and Kitchener Streets, the woman trapped on her car had been there for about an hour before the water receded enough for the swift water rescuer to wade to the truck, give Greg Twidale a lifejacket, and then wade towards the car with another lifejacket. The woman put on the lifejacket and waded to the truck. She thanked Greg for his help and waded from the water to safety. At the same intersection, Chris Skehan had been holding onto the light post for 30 to 40 minutes. Once the water was around his ankles, Chris saw a QFRS swift water rescuer coming to help him. Once out of the water, Chris was checked by a paramedic and spoke to a police officer about what had happened. Chris returned to his car, which had been flooded but, thankfully, the engine started. He drove back to work.

As the water receded, swift water rescuer Scott Frame was able to reach the fire station. He was sent back out to rescue the family with the baby stranded on top of their four-wheel drive at the flour mill in Ruthven Street. Scott waded through chest-deep water to the car, planning to take the baby to safety first. He asked the man to slide the baby down the windscreen so he could reach it. Once he had the infant in his arms he headed for dry land. Someone watching the rescue offered to take the baby so Scott could return for the adults.

As he and his partner carried the others to safety, he saw six people signalling for help from an office block. He signalled to them, asking for their phone number. They signalled their number and he phoned them, telling them to stay where they were until they could get back to help them.

Just after 3 pm, Toowoomba police phoned the Emergency Management Queensland rescue helicopter base to ask for urgent air support to help find the dozens of people who had been reported missing. Archerfield base manager and senior pilot Mark Kempton was flying a patient to Brisbane for urgent treatment. He could not understand how or why a flood of such biblical proportions could be happening on top of a mountain. He told police that he did not think he would be able to fly into Toowoomba because of the poor weather conditions but he promised to re-assess the conditions once he landed.

The six people trapped in the office block at the flour mill near the junction of East and West Creeks were still waiting for help. Swift water rescuers Peter McCarron and Scott Frame arrived and took them to safety. As the water receded, one of the people in the office block saw what they thought could be a body. Peter and Scott and two other colleagues found a drowned woman with long dark hair, lying face down. She was later identified as Donna Rice. Her body could have come from East Creek or West Creek because she was downstream from where the creeks joined. 'I thought it was one of the ladies I had tried to rescue. She was a similar age and had a similar hair cut. I was devastated,' Peter said. He knew they had more work to do and had to push his disappointment aside to concentrate on saving other people. The rescue team called police to recover the body, and Peter returned to the fire station.

Another body had been found. This one was near the city war memorial in East Creek Park, two blocks from the intersection of Kitchener and James Street. Peter was called out to help retrieve Jordan Rice's body.

When he returned to the fire station, he was told that the two women at Grand Central had both survived. It was hard to believe. Amazingly, the tow truck driver Jason Iacono had written down Hannah's name and car number plate so he could tow the car away. He was able to confirm with the rescuers that both women were alive.

Many people at Grand Central had used their mobile phones to film the flood carrying cars, water tanks, industrial bins and debris through the city streets, and had uploaded the footage to websites. Television news stations worldwide broadcast vision of the destruction.

The floodwater receded almost as fast as it had risen. More than 300 cars were strewn along East Creek and West Creek, with many smashed into bridges and caught in drains under the roads. Firefighter Scott Frame began to search the vehicles along Chalk Drive and under Ruthven Street. As he reached each wreckage, he checked the front and back seats for bodies and radioed back the number plate so police could track the car owners. He searched cars for the rest of the afternoon and well into the evening, but no bodies were found in any of the cars.

Peter McCarron had imagined dozens of people must have been trapped in their cars in the dangerous and chaotic conditions and died. 'For us to only lose two in Toowoomba is pretty lucky, especially with the number of cars. I just don't understand how there were not more people in those cars. It was just lucky. Very, very lucky.'

Withcott

'This is it! Let's get out!'

The town of Withcott straddles the Warrego Highway at the base of the Toowoomba Range. The highway follows a ridge, but as it meanders down the mountain it crosses the headwaters of Gatton Creek.

Withcott has 1,800 residents and several large businesses, including a large factory that makes pumps and irrigation equipment for domestic and export markets, as well as many smaller businesses: petrol stations, medical centres, food outlets, car mechanics, truck sales, antique shops and a pub, all catering for local trade as well as for motorists passing through. Gatton Creek is barely visible in the town and has no creek gauge.

Businessman Ben Burton was up early on 10 January. Before 3 am, he went next door to his business, Withcott Antiques, and sandbagged the front and back doors of the showroom, then sandbagged the front door of his house before returning to bed. Four days earlier, rainfall run-off had caused localised flooding at his business – water had run ankle-deep through a side roller door into the lower showroom and dampened some of the carpet of the main showroom. 'We'd had so much rain in the previous months that I had become addicted to the Bureau of Meteorology site, watching the weather

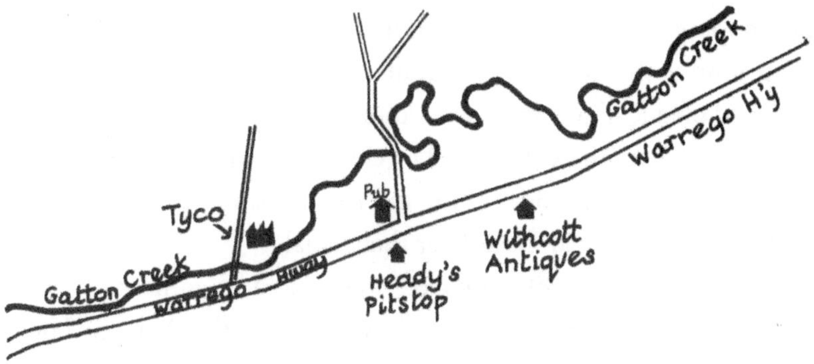

patterns coming through. I had had my eyes riveted on a storm cell coming through. It originated over the ocean and it seemed to track in a direct line to Toowoomba over a few days. I knew we were in for big trouble,' he said. When the intense rain began, Ben told his wife Anthea they were about to be flooded from water running off the Warrego Highway. Half an hour later the highway was underwater.

Rezwanul Huq, a mechanical engineer at another Withcott business, Tyco Pumping Systems, drove to work from his home at Ipswich, 40 kilometres west of Brisbane. He was surprised to see creeks and rivers almost touching the bottom of bridges. Rez, a native of the Bangladeshi capital of Dhaka, was aware of the risk of flooding but he did not know the local landscape well enough to know if there was any danger in this case. When he arrived at work he asked the manager, who commutes from Brisbane, if he had seen water lapping at the bridges and asked if the creeks and rivers could overflow. The manager said he had never seen the creeks so high.

Toowoomba resident Shayne Richardson and her daughter Amanda were driving home that afternoon through Withcott, after spending a week watching an international tennis tournament in Brisbane. Once the tennis concluded they drove to nearby Bribie Island to collect a vacuum cleaner Shayne had bought on eBay. Several roads were cut by floodwater and Shayne carefully avoided them, patting the dashboard of her Honda Jazz and telling her car she wouldn't let him drown. Once at the island, Shayne and Amanda picked up the vacuum cleaner, had lunch, and then headed out through torrential rain hoping to get home before more roads became impassable.

Around the same time, semi-trailer driver Michael Munchow had dropped off a load of kangaroo carcasses in Brisbane and was heading back to Toowoomba with a load of Coca-Cola and lawn mowers on his daily freight trip. Heavy rain and road closures had delayed him and he was running an hour later than usual.

At midday, Tyco's 90 employees were asked to go home because there was water over a small causeway between the Warrego Highway and the factory. Rez returned to his office briefly before going to his car. He reached the causeway – a shallow dip with no concrete sides and no depth markers. A four-wheel drive went across ahead of him successfully, so Rez ventured cautiously into the water. 'As soon as I got into the water my engine stalled. I tried to start it. The car wouldn't start. The front of the car was pushed sideways by the current. I jumped out into knee-deep water. The current was not too strong on my legs. I decided to try to stop my car from being pushed off the causeway.' Rez went to the front of the car and tried to hold the car steady. 'The water had a lot of silt. It was slippery on the ground so I could not push the car backwards out of the water. After 30 seconds the water came up to my waist.'

Long-time Withcott businessman Norm Head left Toowoomba at 12.15 pm to drive down the range to take over his shift at Heady's Pitstop. Norm's son Chris had bought the petrol station in 2001 on the opposite side of the highway to his father's fruit and vegetable business, Tomatoland. Norm leased his own business and worked with his son at the service station, which attracted a strong customer base of local residents, as well as passing trade from motorists on their way to Toowoomba. Chris worked morning shifts and Norm took over from 12.30 pm until closing time each day. When Norm arrived that day, Chris had sandbagged the front door as a precaution, after a minor flood four days earlier that had put muddy water through the shop. He told his father that more rain was forecast and, at about 1 pm, the rain became intense.

A drain on the highway burst. Water around the service station rose up the sandbags and then retreated. Norm thought the danger had passed, but Chris wanted to stay a bit longer to make sure. Within five minutes water flowing down the road and across the apron of the service station was like a choppy sea. Traffic on the highway stopped. Norm went inside to lift computers and electrical equipment higher, and to turn off the power supply. He opened a floor safe and took out a cash bag. Chris worked quickly outside, collecting things and carrying them inside so they would not float away. Suddenly the water was too deep and the current too strong for him to stand up. The doors were blocked with sandbags. He climbed on a heavy steel table against a front window of the shop to try to get back in. He watched his car float away. Then the ice freezer floated away. Chris frantically tried to open the window. It was locked.

Not long after lunch, interstate heavy vehicle owner-driver Paul Pepi drove through Withcott on his way home to Toowoomba in a V8 utility. He had spent the morning working on his truck at Garth French's workshop in Grantham. Floodwater the night before had covered Gatton Helidon Road outside the business, and the two men decided not to risk the truck wheels being flooded. They drove several trucks that were waiting in the yard to higher ground in Gatton, and then headed to Garth's home at Postmans Ridge. From there, Paul Pepi decided to head home to Toowoomba.

The rain was the heaviest Paul had ever seen in 30 years of truck driving. He slowed down but continued up the range until he started to lose traction on the road because of the rainwater flow – it was 15 centimetres deep across both uphill lanes of the highway. He reached a more level section of highway halfway up the range, called 'the saddle', and decided to press on to the top of the range. Two cars passed Paul and disappeared ahead of him around a bend. Behind them, a stream of water appeared across the road.

The road cutting beside him was shaking, big eucalypts crashed to the ground but fortunately they fell uphill rather than across the road. The stream of water crossing the road quickly grew until it was half a metre deep and six metres wide. Rocks and mud slid down the road, wedging under Paul's car and stopping it from moving. His car was pushed backwards and sideways towards the edge of the mountain. There was no guardrail. Paul told himself, 'If I don't get out of here I'm going to be pushed over the range. I'm not going to survive.' He had to get back to the saddle to stop other people getting up there.

Shayne and Amanda Richardson drove through Withcott and were beginning to climb the range when they saw a truck and a four-wheel drive ahead of them go through some water that was moving across the road. They stopped when the utility in front stopped. They saw the water rise around the car in front. Shayne reversed and stopped. The water was soon up to the top of the bonnet. They reversed further back. A small truck drove up and parked behind them so they couldn't reverse any further. They were parked in and had to wait. Within seconds, muddy water was rushing over the windscreen and up the windows so they couldn't see out. Shayne dialled triple zero. The operator asked her how to spell 'Withcott' and what state that was in. Her daughter Amanda took the phone and told the operator they were in a flood like the Rapids Ride at Dreamworld, only muddy. Shayne realised no-one would get there in time to help them. She hung up.

Two of Rez's colleagues, Dave Gesler and Darryl Innocent, were following Rez's car. They saw it stall and jumped from their cars to help. One of the men tried to start the car while the other got a rope from his utility, tied it to the tow points at the back of the car and towed it from the water. By then, large logs were sailing past in the floodwater.

On the range, Paul Pepi realised he had to do something quickly to avoid being pushed over the edge. 'I put the car in reverse. Backed out and spun around. I could hear the water roaring down the creek. I drove back to the saddle.' He parked sideways across both lanes and blocked the road. Paul was trapped on the range for five hours until emergency crews cleared the highway. The two cars he had seen pass him were both buried to their windows in rocks and mud.

In the town, the trucks and cars on the highway stopped and began to back up in both directions. As the water rushing down the highway became deeper, cars moved towards the centre lanes, which were slightly higher than the outside lanes. Floating backwards under the muddy water in their Honda Jazz, Shayne Richardson said that she was scared. Her daughter Amanda, an intelligence officer in the defence force, reassured her: 'We'll be okay. Stay calm.'

The car hit something and started tipping. 'The car felt like it was going to roll and I expected to be drowned. Amanda and I looked at each other and let out a shriek at the same time,' Shayne recalled. Then she remembered reading a newspaper article about a woman who was trapped in her car in floodwater because the electrics failed and the windows would not go down. She started to let down the windows but Amanda asked her to wind them up so the water would not come in the car. Shayne wound them up again. They didn't have much chance of survival if they got out into the torrent anyway.

About mid-afternoon, publican Neil Simpson looked out the front of the Withcott Hotel and saw surges of floodwater coming down the highway like rapids. Neil went immediately to the office to tell his wife Gae. 'I think we're going to get flooded,' he said. Gae told him she'd just finish paying the staff wages and Neil replied, 'I don't think you've got time to finish the wages.'

By then the building was surrounded by water: run-off was flowing fast at the back of the property and knocking over fences. Out the front, the flooded highway cut off their only other escape route. Gae ran with Neil to the front of the hotel and saw waves of floodwater pouring down from the range highway and flowing through the town. The water rushed under the hotel, which stands on 1.5-metre-high stumps. It bubbled up through gaps in the floorboards of the main function room and Neil worried that if the water rose any higher the old hotel building could be picked up and washed away. There were 20 people in the hotel and they could not escape. 'All we could do was watch and keep our fingers crossed,' Neil said.

Semi-trailer driver Michael Munchow was on the westbound lanes of the highway. The traffic stopped. He phoned his wife to let her know he was stopped in floodwater in Withcott and just as he did he saw Shayne's little blue Honda Jazz floating away and coming towards him, backwards, in water that looked about two metres deep. 'I watched the car float from more than 100 metres up the road,' he said. Michael saw the car tip as it hit a gutter. He thought it would go over.

The car righted itself and kept floating towards his prime mover and 15-metre trailer. 'I said to the missus, "Holy shit, they're going to hit the front of the truck here,"' he said. 'As it came closer it started swerving out towards the left, as if it was going to go around the truck.' Michael quickly took his boots off. He told his wife, 'I'll have to go, love – I think I might have to get in and take a swim to get some folks out of here.'

Antique shop owner Ben Burton didn't see the wave coming. 'There was nothing, and then all of a sudden our block of land was totally covered in water and our buildings were taking water. I was drawn outside to see what was going on. I was taking photos. The roller door had been forced in.' Water started rising very quickly inside the shop and within seconds Ben's wife Anthea was waist-deep in rushing water. Although she could swim, the current was sweeping her across the shop. All around her, china was breaking, furniture was falling, glass was smashing. She screamed for Ben to help her as she was pushed towards the back door. Ben could not move against the current to get in the front door so he went to the side door just in time to catch Anthea as she came out. Ben helped her get to a downpipe and told her to hang on.

He saw a tall bookcase of antique books become wedged in the doorway. He realised the obstruction would force the water higher inside the shop. He had to get it out and let the water move freely. He grabbed handfuls of Anthea's antique reference books and threw them into the current. 'Don't throw those away!' she cried. It had taken 30 years to collect them, but Ben didn't stop.

Once the bookcase was light enough, Ben managed to twist it so that it could move out the door. It floated away, followed by a procession of antique furniture from the shop. Inside the shop, more furniture was being lifted from the floor, falling over, crashing into the water and rushing out of the door.

Neil Simpson saw the Honda Jazz carrying Shayne and Amanda Richardson twisting and turning as the churning water pushed it past the hotel. The women were screaming in terror. 'The car hit the gutter of the road opposite the hotel, hit a road sign on the median strip and knocked it out. It just looked to me like the car was going to tip over,' Neil Simpson said. 'It was horrifying to not be able to help them. Everyone was just standing on the balcony of the hotel in awe.' Neil hoped the water wouldn't rise any higher. 'It would have been disastrous if it had come higher because the traffic was backed up for two or three kilometres – there were a few hundred cars trapped,' he said.

At Heady's Pitstop, Chris started hitting the window to attract his father's attention. Norm abandoned the safe. He couldn't open the window; he didn't know where to find the key. He then heard banging on the back door of the shop, opened the door and saw the tenant who rented a house on the service station site, Brad Burton, and let him in. Brad asked him, 'What the hell is happening?'

They had to get Chris in through the window. Brad found a hammer and smashed the security lock. At last, the window opened. Chris stepped inside and the table was immediately swept away. Chris grabbed his laptop and mobile phone. They could hear water hitting the back wall of the shop and bowing the bottom of the door inwards. The wall gave way and exploded inwards. Chris shouted, 'This is it! Let's get out!'

In his truck, Michael had to do something fast to stop the Honda Jazz. 'I got off the phone. I looked. All I could see was a power pole there beside the trailer. I put the truck in reverse and jack-knifed. It was just sheer luck, the angle the car floated down and caught on the truck and wedged up against the post,' he said.

Inside the car, Shayne and Amanda realised they had stopped moving. Their car was wedged between the passenger side front wheel of the truck and the post. As he climbed from his truck, Michael could see the current was deadly. 'I was trying to avoid getting into the water because the current would have taken your feet out. I climbed out the passenger door and climbed along the bunk cabin onto the fuel tank of the truck. I had one foot on my fuel tank and one on the roof of their car.'

At Heady's Pitstop, the flood wave filled the shop. It was impossible for Norm, Chris and Brad to get out the front door. 'The only exit route was to get out the back and into the house. A washing machine was wedged in the front door and water splashing over the machine was going up to the ceiling,' Norm said. They all climbed over the washing machine and into the kitchen, where the water was up to the windows.

Michael knocked on the car window to ask the car driver to put the window down. Fortunately the electric windows were still working. Michael shouted over the noise of the water, 'Let's get your stuff and get out of here!' Michael helped Shayne climb out through the driver's side window and climb along the outside of the truck and in through the passenger door. Amanda then climbed out and into the truck as well. Both women were shaking with fright. Michael climbed back into the truck. From the safety of the cabin, Shayne and Amanda watched in horror as the water began flowing over the top of the car and in less than two minutes the little car was swept away from the post. Shayne and Amanda had escaped just in time.

In the house behind Heady's Pitstop, Chris Head and his tenant Brad climbed out of a window on to a side fence that was protected from the main current. Norm stood on the window ledge. From here they could see cars floating backwards down the highway bumping into each other. Norm saw a truck driver helping two women from a flooded car into his truck. The roar of the water was deafening. 'The front windows of the shop blew out and we were watching our stock floating away,' Norm said. At the height of the flood, the house lifted off its stumps briefly and came back down.

Somehow, the building stayed together. 'It was just survival. There was nothing you could do. We had tried to save everything earlier. We were just hoping it wasn't going to get any worse. Once we saw a drop in the water level we realised we were going to be okay.'

Ben and Anthea Burton took refuge at their house, which was next door to their antique shop. The shop had shielded the house from the main force of the flood, reducing the inundation to less than half a metre deep inside. Ben and Anthea sat down to take stock of their situation – their business was destroyed and their house had been flooded, but they were both unscathed. Together they walked to the Withcott Primary School where an evacuation centre had been hastily set up. The school principal invited them to stay at his house overnight.

When the water receded from the highway, hundreds of people who were stranded during the afternoon went to the pub for food and drinks and to find out what roads were cut and when they might reopen. Power and phones were now working. At the hotel, Neil and Gae Simpson and their staff helped people who were drenched and freezing to get dry and warm. 'We didn't lose power. People were hungry. We just dug out whatever we could.' The hotel became a disaster relief centre, with food being given out as fast as it could be cooked. Media reports began to filter through that people had died in Toowoomba and the surrounding area.

Neil was thankful that he and his wife, and their staff and customers, had been spared. 'If the hotel had floated we would have ended up down Gatton Creek, and being old, the building would have probably been demolished,' he said. 'Police were fearful another wave of floodwater could be coming through. They told everyone to get their vehicles out.'

By 10 pm one lane of the up section of the highway was cleared, and police escorted cars and trucks up the range to Toowoomba.

In the truck, Michael Munchow and Shayne and Amanda Richardson had been stranded for almost eleven hours. Finally, the truck could make its way slowly up the range. Michael's semi was too big to negotiate the suburban streets of Toowoomba so he drove across town to drop off the truck, collected his ute, and drove Shayne and Amanda home.

No-one died in Withcott that day, but dozens of people made very narrow escapes.

Postmans Ridge

'I don't think I can do this. Mate, I'm going to have to let you go, big fella.'

Three valleys on the edge of the Toowoomba Range form the headwaters for three more seasonal creeks between the Range Highway where Gatton Creek rises, and Murphys Creek, ten kilometres to the north. For most of the year the creek beds are dry gullies which come alive only after storm rain and carry run-off quickly to the valley floor. Here they converge and begin their 140-kilometre easterly journey to the Brisbane River to empty into Moreton Bay.

East of Withcott the first settlement is Postmans Ridge, named after the ridge that extends from the mountains and channels water either side of the rocky outcrop. South of the ridge lie Gatton Creek, Little Oakey Creek and Rocky Creek, and to the north is Six Mile Creek. Cattle-grazing properties here have been gradually subdivided into smaller acreages of creek flats and sloping eucalypt scrub, and developed into rural residential properties. Many houses built during the past 30 years have been built on the creek flats and closer to the creek as the district became more closely settled.

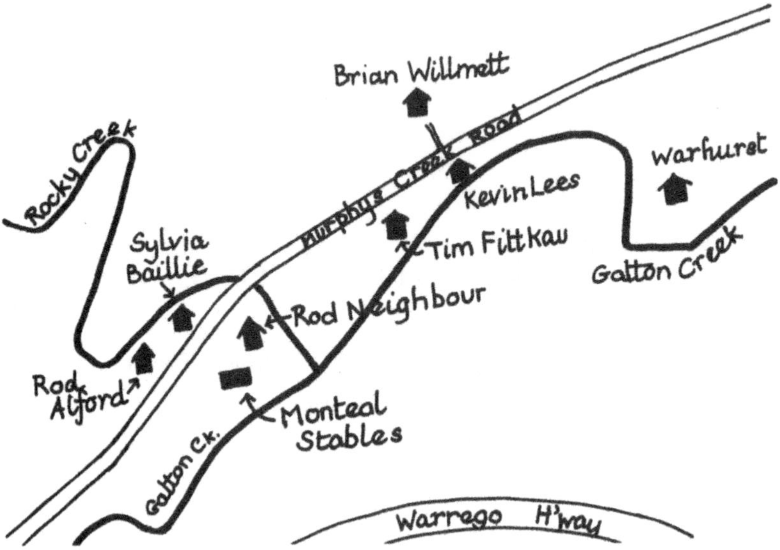

Turning north from the Warrego Highway, Murphys Creek Road winds along undulating creek flats. This narrow country road is dotted with dozens of properties that draw their water supplies from Rocky Creek and Gatton Creek, which converge here and meander along about a kilometre north of the highway. It's here that Gayle and Gary Teal operate a small racing stable, Monteal Racing, where they train and breed thoroughbreds for the local racing industry. The round yard and stables are situated on the creek flat backing on to Gatton Creek, with Rocky Creek running alongside the property.

Retired grazier Sylvia Baillie lived across the road, having moved to the district just under ten years before. She'd sold the family grazing property in northern New South Wales and moved to the Lockyer Valley to be within range of some of her four children, as well as her close childhood friend Janette Barnes at nearby Murphys Creek. The small brick house by the creek was just what she was looking for – a quiet area where she could be independent, a small property with its own water and a hill where she could see cows grazing. She kept fit by walking her border collie Belle on her neighbour Brian Willmett's grazing property, crossing the creek at a rocky ford a few metres upstream of her house and setting off across the paddocks.

She watched over Brian's cows and reported back to him any animal that needed attention. A few years earlier, when a young cow had trouble calving and was lying in the paddock unable to stand up, Brian reluctantly planned to shoot the animal because he had to go away for work and couldn't tend her. Sylvia volunteered to carry food and water to the animal and two weeks later the cow was strong enough to stand up again. Brian named her 'Sylvia'.

Opposite Teal's place, across Gatton Creek, is the Warhurst's family property. The house was set on the creek flat with Gatton Creek flowing in a loop around two sides of the property. Bruce and Wendy Warhurst had bought the hobby farm to give their four sons a rural upbringing. The couple ran the local scout group and were well-known in the district for their youth work and bush skills. One of the couple's four adult sons, Paul, still lived at the property with his wife Samantha and their two-year-old daughter Hailey.

On 9 January the property was becoming so muddy that Samantha drove to Toowoomba to buy gumboots for her husband. She tried several shops in Toowoomba, but none had any.

The same afternoon Sylvia Baillie's daughter who, with her family, had been to visit Sylvia, returned to their home in Brisbane. Family friend Kelly Wilson, the daughter of Janette Barnes, also dropped in to check on Sylvia because of a minor flood a few days earlier that had covered the bridge on Murphys Creek Road near Sylvia's house. When she arrived, Kelly was worried by the level of the creek and the swift current and decided to stay with Sylvia overnight. As a precaution, Kelly helped Sylvia pack her photo albums and prized family history documents into suitcases, and put them near the front door in case they needed to leave in a hurry.

During the evening they heard on the radio that another 100 to 300 millimetres of rain was predicted for the following day. Sylvia went to bed but Kelly stayed up all night. She put a marker post in the garden and listened to the roar of the water grow louder and then fade away as the water level rose and fell. Kelly ran outdoors frequently to check the height of the creek and the marker post, sometimes every ten minutes. By midnight, the water was just over the creek bank and flowing across Sylvia's backyard, rushing at 60 to 70 kilometres per hour just three metres from her back door. Kelly determined that if it came within two metres of the back door they'd evacuate through the front door and go to the car that was already parked on higher ground at the neighbour's house. By 3 am the water level started to fall and continued falling for several hours.

Further along the same road, Kevin Lees and his wife Eileen were also alert to the danger of flooding, and took turns to sleep while the other checked the creek. The couple had lived in the Lockyer Valley and Toowoomba area for 32 years, but had moved to Postmans Ridge in 2005. Their property straddling Gatton Creek had not flooded in living memory, but rain had swelled Rocky Creek to its highest level a few days before, rising to half a metre below their floorboards. As more rain fell, Kevin became anxious. He knew he would need to be prepared to evacuate because of his chronic emphysema, which meant he could not walk far or fast – even breathing was difficult as he needed an oxygen cylinder almost continuously. Their neighbour Tim Fittkau's house had also been above flood level but it had been inundated for the first time a few days earlier. He and his family were staying in Toowoomba while their house was awaiting repairs.

By morning, Rocky Creek had receded back within its banks but there was water still more than a metre over the Rocky Creek bridge on Murphys Creek Road near Sylvia's house. Sylvia and Kelly drove to Withcott to buy milk and some bread rolls for breakfast. Kelly was still worried about the predicted rain and decided they would pack the suitcases of photos into Kelly's car. Kelly then left Sylvia's place and went home to have a few hours' sleep and to check the Bureau of Meteorology website. She promised to return by lunchtime.

When Sylvia's neighbour Rod Alford left for work at 8 am, Rocky Creek was the highest he and his wife Wendy had seen it since they moved to their two-storey brick house in 1999. Once at work, as regional operations manager of Workplace Health and Safety for the south-west region, he logged onto the Bureau's website and saw several storms converging. Twenty years of disaster management planning meant he was keenly aware of the looming danger. He monitored the site during the morning, and just before 12.30 pm he decided to go home. Halfway down the range, the rain became extremely intense, the heaviest he'd ever seen. The rain on the ground was much heavier than the intensity indicated by the radar.

Two kilometres downstream, heavy vehicle mechanic Garth French checked the level of Gatton Creek several times during the morning. Garth was concerned for his elderly neighbour Lizzy Crust across the road, because her house was 20 metres from the high bank of the creek. He dropped in to let her know they might need to evacuate her later in the day if the flood worsened. 'Lizzy reckoned it was her house and she wasn't leaving,' he said. Garth was not concerned for his own house, which was 200 metres from the creek, because when it had been built in the early 1990s the land was built up so the foundations of the house were half a metre above the record 1974 flood level. Their dogs were barking madly during the morning so he tied them up to verandah posts at the back of the house.

Across the road from Sylvia's house, Gayle and Gary Teal were helping a neighbour fill sandbags when they saw Gatton Creek suddenly break its banks at the back of their property. Gayle ran to the lowest paddock and took a horse to higher ground. The water was rising before her eyes. She ran to the stable, went to the lowest enclosure, put a halter on the horse as fast as she could and led him to safety. She returned for each of her horses.

Helicopter pilot Brian Willmett was at home, having time off after spending several weeks evacuating residents from the flooded towns in western Queensland and dropping food to isolated people on the Darling Downs, west of Toowoomba. On this morning, his mate Mick, a nurseryman, went to visit him. They set off down the driveway in Mick's car to check the local creeks.

Nearby, Samantha Warhurst was determined to try again to buy gumboots for her husband Paul, whose work boots were soaked. She asked her father-in-law Bruce and his wife Wendy to go with her because she was uneasy about the risk of flooding. Bruce decided not to go because he wanted to keep an eye on their horses and dogs, so Wendy set off for Toowoomba with Samantha, Paul and their daughter Hailey.

Garth French, with his wife Wendy and son Scott, returned to check Gatton Creek in the early afternoon and timed the creek rising. 'It was coming up a metre a minute. We were timing by the watch and measuring the height by the roadside posts. That's when we went round and said, "Lizzy, it's time to go",' he said. The water was less than half a metre below the floorboards of Lizzy's house. They had half a minute to get her out. Lizzy was still unwilling to leave, so Garth told her she could go in the back seat or in the boot of the car – it was her choice. She chose the back seat.

Garth and Scott returned to their house to find their dogs were barking madly, swimming round and round the verandah posts. Scott set them free. Wendy French drove Lizzy to higher ground a little further along the road.

At about midday, Kevin Lees emptied the rain gauge in his yard. They'd had 50 millimetres that morning. The rain continued and after a while became even more intense. After half an hour the rain gauge that held a maximum of 150 millimetres overflowed. Kevin told his family, 'We're out of this place; it's going to be the worst flood in history.'

They quickly got their visitors, grandson Drae Kark, 18, nephew Clem Lees, as well as family friends David and Wendy Patterson, to leave the house. Everyone ran outside. Drae and Clem drove their cars, which had been hitched to a caravan and a trailer, up the driveway and across the road into Brian Willmett's property. Kevin set off up the driveway on his mobility scooter because he knew he could only go as fast as his scooter would carry him. Kevin's wife searched desperately for her car keys. By the time Kevin was halfway up the driveway he turned around and there was a metre of water going through the shed and half a metre through the house. Eileen gave up the search for her car keys, put on gumboots and ran up the driveway.

High school student Hugh Sedger was at home on his family's property in Murphys Creek Road preparing for a job interview. His parents had both gone to work in Toowoomba. The rain that had been falling for most of the morning suddenly became more intense at about noon, and it rained hard for about 45 minutes. It was the heaviest downpour Hugh had ever seen. Within 15 minutes, water was running down their land and flooding the downstairs section of the house. Hugh quickly lifted everything he could off the floor, took the dogs upstairs and sat on the large front verandah. From there he overlooked the Warhurst's property across the road. He saw Bruce Warhurst open some gates to let their horses out and then run back behind the house. 'Within about a minute I heard a massive roar coming down the hill. I phoned Mum and told her the neighbour's shed was being ripped apart and cars were going down the creek.'

Hugh decided he had to leave the house. He took the dogs with him. By then the run-off water was flowing so fast across the front of the property that his only escape route was cut off. He had to brave the water with the dogs. 'I was washed over the front fence. I can swim but it didn't matter if you were the best swimmer in the world, you still had no hope against how strong the water was – it was cruising at 60 to 70 kilometres an hour, knocking big trees over, everything in its path,' he said.

By noon, the rain at Kelly Wilson's place at Murphys Creek suddenly became torrential. 'I was concerned the colours on the Bureau's radar were not representing what we were getting. The colours were indicating heavy rainfall but the rain here was like an enormous fire hose – the radar wasn't showing what I thought it should be showing.' The rain eased off for a few minutes but then became torrential again. The ground could not take any more water; everything that fell now would be run-off.

Urgently, Kelly phoned her son, who was in Toowoomba, and warned him not to attempt to get home. She told him, 'Don't come back here until I phone you. A bomb is about to go off.' Kelly knew she needed to get back to Sylvia. She tried to get out of her property but the road was flooded and she couldn't. She phoned Sylvia to warn her.

As Rod Alford arrived home from Toowoomba and walked indoors, he saw water raining from his ceiling – the rain was overwhelming the gutters and pouring into the house. Looking out the large windows overlooking the creek, he saw the water level covering the highest of a series of retaining walls down to the creek.

Next door, Sylvia was on the phone to Kelly but hung up to answer the door, promising to call back. It was Rod, and he told Sylvia that the water was at her back step. 'Come to my place, it'll never get me,' he said. 'You're not safe down here.'

Sylvia told him, 'Okay, I'll get my photos.'

Sylvia phoned Kelly back at 1.52 pm. Kelly told her they'd had 100 millimetres in 30 minutes.

'There's a whole lot of water and it's coming your way,' she said. 'Get the dog. Get your bag. Get your keys. Get in the car and go up to Dianna Court and don't move until we get there. As soon as we can get out, we're coming.' Kelly made Sylvia promise she would go immediately. 'She promised me she would go,' Kelly said.

Rod Alford ran home from Sylvia's house and saw horses running up the hill.

> I felt a vibration. When I was looking out the back windows I saw a wall of water – not coming down my creek – it was coming from the northwest over the back of my hill. The water was moving so fast and was so high it couldn't follow the creek. The creek meanders at the back of my place. The water followed the mountain range down and channelled it down the hill towards my place and Sylvia's place. It was a brown wall with what looked like roofs, shed doors, washing machines, fences and gates. It was several metres high and moving at 85 kilometres per hour. I uttered a series of four letter words.

Hydrologists later verified the wall of water was 9.8 metres high.

Next door to the Teal's racing stables a new family, Rod and Helen Neighbour, and their son Alex, 18, had moved in three weeks earlier. They hastily packed their car and tried to drive to the highway to get to safer ground. Traffic was stopped and they could not get from Murphys Creek Road onto the highway. Gatton Creek was dangerously high. They turned around to return home and saw Sylvia's house becoming engulfed in water – and Sylvia at the front door. She had left her car and gone back to her house. Alex wanted to run to Sylvia's rescue but his father stood in his son's way and told him to get ropes. Alex ran to the backyard near the Teal's stables, shouting for ropes. Gayle heard him calling but she didn't have any – only leading reins, which would be too short. She told Alex to look for an extension cord or speaker wires – anything that looked like rope. He grabbed some cable from the shed and ran back towards Sylvia's house.

Waves of floodwater were hitting the side of the brick house and running across the front yard, cutting her off from the road. Sylvia came to her front door, where the water was a metre deep. She screamed for help. It was 2.20 pm when suddenly the force of the water broke the corner of the house away. The walls collapsed and the roof fell heavily into the water. There was nothing anyone could do. Alex arrived in time to see the house cave in; he threw down the cable in despair.

Rod Alford ran outside. The wall of water had already hit Sylvia's house. It had been three minutes since Rod had told Sylvia to leave her house. He was desperate to know if she had escaped. 'I heard a couple of screams. Neighbours were already on the road. I said, "Sylvia's not in there, surely?" They said, "Yes." I ran in to about waist-deep. Her house exploded in front of me and was gone. Just gone. The water washed it across the road into the trees, not down the creek.' Rod looked back at his own house. Half a metre of water was running through the ground floor.

Samantha and Paul Warhurst were driving up the Toowoomba Range, a four-lane highway with a wide median strip between the two up and two down lanes, when mud and rocks began falling from the steep-sided road cutting. Rocks up to half a metre in diameter rolled down the road and hit the car's wheels, stopping it from moving. After a short time, water was flowing quickly down the highway, cascading down the mountain. The rocks, which had surrounded the car and trapped them, now became protective, breaking the force of the water and saving the car from being swept off the highway. As they sat stranded in the car, Wendy phoned her husband and told him they were trapped. Bruce phoned back a few minutes later. It was 2 pm. Bruce told his wife not to try to get back home because the roads would be flooded. He said he would come to rescue them as soon as he could.

Across the road, helicopter pilot Brian Willmett saw a sudden huge rise in the creek behind Kevin's house. 'The water was four or five metres high and moving at about 20 knots,' Brian said. Kevin's neighbour Tim Fittkau, and his brother-in-law Gary Hodgkinson, had returned that morning to Tim's house to rip up the sodden carpets and continue cleaning up from the flood the day before. Tim and Gary saw the creek rising fast and went to the road where Tim saw Kevin in trouble. He ran to help. Brian grabbed Kevin by his right arm; Tim grabbed Kevin's left arm. Kevin's nephew Clem appeared and took hold of his feet. 'We dragged Kevin off his scooter and his scooter was washed away,' Brian said. The loss of Kevin's scooter meant he was also separated from his oxygen cylinder.

Brian told Tim they had to get to higher ground. 'As we were taking Kev out, the power pole in front of his house fell and the wire hit the water 30 metres from us and sparked and blew all the fuses. We were in half a metre of water that was really running fast, dragging him across the current, and struggling to stand up ourselves.' They reached the road but were coming to a barbed-wire fence. Tim's brother-in-law Gary was in his car on the road and saw that the men would not be able to get Kevin over or through the barbed-wire fence. He rammed the fence with his car to knock it over. Once the fence was on the ground, Brian, Tim and Clem were able to drag

Kevin into the paddock to higher ground. 'We dragged him 70 or 80 metres and we were physically wrecked. Kev was really heavy and the water was getting faster and higher,' Brian recalled.

As they struggled through the water, Clem slipped over. Tim reached out to Clem to help him stand up. When Tim and Clem stopped pulling Kevin through the water, the current became too strong for Brian to drag Kevin alone.

Brian's legs were numb and he was breathing hard. He told Kevin, 'I don't think I can do this. Mate, I'm going to have to let you go, big fella.' Kevin told Brian, 'Mate, save yourself. Just let me go if you can't do it.'

Clem managed to stand up again and the three men were able to make headway as they dragged Kevin against the current. Just then Brian heard a loud cracking noise behind him. 'I looked around and I saw Tim's house breaking off the slab. I said, "Mate, is that your house?" And Tim said, "Yeah mate," and kept pulling Kev along.'

Brian, Tim and Clem all rallied their last reserves of energy to drag Kevin above the waterline and let him down on to the grass. The force of the water had dragged Kevin's trousers off and he had been separated from his oxygen supply. He was gasping and his face was blue. Brian looked back and saw Eileen. He had to go to help her but he didn't like Kevin's chances of survival. 'When I left him at the edge of the water I didn't think he'd be alive when I came back.'

Rod Alford ran to his garage and tried to start his English MG sports car. As the motor started, another wall of water, bigger than the first one, hit. It was moving as fast as the first wave. Rod heard logs smashing into the side of his house. The back door of the garage gave way. A torrent gushed suddenly towards him. The roller doors exploded.

His back wheels found traction and he backed up the driveway. Rod got out of the car and ran back into the garage to try to save his son's Mustang. It was already floating. He had no hope of saving it now. He swam around in two metres of water, trying to catch tools and car parts that were being swept away. The water rose another

1.5 metres and Rod realised it was too dangerous and gave up.

From her yard, Gayle Teal had seen the roof of Sylvia's house subsumed under the water. She was stunned, but pulled her mind back to her drowning horses. She had to save whatever life she could. The water had risen even higher in the few minutes she had been gone. She ventured back in and worked as fast as she could to save more of her horses, the water increasing in depth and speed each time she returned.

By the time she returned for the last horse, their prized stallion Hayil, a 15-year-old Group One winner at England's famous Royal Ascot Racecourse, Gayle was wading in chest-deep rushing water. 'My husband told me not to go back for the stallion. As I looked at Hayil, he looked around at the water and looked back at me. I had to at least open the gate so he had a chance to swim if the water got too deep. He was already shoulder-deep and he was at the highest point in the stable.'

Gayle climbed along the fence and down across the alleyway into deeper water to get his rearing bit. It was underwater, but she found the hook and it was still there. By the time she grabbed it, put it on him and returned to the gate, the water had risen to her shoulders and the stallion had to lift his nose to keep his head out of the water.

'I did think I was going to die at that point because the water was rising so fast and I knew the water would be over my head by then in the laneway,' Gayle said.

> I panicked. I stopped and took a couple of deep breaths. The horse waited for me. I realised that if I curled my arm around the top railing of the fence I could lead him out the gate. I opened the gate and gave him enough rein so he could swim if he felt frightened. He took tiny steps and followed me from the stable, out of the water and through a paddock of mares that we had to breed with him. He neighed once. I gave him a little nod with the rearing bit. I told him, 'Not now,' and he kept walking forward.

From the road, Rod Alford heard the chilling screams of two horses whinnying in terror, and as he turned to look he saw the horses struggling as they were swept downstream behind his house. He ran into the water and swam out far enough to grab one of the horses by the mane. He couldn't touch the ground but directed the horse towards shallower water. The horse's feet found the ground first, and carried Rod out of the water onto Sylvia's backyard.

As Kevin Lee lay gasping for air, his wife Eileen struggled to wade through the current in her waterlogged gumboots. She was crossing the fallen fence when her feet got tangled in the barbed wire. Brian Willmett and Clem ran back to her. Eileen was in the water. 'I just got there and caught her, otherwise she would have been gone,' Brian said. Brian and Clem dragged her through the water and put her down next to Kevin in the paddock.

The Lees' friends, David and Wendy Patterson, were also trying to get across the fence. Tim ran to help. 'I started pulling them across but the current swept them from my grasp.'

Wendy was swept away across the paddock into deeper water and hit against the heavy fence timbers at the corner of the paddock. 'Hitting the box stay saved her life. The top wooden rail held her. David went straight after her into deeper water to go to her,' Brian said. The fence was completely submerged. Brian quickly weighed up whether to risk going in to get them. He looked at the level of the water for half a minute. It had stopped rising. They would be alright.

'I could see they were not going to go any further so I was yelling at them to stay there. The water was so loud they could not hear a word I was saying so I was gesturing with my hands up giving them a "stop" sign and signalling to them to reach for the branches of the tree. They understood. They grabbed the branches of a silky oak tree above them.'

Hugh Sedger grabbed a post to prevent himself being swept away as he waded across the front paddock of their property with his dogs. He reached the safety of the road and joined some other local residents who had also fled their houses. They were shocked as they saw the floodwater rise up the Warhurst's house in a couple of minutes. The walls gave way and bowed outwards near the floor until only the roof was above the water. The house broke apart and the roof floated away. 'Everyone was crying. Everyone was watching Bruce Warhurst's house get ripped in half and getting taken down the river. Everyone was completely shocked,' Hugh said.

Two Queensland Fire and Rescue swift water rescue teams were driving through Postmans Ridge on their way to Murphys Creek to help locate two people who had been swept from a house. Technical rescue coordinator Nathan Chadwick heard on the UHF radio that there was a seven-metre wall of water coming down the Lockyer Valley, but he was still shocked when he heard the loud roar of the water and then saw the flood front. 'It was very similar to the footage you see of a tsunami, except those tsunamis seem to move a lot slower than this was moving. This was a wall of boiling, brown, highly aerated water moving huge shipping containers, water tanks, big gum trees like they were nothing. The ground was dry and then this wall would hit the ground and consume everything in its path.'

It was moving at 60 to 70 kilometres per hour and quickly rose to four metres over the road. The crew saw the water engulf houses along Postmans Ridge Road. Nathan and his colleague, senior technical rescue instructor and station officer Phil Paff, drove to a house that was in the firing line.

Nikki Hore and three children – her daughter Rebecca, 19, her son Cody, ten, and Cody's friend Bailey Neumann – were at home but didn't realise they were in danger. They were 500 metres downstream from the Warhurst's house. Nikki and her husband Nigel Hore had built the house in 2005, and no-one had warned that the small, dry creek behind their property might be a flood danger. Nikki had given the children some lunch, noticed her driveway was being flooded, and went to take photos.

'I was down at the creek. I turned and looked at the house and I could see Hegarty's house behind our place flooded up to the gutter,' she said. 'I was freaking out and watching it in amazement. I saw

Warhurst's swimming pool and a camping trailer going past. I looked back at the house and the boys were gathering up the chickens. I saw water was coming down the hill and ran to the house to get the boys inside. I saw the fire and rescue truck come into our driveway. They said, "People are dead. We need to get you out."'

As Phil spoke to Nikki he saw a house go past in the creek behind her. Nikki got lifejackets for the boys. 'It was at its worst when they first arrived. That's when the creek broke its banks.'

Phil Paff was already in his wetsuit. Nathan had no time to change from his overalls and boots. They raced to rescue the frightened children. 'I've never seen terror like that in my life. There was genuine fear in their eyes. Absolute sheer terror,' Nathan said. 'If we had waited for another 30 seconds it could have been too late. We had an inflatable boat on the roof of the truck. Phil swam across along the fence. He tied the rope off. I used the rope to swim across with the boat.'

Nathan then swam back to reposition the rope so the boat could be guided back across the creek. Phil got the boys in the boat and held onto the rope to prevent the boat from being swept away. They returned for Nikki and her daughter Rebecca.

Once they were out safely, Nikki phoned Bailey's mother to ask her to send her husband Jeff Neumann in the truck to take Bailey home. She and the children watched as the water continued rising. It came up to ten centimetres below the floorboards before it started going down again.

Rod Alford phoned his wife Wendy and told her Sylvia and her house was gone, and that he believed their house was going to go as well. He told her he was standing out the front on the road in the water and hoped he would be alive to see her later that night. Wendy told him, 'I'll try and get home as urgently as I can. It's flooding up in town, you wouldn't believe it.'

Everyone at that section of the road was trapped between Gatton Creek and Rocky Creek. They all stood on the highest point of the road, but even then the water was waist-deep.

About two kilometres downstream at his house, Scott French had released the dogs. But in those moments the water had risen so fast that now he and his father were trapped on their property. The only way to escape the water was to climb on to the roof of their house or shed. They could see the shed was taking the brunt of the force, so they decided they'd be safest on the roof of the house. 'I knew the extension ladder was behind the shed, so we got around there and found the ladder, dragged it to the house and climbed on the roof,' Garth said. He warned his son that if the house did get destroyed he should go with the flow of the water rather than trying to fight the current.

From the roof they saw the torrent tearing huge trees out of the creek. 'It was like thousands and thousands of rifles going off because the trees weren't just snapping in one instant. They'd creak and break and crack a thousand times before they gave in and fell over, and then you could hear them smashing and breaking under the water,' Garth said.

With time to think, Garth's mind turned to where the water was heading – to Grantham where his heavy vehicle mechanical workshop was on the highway, between Marty's service station and the convenience store. His phone had got wet. He tried to make a call but the screen was blank. It wasn't working. He couldn't contact the people in Grantham to tell them what was coming. Garth looked around. He felt helpless about the disaster unfolding around them but there was one thing they could do – clean out the gutters. Garth and his son worked their way around the house, grabbing handfuls of wet leaves and throwing them into the floodwater below.

Everyone who had seen Sylvia's house collapse immediately started looking for her along the creek, hoping they could rescue her. They found stunned animals and helped them from the water, but no sign of Sylvia.

Once the water went down a little, helicopter pilot Brian Willmett went back in to help Wendy Patterson up the paddock to higher ground. Her legs had been gashed by the barbed wire of the box stay, but she and her husband David had both survived. The next priority was to get oxygen for Kevin. The caravan that had been driven up to Brian's property moments before the flood hit had an oxygen bottle inside, and Kevin was stabilised.

Sylvia's friend Kelly Wilson at Murphys Creek was desperate to get someone to check on Sylvia. She asked her husband and her brother to go. They were gone for what seemed like a long time but when they returned, Sylvia's car was not with them. Sylvia was not with them. Kelly was very worried and the men told Kelly to sit down. She refused. They told her Sylvia's house was gone – and that Sylvia had been inside her house.

Bailey's father Jeff Neumann arrived in the truck with his bobcat on the back. Nikki and the children climbed in. As the fire crew turned the fire truck off the driveway to leave the property, it became bogged. Emergency calls were flowing in but the rescue team had no vehicle to be able to help anyone. Jeff unloaded his bobcat and tried to pull the truck out, but then the bobcat got bogged. He then tried to tow the truck out with a rope. The rope broke. They needed something stronger.

Nikki's husband had a crane sling in the shed, which had escaped the flood. Jeff attached the crane sling to his truck as a towrope, and pulled the fire truck out of the bog and onto the road. Nikki was relieved – the swift water rescuers, Nathan and Phil, would now be able to save more people.

Jeff, Nikki, the rescuers and the children all gathered at their front gate where QFRS had set up a command post, and while they were talking Jeff's phone rang. It was a mate in Murphys Creek asking him to help rescue a woman from the creek at Rick Luchich's place. Jeff and two of the rescuers set off for Murphys Creek.

Once the water receded enough for Nikki to go back to her house, she gathered food for the rescue crews and the children, who were all hungry. She packed clothes for her family, tied up their pets and took food back to the command post for the rescuers.

Debris was scattered along the creek and along the road. Hugh

Sedger went for a walk down the creek to survey the damage. Dead cows and horses were lying around, dozens of cars were mangled and lying in the creek and up trees, boats were cut in half, metal water tanks had been crushed, and injured animals were groaning in agony. Hugh saw a horse in the water screaming and gasping for air. 'The water was up to its head. Its legs were tangled in barbed wire. When it got out I saw it had half a leg missing.'

At Sylvia's place, all that remained of her house was the concrete slab and floor tiles where the bathroom had been, as well as a couple of rose bushes in her garden. At the Warhurst's place, the house was gone – even the stumps had been torn from the ground. Three concrete steps leading to the front door and the concrete floor of the garage were all that remained. Brian was missing but his family did not give up hope that he might be found alive.

As the QFRS rescue crew moved along the road checking on people in each house they counted six houses had been swept away. Eleven people were missing. They needed to provide shelter for the residents whose houses had been lost. They cut the lock on the local hall to let people in. Local residents brought food and drinks, clothes and bedding for the survivors.

Helidon

'There's a big yellow storm up on the range behind you. I'd advise evacuation.'

The district around Helidon is famous for the ancient sedimentary pink-and-white Triassic and Jurassic sandstone formed in the valley floor, as well as basalt and granite that have been quarried for more than a century. The sandstone is known worldwide as a fine building material and has been used for public buildings such as cathedrals and universities, as well as for commercial buildings.

The Helidon district is also widely known for the carbonated mineral springs, which emerge through fault lines in the Great Artesian Basin.

After flowing through Postmans Ridge, Gatton Creek runs east and joins Lockyer Creek, which then continues towards Helidon and converges with Murphy's Creek. About five kilometres north of the junction, Alice Creek also joins into Murphys Creek. Alice Creek drains a large mountainous catchment area from the ranges near Ravensbourne National Park, which greatly increases the flow in Murphys Creek.

As Lockyer Creek approaches the town of Helidon, it runs along the western edge and under the Warrego Highway, meeting with Sheepstation Creek 100 metres upstream of the bridge. As the creeks

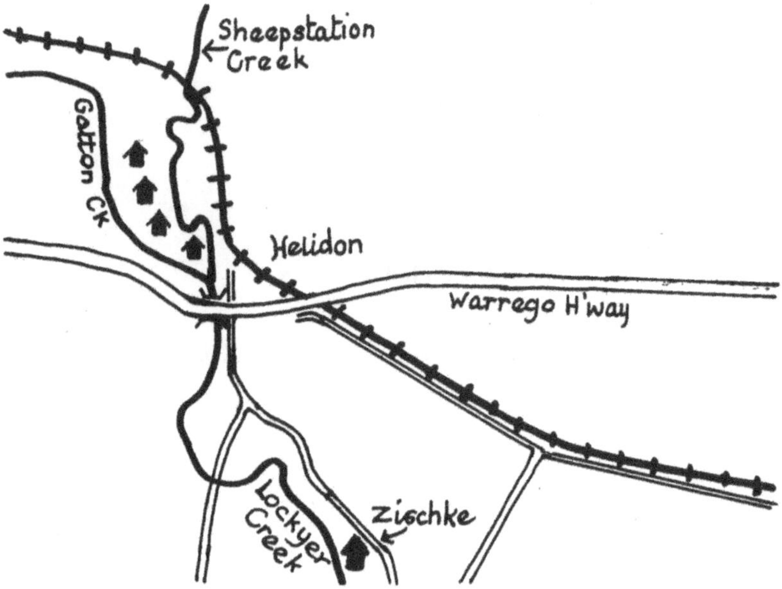

converge, several small acreage properties lie between them on Dip Road; they were all positioned well above the record 1974 flood level. The only regular localised flooding was of a park and rest area for travellers on the creek flat beside the highway.

David and Diana Colleson run a strawberry farm in Dip Road, taking advantage of the rich alluvial soil. Across the road are electrical lineman Lloyd Warr, a keen collector of antique chainsaws, his wife Jean, and their son Russell. Next door to the Warrs are Bendigo Bank employee Rick Emmerson, his wife Bronwyn, and their two daughters, final year Bachelor of Commerce student Angela, 19, and school student Rebecca, 16. Rick and Bronwyn Emmerson went to Toowoomba to work on 10 January, leaving their two teenage daughters, who were on holidays from university and school, at home watching movies and relaxing.

Lloyd Warr set off to Dalby where he worked as an electricity transmission tower builder, and his son Russell drove to Toowoomba to work at Allied Mills in the CBD. Lloyd reached the bottom of the Toowoomba Range and saw a sign saying that the road from Toowoomba to Dalby was closed. He would not be able to get to work. Lloyd turned around and headed home again. Once he arrived back in Helidon, he began mowing the lawn.

Looking at the storm cell on the Bureau's radar, amateur weather watcher Neil Pennell thought about phoning the Helidon police to warn them. He rehearsed in his mind what he would say: 'I'm looking at the radar on the internet. There's a big yellow storm up on the range behind you. I'd advise evacuation.' Neil picked up the phone to dial Helidon police. He hesitated. They would think he was crazy. He put the phone down again. Still concerned for people about to be struck by the storm, Neil asked on the online forum who should be told to get the message out.

Weather forum member Dave was also anxious. He posted at 1.49 pm: 'There is nothing really that we can do is there? This is why I wanted to see some sort of heads up for everyone in South East Queensland a few days ago, because it is hard to justify sounding the SEWS [Standard Emergency Warning Signal] just for that part of Lockyer Creek (for example) if they have no telemetry telling them just yet that there is a huge wall of water coming down the creek in that area.'

In Toowoomba, Rick Emmerson phoned his daughters Angela and Rebecca at about 2 pm to let the girls know his office in the Bendigo Bank in the Toowoomba CBD had been flooded. He asked the girls to check both creeks. Angela and Rebecca got dressed and walked to Lockyer Creek – it was two metres below the creek bank. They walked across to check Sheepstation Creek – it was also within its banks.

Call centre operator Kelly Zischke felt uneasy about the weather conditions in Toowoomba and left work early at 1.30 pm instead of 2 pm to return to her farm at Helidon beside Lockyer Creek, a kilometre downstream of the bridge. As she left Toowoomba, she crossed the intersection of Kitchener and James Streets, and saw that East Creek was level with the height of the road surface. There were no signs that the roads were closed. As she drove down the range, water was running down the side of the highway and across the road.

As she drove through Withcott the rain intensified. She stopped and phoned her husband Gavin, a pumping and irrigation mechanic. Gavin told her to try to get home.

She pressed on, crossing the bridge at Helidon. The creek was swollen but within the banks. When Kelly arrived home at their farm beside Lockyer Creek and walked to the creek with Gavin, it was still within its banks. Gavin expected he would be called out during the night to fix flooded water pumps along the creeks so he needed to get some rest while he could. He and Kelly went indoors.

Lloyd and Jean had lunch and went to check the levels in the creeks at about 2.30 pm. It wasn't raining. Suddenly, Sheepstation Creek began to flow over the causeway and then to overflow the creek banks and flood the strawberry farm. Lloyd kicked off his thongs and ran home ahead of Jean to release their parrots from large outdoor cages. Jean followed him, kicking off her shoes as she went, so she could run faster.

As Angela and Rebecca headed back to their house, they saw Lockyer Creek had broken its banks and was halfway up their backyard. 'I said to Bec, "Is that water?" She said, "No, it's just reflection off the grass." We got a bit closer and it *was* water and it was moving,' Angela said. 'We were super excited. We raced back inside and rang Dad and said, "Oh my God. Guess what! You'll never guess: there's water in the backyard!"'

Lloyd didn't have the keys to the birdcages. He ran inside. By the time Jean found them, it was too late to go back to release the parrots: water was already building up against the windows. Panic set in. Lloyd guessed the flood could not rise to more than a metre deep, so if they quickly moved things higher, they'd save most of their possessions.

It was still dry inside. Jean put their photo albums up higher. She unplugged the hard drive of her computer containing 30 years of family history research. Water was now coming in to the house. They were standing in ankle-deep water and Lloyd was worried that it was still rising fast. He didn't know when it would stop. They had to get out. Now.

He told his wife, 'I need you to get outside the house now.' Jean put the computer down and grabbed her handbag. Lloyd went to shut doors through the house. As he returned, the laundry door caved in. Jean told her husband she was terrified and Lloyd admitted he was too. Lloyd knew if they were caught in the house now they'd be trapped. They had to get outside fast. They could see more than a metre of water making their glass sliding doors bulge inwards. Lloyd told his wife, 'Grab your handbag and climb out the window.' He bashed on the flyscreen and pushed it out with his fists.

Jean climbed out and grabbed a verandah post, and Lloyd followed her. Jean shouted, 'What are we going to do now? We're going to drown!' Lloyd told her, 'No we're not. Hang onto the verandah posts and we'll float up to the roof.' Within a minute the water had floated them up until they were level with the gutter.

Angela and Rebecca saw their father's orchid nursery sheds washing away. Their father told them on the phone to stay inside. The girls put towels at the doorways to prevent water coming inside the house. Water began bubbling up through the wooden floors. The girls told their father the water was getting higher. He told them to get in the car and get away. Angela told him, 'Well, that's not an option – my car just washed down the driveway.' He then told them to get furniture, pile it up on the verandah and get on the roof. Angela told him there was a metre of gushing water out there and she wasn't going out. Then she said there was 30 centimetres of water inside the house. The phone went dead.

On the Warrego Highway, truck owner-driver Michael Woodham saw two trucks in front of him stop at the Helidon bridge in the left lane. The bridge was clear of water but the road on the western side of the bridge was a metre under water. Michael stopped his truck behind the other trucks. A white four-wheel drive and a bronze Mercedes Benz in the right lane continued over the bridge. In the four-wheel drive was Toowoomba Turf Club racing steward James Perry, who was driving home to Toowoomba with his wife Jenny Thorncraft, and their son Edwin (Teddy), nine.

They had driven past two teenagers desperately waving down traffic to try to stop them going across the bridge into the fast-flowing water on the other side. The two young men, Gavin Anderson and Anton Wilkinson, had been watching the flood from near the Helidon bridge when they saw the water rise so high that it began to cover the eastbound lanes of the highway. They realised it would be only a short time before all four lanes were submerged and drivers coming from the eastern side would have no warning that there was water flowing fast across the road. Traffic from the west had stopped so they were able to run across the bridge, jump a barrier fence, cross to the eastbound lanes and warn traffic.

They began waving frantically with both arms. Looking across the bridge, they could see all four lanes of the highway were already submerged. A truck and some cars ignored them. A white car went past them, slowed down and continued into the water. It stopped. The teenagers saw the driver crawl out the window and start waving, signalling for help. Gavin and Anton could see it was too dangerous for anyone to try to get to them. 'They were 45 metres out in the water. There was no way we would have made it out there, even with a rope on. The current was just too strong,' Gavin said. They kept watching and saw the driver climb back into the car.

Within a couple of minutes the force of the water had increased so much that it pushed the car off the highway. The car went underwater and popped up 150 to 200 metres away. As it floated across a paddock of young trees, truckie Michael Woodham radioed to trucks ahead of him to come back to help. Michael and the other drivers got out of their trucks. They could hear the roar of more water coming down the creek, so they ran back to their trucks and moved them further back from the bridge. Then they ran to the Mercedes, which had stalled in the water, and pushed it backwards up onto the bridge.

They were just in time: a huge surge of floodwater, estimated to be almost five metres high, came down the creek carrying trees, vehicles, house roofs and sections of buildings. 'It was like in movies when someone calls on the wrath of God and a wall of water comes,' Gavin said.

At their house between Lockyer Creek and Sheepstation Creek, Angela and Rebecca knew they would have to try to save themselves. They followed their father's last instruction. They took a TV cabinet and chairs but they couldn't hold them on the rails and lift themselves on to the roof. They gave up, letting the furniture float away, and instead went back inside to try to get their cats. They closed the doors in an attempt to keep the water out of the house. 'I thought we were going to die,' Angela said. 'Bec told me, "Calm down. You're older. You have to work out what to do." We tried sitting on our beds. Our beds started to float.'

Realising they would have to try again to get on the roof, but not knowing how long they would be up there, they decided to get some water and food supplies. They took a bottle of water and a sealed packet of crackers, as well as one of the cats, and put them all in a large plastic storage crate. The water was already so high they did not have time to get the other cat. They had to get outside.

The back door of the house had shattered. Inside the house, the water was now more than a metre and a half deep. With the water pressure inside and outside equalised, the girls were able to open a glass sliding door. As they left the house, Angela and Rebecca adopted Plan A: to get to the roof. If that failed and either of them was swept away, Plan B was to grab on to one of the many trees surrounding the property.

They climbed on to the verandah railing, which was by then underwater, and held on to the gutter for support. From there they saw their neighbours, Lloyd and Jean, on the roof of their house and waved to them.

The girls threw the food and water on the roof and lifted the cat from the floating plastic crate so it could climb up. The girls tried but could not lift themselves onto the roof so they decided to walk around the house on the verandah railing to get out of the direct flow of the current. Halfway along the house, Angela lost her footing. She had reached the front steps. Holding the gutter and kicking her way across, she then shouted back to her sister, 'Bec, just be careful, the stairs are here. Bec said, "What did you say?" just as she took the step and she almost fell in the water,' Angela said.

A Queensland Fire and Rescue Special Operations Unit truck arrived at the bridge, which was by then submerged by the rushing torrent. Officer Brad Mills and firefighter and rescue technician Andrew Neil had been dispatched to rescue Rez Huq and his colleagues who were isolated at the Tyco pumping and irrigation factory at Withcott. As the rescue crew drove west from Brisbane with their lights and sirens activated, Andrew and Brad switched their radio frequency from the Brisbane channel to the Ipswich channel. They were both highly trained for swift water rescues, urban search and rescues, vertical rescues, trench rescues and confined space rescues. As they approached Helidon they heard a call over the Firecom radio that a car had been swept off the road near the bridge at Helidon.

James Perry phoned triple zero at 3.12 pm but the call dropped out. He tried again two minutes later and this time the call was transferred to the Brisbane police communications room. James asked for urgent help, saying he could see a QFRS vehicle but no-one was coming to save them.

Channel 7 reporter Erin Edwards was in a news helicopter overhead. The crew had filmed Murphys Creek raging down the escarpment, converging with Lockyer Creek and now flooding the western edge of Helidon. She saw a blob of white in the vast expanse of floodwater and debris. Could it be a car? The helicopter descended to get a closer look. They saw three people sitting in the car waving.

The people, James Perry, his wife Jenny Thorncraft and their son Teddy, climbed onto the roof of the car and held onto the roof rack. The car floated slowly along in a paddock of young trees. Michael Woodham watched as the car drifted into the main stream of the creek. 'I saw them sitting on the roof of the vehicle huddled up. Powerlines were crackling above us.'

Hundreds of people, including local residents and dozens of stranded motorists, had gathered to see the spectacle of the creek in full flood. Michael saw the white floating car with the people on top heading for the bridge over Back Flagstone Creek. He was very worried and wanted to keep an eye on them. 'I could see the powerlines flicking into the water and splashing. We jumped in a car and went to Zischke's until the helicopter came to pick them up. We couldn't rescue them. The water was too dangerous.'

Kelly and Gavin Zischke were alerted to the flood when neighbours knocked at the door. The creek had risen several metres and was threatening their shed. Gavin ran to it and tried to start the tractor. The battery was flat. Kelly could see the water rising around the shed and she yelled for him to come out. Gavin waded out and Kelly saw their dogs swimming in their fenced yard. She shouted for Gavin to let the dogs out.

The first surge that went down the creek was like big crashing waves, then it filled up backwards and rose up. A helicopter landed opposite their property, on a small island with trees.

As Andrew and Brad arrived at the scene, the bridge was completely underwater and Lockyer Creek was flowing a kilometre wide. Lockyer Creek gauge shot past the major flood level of eight metres, and sent its final reading of 12.74 metres to the Bureau at 2.53 pm. The flow gauge measured 3,000 cubic metres of water per second flowing down the creek, augmented downstream of the bridge by another 1,000 cubic metres per second from Monkey Waterholes Creek. The water continued rising and destroyed the gauge. The debris left behind showed the water level had risen to 13.88 metres at about 3.10 pm.

Brad went to the water's edge to do a situation report while Andrew started to pack equipment they might need. Brad called Andrew to the water's edge. The car was a kilometre downstream. 'The people on the car weren't in the full force of the current but they were on the other side of the river from us. We realised there was nothing we could do from where we were.'

Andrew and Brad had to think quickly. They had lifejackets, but no way to reach the stranded car. The only helicopter in the air was a media machine with no winch. Andrew Neil, who has 30 years' experience in surf rescue, volunteered to be dropped from the helicopter without a winch, into the floodwater next to the car, taking three lifejackets with him for the people on the car. It was a risky option but they would try.

Local fire and rescue officers had set up an incident control centre near the bridge. The officer tried to contact the media helicopter hoping it would be tuned to the Firecom channel. Channel 7 pilot Greg Rogers answered the call from Firecom – he was on their channel. Andrew and Brad quickly got prepared. They changed into wetsuits, helmets, booties and gloves, and took a throw bag and rope. Brad and Andrew climbed into the helicopter and were lifted into the air.

Andrew Gurr was among the crowd that had gathered near the bridge. He had never seen the creek so high. Once he realised the water was heading for Grantham, he became concerned for his elderly mother Jean, 88, who found it difficult to move around. He knew she would be sitting in her lounge room watching television, unaware of the looming danger. Andrew tried to phone her but there was no answer. He drove towards Grantham but was stopped at a police roadblock and had to turn back. He returned home and phoned triple zero. He gave his mother's name and address, and explained she would need help.

James, Jenny and Teddy held on to the roof rack on either side of the car as the vehicle drifted through a plantation of young trees. As they went downstream, the water level was so high that an overhead powerline was dipping into the water. The family had to move on the roof to get themselves lower so the dangling powerline would not touch them.

As the white car slowly floated towards the main creek channel, the water became rough and Jenny could see thick high-voltage powerlines in the water. Jenny and James decided they must jump from the car and dive under the powerlines.

When Jenny surfaced, she said she 'looked around again and saw that James had hold of the vehicle and had Teddy between him and the car. I made eye contact with James and then had to dive deep as there were more powerlines in front of me and I didn't want to be electrocuted by them. That was the last time I saw James.'

As she surfaced a second time, Jenny was carried along very fast by the current and was struck by waves. 'I got dragged under a number of times and made sure that I was facing away so that I didn't get slapped in the face with waves. I was out of control for a while and then calmed down and decided that I had to swim across the current but not too fast as I did not want to exhaust myself.'

Although she did not know how fast she was moving, Jenny saw people on the banks of the creek running to keep up with her. She needed to grab onto something. 'I saw a tree sticking out of the water so I thought I would line myself up with it and try and grab it,' she said. 'I hit the tree really hard and got knocked a bit silly. I then went under and thought, "I'm not coming up again." But she did resurface and decided that rather than try to grab a tree, she would try to get caught up in branches. As she neared another tree, she was swept through the branches and slowed down enough to grab onto a branch and pull herself up. 'I remember that the water was travelling over my face and I just held on as I knew that it was my last chance.' She had been swept 1.8 kilometres downstream from the highway.

From the air, Brad and Andrew could not see the car. 'We saw nothing. They were gone. The car was gone. The people were gone,' Andrew said. 'We thought hopefully we could spot them in the water. We started searching, a low-level search down the river for a couple of kilometres. As we were coming back, I spotted her in the trees, clinging to a small bunch of trees.'

At Lloyd and Jean's house, the water rose high enough for them to reach the gutter. Lloyd grabbed it and told Jean to hold on, too. When she did they both received an electric shock. Jean let go with both hands and started to float away. Lloyd grabbed her and told her to hold the wooden facia board under the gutter. Lloyd knew what to do. As a linesman, he had had many electric shocks. 'I knew the power to the house would have to go off soon. I kept touching the gutter and getting more shocks until the power was off.'

Once it was safe, he climbed on to the roof. Jean tried to lift herself up on to the roof too, but one arm was trapped under her body. She got back in the water and put both arms in the air, and Lloyd lifted her onto the roof.

Angela and Rebecca continued walking along the submerged verandah rail towards the garage at the far end of the house. They decided to try to get on to the roof by climbing a steel-framed breezeway between the house and the garage, but they couldn't lift themselves onto it. The surface of the water was, by then, level with the roof of the garage. Holding onto a strong vine that was growing on the breezeway frame, they swam to the garage roof, rolled onto it and climbed back across the breezeway and finally got on to the roof of the house. Once there, they saw their furniture and other goods floating away. 'There was nothing we were going to be able to do about what we were losing. We were thinking about things that we were happy we were losing because we didn't want to be sad while we were sitting on the roof,' Angela said. Finally the water seemed to stabilise. It had risen to just below the gutters.

Terrified of heights, Jean sat near the gutter. She saw her husband's shed implode. His collection of hundreds of antique chainsaws was gone. She saw their caravan float away but then it snagged behind a clump of bamboo. The water continued to rise and she had to move further up on to the roof. Lloyd's priority was to find things that would float, in case the water came higher and they had to leave the roof. 'I didn't know where it was going to stop,' he said. 'I got a dining room chair, a plastic chemical drum and a cupboard to help us float. I tried to get some polythene pipe and a couple of hoses to tie the other things together, but missed them as they gushed past in the floodwater.'

Jean looked at the water. 'It was running fast. It was like soup. I didn't know whether I had the strength to survive if we did have to get off the roof.' Lloyd and Jean agreed to try to swim to the canopy of a large pecan nut tree if they were swept off the roof. With their plans made, Lloyd sat beside his wife. He told her, 'I can feel people are dying.' He had never felt this before. 'I could feel it in my body. It was frightening. I just knew that other people were dying.'

Jean knew he was right. Jean asked her husband if they were going to die. He told her, 'Not if I can help it.'

The flood was at its highest point as the news helicopter with the rescuers on board started low-level searching down the river and spotted Jenny clinging to a tree. The helicopter was running low on fuel, but Andrew and Brad could not leave her there. They had to try to reach her. They saw a small island of land in the flow of the floodwater. It was 4 pm when the helicopter dropped them on the island, a knoll with large trees on it, and left immediately to refuel. Andrew and Brad could see the woman. She was still clinging on. They assessed how they could safely get to her.

They tied a rope to one of the trees on the island. Andrew was the stronger swimmer of the two and he swam to a position downstream of Jenny in case she let go of the tree. Brad assessed their options and decided there was a chance they could get to her. Andrew swam back to shore and the two men set off to swim to Jenny.

She was upstream of them, but they approached her by going downstream and crossing the current, over to where they could see a back eddy of water that was flowing to where Jenny was hanging on 50 metres upstream. 'She could see us coming. We yelled to her and she said she could hang on. She was devastated, crying,' Andrew said. Jenny told them what colour clothes James and Teddy were wearing, and where she had last seen them. The rescuers radioed the information back to searchers who were working their way along the side of Lockyer Creek. The water level was beginning to fall and an island started to form upstream of the trees where Jenny was clinging on. Andrew set off swimming towards her. He put a lifejacket on her and swam back with her to higher ground, while Brad searched for Jenny's husband and son and used his waterproof radio to call for a helicopter to collect them. A New South Wales Rural Fire Service helicopter on standby at the Gold Coast was dispatched.

After three hours the water level stabilised and started to fall.

Lloyd Warr watched it recede down the house and off their yard. In half an hour it was gone. Lloyd climbed off the roof. He walked around the house. Inside, all the ceilings had fallen in and silt and debris were a metre deep inside the house and around the outside of the house. He found his large fibreglass esky. He saw a teddy bear and picked it up. He needed to save whatever could be saved – even if it was only a teddy bear. 'I put him in the esky. The poor little fellow wanted saving.'

He found a dining table and moved it close to the house. He asked Jean to get the chair off the roof and slide it down, and Lloyd then put it on the table. Jean sat near the edge of the roof and wiggled down to the gutter, felt with her feet for the back of the chair and slowly lowered herself onto the chair. She stepped down on to the table and on to the ground. Lloyd told her, 'Don't look back in the house. Don't look around. We'll just walk out.'

Lloyd held her hand, and with the other he dragged the esky with the teddy bear inside. The couple walked across the bridge over Sheepstation Creek to the crowd of people near the pub who had been watching the flood.

The Zischkes were amazed by how quickly the flooding subsided. 'It went down a lot quicker than it took to rise. It was like someone had pulled the plug from a bath and it was just sucked away. It went down within ten minutes,' Kelly said.

Volunteer New South Wales rural firefighter Kendall Thompson was on standby at Coolangatta. He was assigned to a crew that was being put together to relieve exhausted local helicopter rescue crews. There was also Ned Lee, a pilot from New Zealand, a crewman Kris Larkin, also from New Zealand, and a pilot from Sydney, Matt O'Brien, to fly as co-pilot. The crew met just after midday and began removing fire-bombing equipment from the helicopter to prepare the aircraft for swift water rescues. The team decided to practise a winch rescue at the beach while they waited to be assigned rescue tasks. Kendall had never performed a winch rescue but he had been winched from a helicopter into fire zones with equipment to fight fires. Before they began their practice rescue, a call came in for them to urgently fly to Helidon.

When they reached the town they found Andrew Neil and Brad Mills with Jenny Thorncraft, picked them up from their island and flew them all to the Warrego Highway. Ambulance officers attended to Jenny's injuries and a woman from the fire brigade wiped her dry. Jenny thought that she had lost both Teddy and James.

Brad and Andrew went with the New South Wales helicopter to continue searching for James and Teddy. While they were in the air, they were asked to check a report that a second wall of water was on its way down the creek system. They quickly surveyed the creeks and found the report was unfounded. By then the New South Wales helicopter had to fly to Toowoomba to refuel. The helicopter dropped Brad and Andrew off in Grantham to lighten their load so that the aircraft could carry more flood survivors.

Once the water receded, family friend Malinda Schulz discovered Angela and Rebecca stranded on the roof. Malinda found a ladder among the debris and helped them down. The girls walked through mud up to their thighs. Angela began to go into shock, shaking and crying with relief that they had survived. They were taken to Malinda's home and had warm showers and phoned their mother. Angela took the phone and only managed to say, 'Mummy!' before she burst into tears.

Malinda took the phone from Angela and told Bronwyn Emmerson that she thought they had lost everything. Bronwyn replied, 'No, we haven't lost everything. We still have our girls.'

Lloyd Warr's first priority was to find somewhere he and his wife could have a shower. 'We stunk. It's not a smell that you can describe – a dirty, muddy mix of manure and sewerage. It was a bad smell.' Their next problem was having no underwear. Clothes had been donated but there was no underwear. 'Mixing with all these other people, you feel only half dressed.'

Malinda went to the evacuation centre that was being set up at the Helidon RSL hall. Angela and Rebecca went with her and spent four hours in the kitchen making sandwiches for flood survivors coming in.

Andrew Gurr went out in his car again and tried to get to Grantham to find his mother Jean, but the roads were still blocked so he had to return home. Three hours had passed and still there was no news from the police, and no phone call from his mother to say she was alright.

By evening, he was very anxious. His mind replayed their last conversation, when his mother told him how the Bluecare bus she was travelling in had stalled in floodwaters at Grantham and had to be towed out. She was worried about being flooded. Andrew had assured her there was nothing to worry about: she'd be perfectly safe in her home. Now he felt guilty. His mother had moved from Western Australia in 1990 to be near her children and grandchildren, but she was most comfortable at her own house. Andrew realised she should have been with his family. But, he rationalised, she was always happier in her own home. He had to keep searching.

Andrew went out again, this time to the evacuation centre in Helidon. There he found a police officer and saw dozens of people arriving from Grantham. 'I realised something really bad had happened. There were so many people there but no-one had contacted me. I had hope that she would be found, but I was feeling very ill.' After a sleepless night, Andrew returned to the evacuation centre several times the next day but there was still no sign of his mother and no-one had news of her.

Weather watcher Neil Pennell saw the news that evening. The footage from Toowoomba told him a lot of people had died. He posted again to the Weatherzone forum at 10.08 pm, lamenting that he should have acted on his gut instinct earlier in the day and phoned the police in Helidon. 'It's not hard to imagine what the response would've been. When I saw the plot of the creek height a little while later I felt ill. Maybe I should've called anyway. I might have felt a bit better now. All I know is those people clinging to the roof of that car deserved a better warning than the one they got today. I fear what tomorrow's news will tell us about today's events.'

Carpendale

'We're really busy. We can't come to you.'

Between Helidon and Grantham is the district of Carpendale, a flat patchwork of large vegetable farms growing a profusion of lettuce, broccoli, cauliflower, potatoes, onions and other vegetables in straighter-than-straight rows that line up for an instant as you drive past. The topsoil here is metres thick – a rich, volcanic loam highly prized by market garden farmers who have ploughed, sowed and reaped several crops each year for generations.

Underground aquifers hold a vast water resource, which is tapped by hundreds of bores drilled into the sandstone and basalt rocks beneath the valley. The bores pump water to the thirsty crops above, supplementing the irregular flows in the surface water through a network of creeks flowing from the Great Dividing Range on their way to the east coast.

As Lockyer Creek sets out on its ten-kilometre journey from Helidon to Grantham, the creek channel bends in a semicircle just downstream of the Helidon bridge. Monkey Waterholes Creek flows into Lockyer Creek, which continues almost straight for five kilometres. To the north of the creek is an expansive floodplain, while to the south of the creekline the landscape rises towards the foothills of Mount Whitestone.

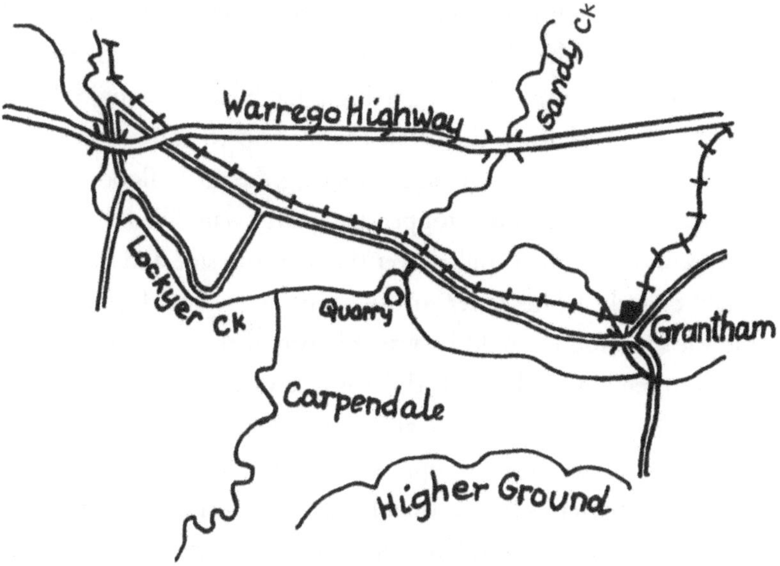

Just over two kilometres upstream of the town of Grantham, the creek channel makes a tight left semicircle before retracing its course and passing a kilometre south of Grantham. The semicircular bend curves around what once was a low-lying creek pocket that flooded regularly during the summer rainy season. The pocket of productive farmland grew potatoes, melons and other crops for decades. In the record flood of 1974, floodwater flowed across the pocket and continued down the creek past Grantham and slowly backed up Sandy Creek, gradually inundating houses in Harris Street, the lowest part of the town, as well as some homes bordering Sandy Creek.

During the 1980s, miners began extracting loam, sand and gravel from the creek pocket. Successive miners operating the quarry gradually built up an earthen wall to prevent minor floods in the creek from pouring into the open cut sand quarry and destroying excavation machinery. From the mid-2000s, the wall was built up even further until it was higher than the northern bank of the creek. Landholders grew concerned that if there was ever a major flood their properties would be in danger, instead of the main flow following the creek bed as it had always done.

Local resident John Gallagher wrote to the council about five years earlier informing the chief executive officer that the earthen bank around the quarry was becoming so high that he feared a major flood would be diverted from the creek channel on to agricultural land that was dotted with hobby farms. During the 1996 flood, he had seen that the floodwater overtopped the quarry wall, filled the central pit in seconds and then spilled over the opposite side and flowed on down the creek. In his letter to the council he warned that people could die and houses could be washed away if the earthen wall was allowed to remain in place. He did not receive a reply to his letter.

Landholders opposite the quarry also grew anxious. Tom Friend saw the low pocket on the opposite bank of the creek gradually become several metres higher than his property on the high bank of the creek – it threatened his house and the hobby farm where he keeps cows and a menagerie of smaller animals: pigs, ducks and chickens. Tom had farmed the low pocket years before, growing lucerne, and he knew it was a floodway. The farming flat, once four metres below the bank of the creek, was now up to five and a half metres above the bank. When Tom walked across his paddock he could look back towards the quarry and see that if there was a major flood that rose above the creek channel, it would flood his property.

On several occasions he spoke to the on-site manager about the risk to his property. In the major 1974 flood, he had seen the water level reach as high as the gate of the quarry at the top of the creek bank, but it did not flow across his land. It would take a flood of major proportions to cause a problem – he didn't think it would happen, but if it ever did his property would be directly affected.

Next door to Tom Friend, on Quarry Access Road, electrical contractor Jonathan Sippel was becoming concerned about the risk of flooding. On Boxing Day he was worried when he saw Lockyer Creek rise until it was only 1.5 metres below Kapernick's Bridge, a kilometre upstream of the quarry. He phoned local councillor Peter Friend, Tom's brother, and asked him if there was a risk of flooding at his property. Peter Friend drove to the quarry and met Jonathan there, showing him the sign on the quarry gate that marked the height of the 1974 flood. Jonathan was calmed. His property was well above the record 1974 level.

On 5 January Jonathan and his wife Annaka took their children, Henry, three, and Ned, nine months, for a holiday to the beach. A fortnight's rest would do them all good. The day after they arrived they heard a weather forecast for 300 millimetres of rain in south-east Queensland for the following weekend. Jonathan had a gut feeling roads would be cut by floodwater unless they went before the rain started. They packed up the next morning and headed home. During the weekend Jonathan kept monitoring the creek, walking across a few times each day to see how high it was flowing up the banks.

The ground underfoot at Jonathan and Annaka Sippel's property was soggy. They drove to Toowoomba the next day, 10 January, to buy gumboots for themselves. They returned home for lunch, put their boys to bed for their afternoon sleep, and relaxed together watching a movie.

Across the road from Tom Friend's house, retired couple Graham and Helen Besley were in their farm office, putting the finishing touches to a new webpage when the power was cut. It wasn't raining so they decided to go for a walk.

Adjoining the quarry and immediately upstream is the farm Tony McIntosh rents from his cousin, an irrigated property relying on water from a weir in the creek. Looking across his paddocks towards the creek just after 2 pm, Tony could see the water level near the top of the banks and hear the rush of the water. By 2.25 pm the creek was level with the top of the banks, and the water was turbulent as it rose higher and surges rolled over the surface.

On Gatton Helidon Road, traffic was moving normally. Grantham resident John Mahon, who had run local butcher shops for 35 years, was on his way from Helidon to Grantham between 2 pm and 2.30 pm when he saw Lockyer Creek banking up, upstream of the quarry. He could see water above the creek banks and a large amount of debris and logs that appeared to be above ground level and staying still. He drove two kilometres to his house and looked south towards Lockyer Creek. He could not see any debris or even water in creek.

By 2.30 pm the floodwater upstream of the quarry was hitting the 380-metre-long western wall of the quarry and flowing backwards across Tony McIntosh's paddocks beside the creek. Tony felt a shudder through the ground, as the root ball of a large tree that was spearing down the creek hit the weir wall so hard that the tree, complete with branches and leaves, stood on end briefly before crashing over the weir.

Opposite the quarry, Graham Besley walked towards the creek, saw it rising fast up the ten-metre-high creek banks, and called to his wife to look. Graham decided they should evacuate. Helen walked home and quickly packed a tin containing their passports, birth and marriage certificates and put them in a basket. She sent a SMS text to her daughter at 2.35 pm saying, 'Pray for us. The water's rising fast.' She added their wallets and medications to the basket as Graham rushed in the door shouting to her, 'We have to get out *now*!'

Jonathan and Annaka Sippel were alerted to the approaching flood by a farmer near Kapernick's Bridge, who phoned Jonathan to tell him Lockyer Creek had risen suddenly and was half a metre below the bridge. Jonathan swore. This meant the creek could come a metre and a half over his farm. His house and his neighbours' houses and animals were all in trouble now.

Jonathan phoned his neighbour Tom Friend, who was away on holidays, to tell him the news and that he would open the gates to let out his cows. Jonathan ran outside and saw water pouring over part of the wall around the quarry. They had to get out.

He shouted to his wife to take their children immediately and drive them 100 metres to Gatton Helidon Road. Jonathan jumped the fence into one of Tom's paddocks to open the gate for the cows. Annaka hastily packed baby food, nappies and clothes for the children, and an overnight bag for themselves. As he jumped the fence,

Jonathan landed in half a metre of fast-flowing water. He opened the gate, jumped back over the fence, and ran to his work ute. Annaka was shaking with fear. She had to get her two boys to safety. She saw one, instantly grabbed him and ran down the few steps from her front door to the ground, stepping into half a metre of rushing water. She waded as fast as she could to the car. Looking towards the quarry, she could see floodwater gushing over the wall. It was eating the wall away – a brown, thick, raging torrent. She buckled the child into his car seat and ran back inside for her other son. She lifted him from his bed, clasped him to her chest and waded as fast as she could back to the car.

At Besley's place, the water was already in the house and swirling around Helen's feet. She ran with Graham to the car and they backed out. It was about 2.40 pm when Helen dialled triple zero and told the operator they were in floodwater. The operator told her, 'We're really busy. We can't come to you.' Helen told him, 'We'll probably drown then, but we're from Quarry Access Road at Grantham. Our names are Graham and Helen Besley.' The operator said they had no-one left to send but that he would talk to her for as long as he could.

Jonathan Sippel tried to drive his work ute to safety but it got bogged. He abandoned it and ran to another car. It started. He drove to the highway where Annaka had already gone with their children. Only a small section of highway was above water and they headed for that.

At the Besley's place, a wave of floodwater flowed up the bonnet of the car and over the roof. Helen believed they would die. She told the triple zero operator, 'A great big wall of water just went over the car. We're climbing out of the car.' As the crest of the first wave passed, the water level retreated to their car windowsills. Their electric windows worked so they put them down and stood on the armrests inside the doors.

By 2.44 pm the water travelling backwards up the creek at Tony McIntosh's farm had risen by several metres, and was covering his lower paddocks and creeping towards the house. As he looked across the creek, it was now flowing at least 1.5 kilometres wide and covering higher paddocks on the other side of the creek. His own driveway was already cut off and the water was beginning to flow into the lower storey of his house. The water level had passed the old tree in the front yard, which marked the level of Queensland's worst flood on record in 1893. At his farm, the major 1974 flood had not come as high as the 1893 flood but this was now surpassing it and writing a new record. Within ten minutes, the huge expanse of water had risen by another metre and was rising inside the house.

Graham Besley had a coil of rope and he threw it across the top of the car so he and his wife could each hold on to one side of it. As the water got deeper they stepped up from the armrests to the window-sills, still holding on to the coil of rope. Another wave of water hit the car and flowed over the top. They were soaked but they managed to stay on the car by hanging on to the rope.

More waves came, about a minute apart, for about 20 minutes. These lifted the car off the ground and carried it off the driveway, through a line of palm trees, over a barbed-wire fence and into a paddock. The triple zero operator encouraged them, telling them, 'You'll be okay. You're doing so well.' He encouraged them to keep holding on.

On the highway, Jonathan and Annaka and their children were just out of the water but with the level still rising, they had to move the cars further along the road. Their neighbours, Neville Mallon and his wife Charmaine, were also on the highway with their cars. Jonathan wanted to try to get his electrical tools from his work ute, which meant he would have to wade back home. He was not sure if he would make it back. He told his wife, 'If I don't come back, move the car further up the road.' Neville also waded back to his property to try to save his tractor.

By about 3 pm Lockyer Creek was flowing over Kapernick's Bridge. At Tony McIntosh's farm the water level peaked within a metre of the second-storey floor of his house, eclipsing the record 1893 flood by 1.5 metres. Then, all of a sudden, it began to drop. He needed to warn people.

Tony phoned local farmer Derek Schulz at 3.16 pm, because Tony knew farm workers could be in the paddocks and that they would be in danger if the creek broke its banks. Derek was away on holidays and initially suspected Tony was drunk, but Derek phoned another local farmer who confirmed Tony's account. Derek then phoned his workers to warn them to leave the paddocks and go home, stopping to warn people at Grantham on their way. Tony phoned Gatton police at 3.22 pm to tell them there was a huge amount of water flowing down the creek and urge them to evacuate people from Grantham. The police told him they were very busy, with the heavy rain flooding roads and houses.

Across the creek, a farmer who noticed the creek rapidly rising phoned a woman in Grantham who was looking after his three young children, aged seven, five and three. Alerted by his call, Wendy Hodda hurriedly got a ladder from the garage to put her own young son and the three children on the roof. Wendy's elderly Dutch-born mother Regina could not climb a ladder, so Wendy placed a chair on the kitchen table and helped her up. When the old woman sat on the table Wendy told her, 'Mum, I really want you to go up there, onto the chair.' The old lady did not want to go any higher. 'Wendy, this is far enough. If the water gets any higher than this, I'll swim.'

As Wendy looked out through the window towards the wooden picket front gate, it burst open and the muddy torrent swept through. Wendy hurried outside, closing the door behind her, and climbed the ladder as fast as she could with the youngest child in her arms. After five minutes the torrent was at least three metres deep. It would be a miracle if her mother survived. All she could do now was pray.

Graham and Helen could see helicopters, and Helen asked the operator when they would pick them up. The operator told them, 'They're really busy taking people off roofs. We will get to you.' Helen and Graham looked around and saw the farm greenhouses collapsing, one after another, like dominoes falling over. They were becoming exhausted. They prayed the Lord's Prayer and told each other 'I love you'.

Reaching his house, Jonathan found their puppy trapped in his pen, and lifted him out. He ran to his ute and tried to start the engine again. Water was over the wheels. The engine would not start. He heard a loud, crashing noise and a tremendous roar of water that continued for 15 seconds, as the earthen wall along the western side of the quarry crumbled. Trees, tanks and debris that had banked up now suddenly rushed down the creek and the water around his legs was suddenly pulled away. He saw Neville's tractor sucked sideways by the force into some trees, and he left his work ute and waded back towards the highway. There was just enough room on the road for their four cars to park end to end. They were all surrounded by water.

Downstream of the quarry wall, a wave of floodwater knocked Graham and Helen Besley off the roof of their car. The phone was washed away. Once she was swept off the car, Helen Besley swam towards the wreckage of the greenhouses. From there she saw Graham tumbling head over heels in the current. He couldn't swim. The current ripped his shorts off. As Helen saw him being swept past the greenhouses towards open fields, she became frantic. She screamed, 'God save him!' Helen saw the farm's cool rooms, machinery shed and machinery all swept away.

As he was carried along, Graham was swept out of the main current. Although he couldn't swim, he knew how to float, so he rolled onto his back. He closed his eyes and said a brief prayer, thinking he would drown. He stopped struggling. Helen lost sight of him. She climbed higher in the wreckage as the water rose. She saw the side wall and the front wall of their house collapse. Almost all the furniture was then swept from the house. The tin containing their birth and marriage certificates floated past. A mattress floated from the house with one of the quilts Helen had made still spread neatly over it.

The torrent flowed through Besley's farm and then through John and Noreen Gallagher's farm, where it lifted a 2.5 tonne grain feeder and swept it 800 metres towards the creek. Graham floated for several minutes, expecting to die at any moment. When he dared to open his eyes he saw Helen clinging to the wreckage. His floating body had been carried in almost a full circle, around the greenhouses and nearly back to where he had fallen off the car. Helen shouted to him to hold on to the wreckage and climb higher. Graham was exhausted but he held on and managed to climb high enough to be out of the water. Helicopters were still flying overhead. Graham and Helen waved and yelled, 'Over here! Over here! Come and get us!' but they realised they were so covered with black mud that the helicopter crews would not be able to see them.

After 20 minutes of searching the flooded creek in a grid pattern for James and Teddy Perry, volunteer firefighter Kendall Thompson and his helicopter rescue team spotted something on top of a cattle feeder in a wide expanse of water. Descending for a closer look, they saw a small boy. He was badly injured, but alive. He had been carried 6.3 kilometres down Lockyer Creek.

Kendall was winched down to the cattle feeder, where Teddy was scarcely 30 centimetres above the floodwater. Kendall put a harness around Teddy and held him as the winch operator Kris Larkin lifted them into the helicopter. They had no paramedic with them, so Kendall and the winch operator bandaged the boy's legs. One of his legs was bleeding so profusely that Kendall had to put a second bandage on and apply pressure to his wounds to slow the bleeding. The helicopter flew him to the Warrego Highway, where he was placed in an ambulance. His mother Jenny, who had been rescued near Helidon, was in the care of police, also on the highway. The driver of the police car was asked to stop and wait for an ambulance. Jenny told the police she didn't need an ambulance, but the police officer waited anyway. Jenny described what happened next: 'The ambulance then pulled up and a man with a uniform of some type asked me if my son was Teddy Perry. I told him it was and he told me that he was in the back of the car. I then went to the rear of the car and saw Teddy sitting up.'

On the highway, Jonathan and Annaka Sippel saw the floodwater drain away from the road and from their property. In 15 minutes the water was gone. They returned to their house. Annaka sat in the back tray of the ute holding their dogs and looking towards the creek. Jonathan told her, 'Watch the creek. If it comes up, yell, and we'll get out of here.'

Annaka was in panic mode, hoping the still-roaring creek would not come up above the banks again. Jonathan went inside their house to get whatever he could salvage. Thick, slippery mud covered everything below the flood level. It was a mess. Above the flood line, the house was incongruously normal. His cup of tea and biscuit were untouched on the bench where he had left them only about an hour earlier.

Jonathan gathered together baby food and clothes that escaped the floodwater and took them to the car. He drove his family back out to the highway and turned into Flagstone Creek Road, crossed Kapernick's Bridge and headed for higher ground to stay with relatives at Flagstone Creek. At Kapernick's Bridge, the torrent in Lockyer Creek had receded into the creek banks. They crossed over, driving over vegetation and debris.

In the greenhouse wreckage, Graham and Helen clung on for two hours. As the water level receded, they were able to lower themselves down the greenhouse frames and once it seemed shallow enough for them to stand up they made it to the ground. Climbing over mounds of plastic sheeting and debris trapped in the greenhouse wreckage, they walked along Quarry Access Road towards Gatton Helidon Road, and waved down a passing car. Two men saw them and ran and helped them back to the car, took them home and gave them warm showers. Graham and Helen had lost their farm and all their possessions except for the two shirts they were wearing and Helen's shorts. But they had escaped with their lives.

In Grantham, the torrent continued rushing through Wendy Hodda's house, and Wendy's hope that her mother Regina could survive eventually faded. All this time the dog, Stevie, had paddled continuously for two hours. Eventually the water began to subside: after two hours on the roof, Wendy saw the water finally begin to drop. Helicopters were winching families from rooftops and Wendy and the children were all airlifted to safety. Stevie continued swimming until the water went down.

The helicopter crew continued combing the flooded creek for Teddy's father James, but they did not see him. Emergency calls were still pouring in. The helicopter ran low on fuel and went to Toowoomba to refuel, and on their way back, they were called to rescue people in a house that had been swept across a paddock in Grantham.

At Tony McIntosh's farm, the lowest paddocks beside the creek were still underwater as the sun set. When the water finally subsided into the creek, thousands of tonnes of pale brown sand had been dropped on either side of the creek.

The following day a second flood in Lockyer Creek rose as quickly as it had the day before. At Tony McIntosh's place, the level rose to within 200 millimetres of the 1893 flood mark on the tree beside his house. This time, with the quarry wall almost completely destroyed, the flood didn't slow down and back up, but continued across the quarry and down the creek. The farms around the quarry were not flooded and no water ran down the highway into Grantham as it had done the day before. This time, floodwater rose slowly from Sandy Creek backing up slowly and flooding the streets of the town, as it had done in many previous floods.

A few days later, as soon as the flooded roads reopened, Tom and Sandra Friend returned home from their holidays and found their house ruined and their cows, pigs, chickens and geese gone. Tom and Sandra had had a lucky escape. During the clean-up, Jonathan Sippel found his water tanks and electrical cable spools under the railway bridge in Grantham.

A hydrology study later confirmed the earthen wall along the western side of the quarry slowed the floodwater down for approximately ten minutes. Hydrological modelling indicated that, whether the quarry had been constructed or not, the magnitude of the flood was so great that floodwater would have engulfed the section of land between Lockyer Creek and the railway line downstream of the quarry.

Grantham

'Jacob, stay there, Daddy's coming!'

The rural community of Grantham is set on the black soil floodplain of the Lockyer Valley and is surrounded by paddocks of vegetables. Lowset timber houses and a few new brick homes house the population of 500 people. Sandy Creek normally flows no more than a metre wide, through the town and under the town's railway line.

Looking south from Grantham, Lockyer Creek is barely visible as it winds across the flat, wide valley, but when Lockyer Creek is in flood it regularly flows up Sandy Creek into the town, causing minor flooding in the town centre. The Lockyer Creek passes so far to the south of Grantham that no-one thought it possible that it might flood the town, so there was no creek gauge there to warn of flooding in Grantham.

As the drought of the 1990s and 2000s dragged on with barely a good season, and the Warrego Highway was upgraded, businesses shut down. The town's only bank closed along with all the fruit stalls, until only a convenience store, a petrol station and a pub were left. Then the seasons changed and as spring advanced, the crops were lush and the farming sector was buoyant. The rain continued as the wet season took hold through December 2010 and January 2011.

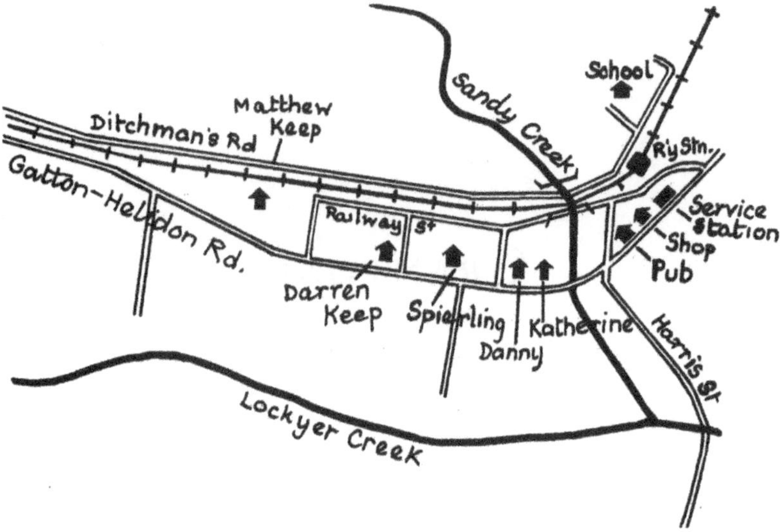

Sandy Creek finally broke its banks on Boxing Day, cutting the roads out of town for a few hours at a time before retreating again. In the following two weeks, Sandy Creek came up three more times. The rituals of sandbagging and closing businesses were becoming routine. Local residents were getting used to driving their cars to the high ground near the railway, which had never been flooded, even in the record flood of 1974. Local rural firefighters were kept busy barricading flooded roads, rescuing people who drove into flooded creek crossings, and attending medical emergencies when the roads into the town were cut.

The families in town have been here for generations in some cases, while others have dropped in, often as farm workers, and stayed. Most of the workers are labourers on the surrounding farms, or they work in local flower farms or retail businesses in town: the convenience store, the petrol station and the pub.

On Sunday evening, 9 January, Sandy Creek was rising again. At Marty Warburton's service station the water was knee-deep in the shop. With all the stock lifted to higher shelves, he sat outside watching and waiting as the water slowly receded. It was just another flood.

During the evening a rural fire brigade truck drove into floodwater and broke down. The officers could not swim. Two firefighting crews from Toowoomba went to the rescue, but couldn't reach the town by road. Toowoomba QFRS station officer Peter Werder and a colleague left the truck and waded two kilometres to town along the road. They reached the rural fire officers and helped them get from their vehicle to the median strip down the centre of the highway, where they could hold onto palm trees. They waited there while firefighter Matt Kendall swam to a local business whose owner had offered to use his backhoe to collect the rural fire officers. They stood in the front bucket and were carried to higher ground on the railway line.

The Toowoomba officers then responded to a call from a family with a young baby in Harris Street, who were trapped in their home. The water was flowing too swiftly for them to cross so they called for a power boat. SES volunteers arrived and transported the family from their home.

Meanwhile, Peter Werder checked on the publican, Lance Richardson, and his family, as well as a second family who lived in a brick house beside the pub. He offered to evacuate them, but both families chose to stay in their homes. Peter Werder was surprised that the offers of evacuation were turned down despite the depth of the floodwaters and the amount of debris.

In Railway Street, retired farmer Frank King was becoming edgy. His house was close to Sandy Creek and he was worried about the hydroponic strawberry and herb-growing operation in his backyard. He had been monitoring the height of the creek by logging on to the Bureau of Meteorology website and walking to the creek periodically to check the height, while the steady rain continued. By evening, he was so worried that he stayed up all night. 'Everything was primed like a loaded gun, ready to go off,' he said.

Local brigade member Danny McGuire was called to tow the inundated rural fire brigade fire truck from the floodwater. Danny and group officer Stuart Damrow, who was in charge of the 11 brigades in the Lockyer Valley, asked police for a compulsory evacuation of the town as they saw the flood levels becoming more dangerous. Their request was turned down. Danny spent the rest of the night door-knocking houses in the lower sections of Grantham along Railway Street and Citrus Street, offering to evacuate people, especially those in recently built lowset houses. Some people evacuated voluntarily. Others chose to stay.

On Monday morning it appeared their concerns had been ill-founded: the rain had stopped and the flood level was falling. But Danny was still worried when he heard there was a forecast of another 200 millimetres of rain in the afternoon. He caught a few hours' sleep and expected another busy afternoon. He asked his wife Llync, also a member of the local brigade, to take their children Garry, 12, Zac, seven, and Jocelyn, five, and go to Toowoomba. Knowing Danny was still on duty and exhausted, she decided to stay and help as much as she could.

In the town, many workers took the day off because they couldn't get out of Grantham. Marty decided not to reopen his service station just in case the water came back up.

As the floodwater receded from the main street, Sandy Halliday reopened the convenience store at midday. She took dozens of phone calls from travellers wanting to know if the roads were passable, and she told them the roads had reopened. Customers crowded into the little shop for milk, bread, papers and lunch. Life was returning to normal.

Private meteorology consultant Anthony Cornelius had watched the two storms converging and was growing anxious at the lack of official warning of the potential dangers for the Lockyer Valley. Since he could not issue a public forecast, he posted to an online weather forum at 12.16 pm. It read: '[It's] concerning for the Gatton-Grantham area right now with that very large storm/rain area moving towards it with no doubt, torrential rainfall! Sandy Creek (in Grantham) has caught quite a few people by surprise and I hope they're prepared for it, but sadly I think most won't know until the water starts lapping up at their homes due to our insufficient warning system.'

With the roads open again, electrician Matthew Keep left his home in Railway Street to drive to Toowoomba. He was caught in a heavy downpour in Toowoomba, and headed back home to Grantham to where his wife Stacy, 24, was caring for their three children: Madison, five, Jacob, four and Jessica, 23 months. Their house was built above the 1974 record flood level, but Matthew was concerned and wanted to be with Stacy, who was six months pregnant.

Stacy's mother Dawn Radke lived with the family and Matthew's mother Pauline Magner, who lived beside Sandy Creek at Grantham, had taken refuge with her son's family because she was worried about her own house being flooded.

Matthew Keep left Toowoomba just after 2 pm and drove down the range, through the towns of Withcott and Helidon. Within minutes of him driving over the Lockyer Creek bridge at Helidon, the floodwater from Murphys Creek, Lockyer Creek, and Sheepstation Creek converged, and the Lockyer Creek river gauge shot up from four metres to 13 metres in 23 minutes. It broke the gauge just after 2.30 pm.

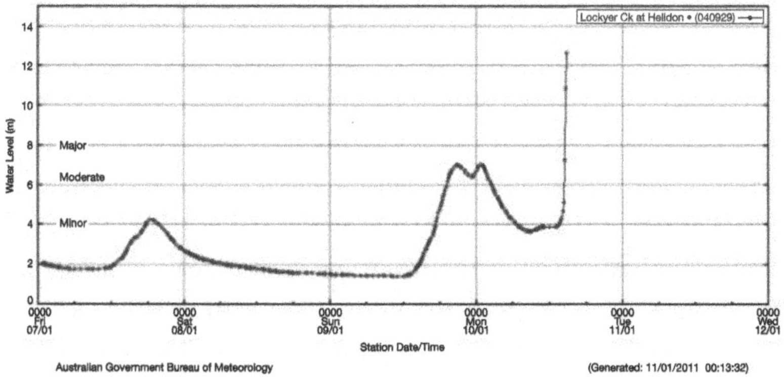

Matthew stopped at the Grantham store to buy chocolates for his children about 3 pm, then drove across Sandy Creek and towards his home. Once there, he went out again to check on his mother's house beside Sandy Creek. The water was now over the bridge. When he returned home, Matthew checked weather websites to find out what the Toowoomba airport rain gauge had recorded. The airport rain gauge is the only one in the city that feeds data to the Bureau, and is located on the western side of Toowoomba. It had recorded only 50 millimetres of rain.

It started raining again. Matthew went back to his mother's house, this time taking Pauline and the three children with him. When they returned home, Matt took Stacy and the children to see how high the water had risen at his mother's house. By then Pauline's backyard was full of water. Matt and Stacy returned home and found the power supply was cut. Matt went to his brother Darren's house to borrow a camp stove so Stacy could cook dinner.

A few minutes after Matthew had left the convenience store in Grantham, Sandy Halliday heard that the Warrego Highway was cut ten kilometres upstream of the town at Helidon. She phoned her sister and business partner Sue Turner, who lives at Helidon. Sue was incredulous and told her sister, 'No, it wouldn't be over the highway. Have you seen how high that bridge is?' But Sue offered to go down and check it out, and joked with her sister, 'You can kiss your pretty arse goodbye if the creek's over the highway at Helidon.'

At about 3.30 pm retired timber cutters Kenly and Fran Arndt were at their house in Gatton Helidon Road when they received a panicked phone call. Kenly was outside helping his neighbour Danny McGuire put a barricade across the inundated highway to prevent motorists driving through floodwater. Fran picked up the phone and heard Kenly's daughter Kym screaming at her, and swearing for emphasis, that they needed to get away quickly because there was a huge wall of water heading for their place. Kym was across the creek on higher land near the piggery and could see fast-moving water coming from the west.

Sue Turner went to Sheepstation Creek, which runs through Helidon and joins into Lockyer Creek. She saw that the level was high but was still rising fast. She phoned her sister and told her, 'Get your arse out of there. There is so much water coming your way.' It was 3.31 pm. Sandy shouted at the customers in the shop to get to safety.

From there the message spread around the town like wildfire. Sue phoned one of her staff, Rebecca Kilah, who was not at work that day, knowing she had young children.

Sue told Rebecca to take her children and leave town, but it was too late – by then all the roads out of town were flooded. Rebecca went to see her father Gilbert Kilah and told him about Sue's flood warning. He checked the Bureau's website and saw that the level in Sandy Creek was low, only 0.2 metres, but Lockyer Creek at Helidon was 12.9 metres. He didn't believe the reading. He then checked the height it had been the previous week and it had been 6.9 metres. He thought the gauge must be faulty but he was wary. He asked his daughter to take her children home and to stay upstairs while he moved her car to higher ground. When he went outside, he saw Frank King and told him the Lockyer Creek gauge was reading 12.9 metres at Helidon bridge.

Grantham meatworker Rob Wilkin had spent the morning helping friends and family clean up from the flood the night before. About mid-afternoon he went to have a sleep before working the night shift at the local abattoir. Before he fell asleep, he heard Gilbert Kilah shouting and got back up to find out what was going on. Gilbert told him that the level of Lockyer Creek at Helidon was nine metres higher than it had been the night before.

Rob was not overly concerned. 'This house has never been flooded and I thought nine metres more in a narrow creek wouldn't be anything across the floodplain,' he said. To confirm his family was not in danger, he went for a drive to check for himself. As he drove round the block he saw a couple of neighbours on the street and knocked at Lisa Spierling's door to let her know. Lisa was baking cakes, unaware of the danger to herself and three of her children: Hahns, 12, Klaus, ten, and Ilsa, four, who were watching television. She wondered if Rob was over-estimating the danger but decided to move her car up the road to higher ground anyway.

Beside the Grantham Hotel, Bess Fraser and her partner Chris Barrett were cleaning up the yard after flooding the night before. Bess lived with her sister, Brenda Ross, whom she helped care for after a stroke in 2008 left Brenda unable to walk. Brenda's partner

Christopher Face was her full-time carer. Brenda's son Joshua lived in a nearby house and also helped to care for his mother. As Sandy Creek rose in the afternoon, Chris Barrett and Joshua moved their cars to the railway yard. Chris returned and took Bess with him to move another car to higher ground. Before leaving, Bess told her sister she'd be back soon. 'We're going up to the railway yard with the car. I'll come back and finish the washing soon.' Bess kissed Brenda and Josh. Christopher was asleep on the couch.

On Gatton Helidon Road, Fran grabbed her keys, her phone and her handbag and bustled outside. She told Kenly that his daughter wanted them to get out: 'She's screaming on the phone. She's hysterical. We better go.'

Looking to the south, Fran saw a rolling wave of floodwater coming from Lockyer Creek. Kenly, 72, was sitting in the front yard in their four-wheel-drive ute that had been retrofitted with two extra wheels, giving the vehicle sufficient strength to carry heavy loads of timber. Fran quickly climbed in. Both knew that Sandy Creek was flowing over the highway by then. The road was closed. They could not escape to the east. Kenly turned right and headed west, towards Helidon.

A few minutes later, Rob Wilkin saw the wall of water coming. 'I saw a five-foot wall of water rolling across the paddocks from Lockyer Creek. It hit home to me that this could be worse than what we thought,' he said. The water was 400 metres away.

Rob thought he would have two or three minutes to get to the railway line – it was enough time to get the Spierling family – if he hurried. He knew there was no time for them to drive their own car so the only way would be to get them in the back of his ute. So, leaving his family in the car and the engine running, he ran into Lisa Spierling's back door, picked up her youngest child Ilsa and yelled, 'Get the fuck out!' The boys, Hahns and Klaus, followed Rob out the door. Lisa stopped momentarily to think what to take. She realised she had no time to find her phone. Looking down she saw her dog, grabbed him and ran to the ute. Once the children were on board,

Lisa climbed in the back of the ute and screamed at Rob, 'Go! Go! Go!'

'As we were reversing out, I saw the wall of water. It looked like a giant chocolate milkshake full of debris. It was rolling at us like a wave on a beach. It was rolling across the paddock. There was no floodwater in front – it was just a wall of water,' Lisa said.

The carload of people headed for the railway line, shouting warnings along the way whenever they saw anyone. Sharon McCray and Ian Day had heard a flood was coming and started running away from Sandy Creek. They didn't realise they were running towards the wave of floodwater. Lisa screamed at them. 'You're going the wrong way!'

Not long after Matthew Keep had left to get a camp stove, Stacy noticed water coming across the paddocks towards their house from the direction of Lockyer Creek. It seemed to be moving slowly. She phoned Matt. Moments later the water was roaring across the road. She and Pauline grabbed bath towels and tried to block the doors and windows with them.

Rob Wilkin saw some people and screamed out the car window, telling them to look down to the end of the road where the water was already beginning to come over the highway. 'People could see the danger coming. They were like stunned mullets. Shocked. Looking at what was coming in disbelief,' he said. Rob's wife and children, with Lisa and her children, sped towards the railway line. There was a gap in the security fence so they had to run along the road to the gap, carrying the youngest children through long grass and weeds, and climb up the railway embankment and onto the railway line.

A block to the south, on Gatton Helidon Road, Johnathon Klaassen, a young farm worker who'd been unable to get out of town to the farm where he worked, was at home, unaware of the looming danger. Johnathon had bought a house in town 18 months earlier. At 3.15 pm his phone rang. It was his brother David, asking him to go and see the flooded creeks around town with him. Not wanting to go out, Johnathon invited his brother to play video games at his house. But his brother persuaded him to go and see the creeks with him instead.

Johnathon took his car to higher ground beside the railway line and walked the few minutes to his brother's house. When he looked back over his shoulder, half the town was under water. He had escaped with minutes to spare.

One of the first houses to be hit by the flood in Grantham was Kathy and John Mahon's five-bedroom brick house on Gatton Helidon Road, at the western end of the town. John was in his shed when he heard a noise and saw what looked like a mud landslide, about one metre high, filled with sticks and logs, hurtling down the road and across the paddock towards his house. 'The water coming down the road met the water coming across the paddock and the next thing it was in the yard and around the house, so fast,' he said. He shouted to his wife Kathy, and their adult daughters Andrea and Jess, to get indoors. John and Jess got towels to barricade the front door but within moments the water was swirling around their knees. Andrea put her children, Liam, five, and Lachlan, three, on the kitchen bench. She and Jess then climbed on the bench. John and Kathy stood on kitchen chairs as lounge and dining furniture, including a heavy timber dining table that seated 20 people, began swirling through the house. Fridges and cupboards crashed over and glass was smashing.

Andrea phoned her husband and said goodbye to him. Jess phoned her boyfriend and told him they were going to drown. Kathy phoned their daughter Rachelle in Brisbane and said she didn't think they would survive. They all held hands and said the Lord's Prayer and kissed one another goodbye. Andrea and Jess got an inflatable toy boat and put floaties on the boys. The water was more than 1.5 metres deep inside the house and about 30 centimetres deeper outside. It was still rising. The family realised they had to quickly get out of the house to avoid being trapped and drowned inside.

On the southern side of Grantham Katherine Godley, 14, was in her front yard when she noticed water from Sandy Creek had broken the banks of the creek and was flooding her yard. A keen photographer, Katherine began taking a video and commenting as she watched the flow of floodwater picking up speed. 'Look at that. Look how fast it is. Shit, that's fast. It's like rapids. It's getting faster. What did they do, open a dam or something? Shit. Go and get a boat. We're gonna drown! We're gonna drown!' Suddenly she saw the front of the main flood from Lockyer Creek pouring across the paddock opposite her house and screamed for her brother. 'Michael! Look at that. Shit, that's coming in real fast now. Michael! Help! I'm going to go upstairs.'

Fifty seconds after she saw the front of the floodwater, it slammed into her house and the other homes along Gatton Helidon Road. The other houses were all lowset and the water instantly engulfed them. Katherine ran up the stairs and got to safety just in time. Just before the water struck the houses, Danny McGuire yelled for his children and his wife to go to the fire truck. He turned the truck around, put his family in and headed for the gate. Another larger wave was now coming from the west, down the highway. 'By the time I hit the gateway the wave had actually hit us. Once it hit the truck all I remember was the truck getting spun around.' Danny phoned triple zero, gave their names and address and told the operator to send helicopters.

As Kenly headed west, the water they were driving through became deeper and deeper. Fran grabbed her phone and called Danny McGuire for help. He told her his fire truck had been washed off the highway. He could not help. Suddenly, Kenly and Fran's six-wheeler hit something head on. It happened so quickly that Kenly had not seen it coming. 'The car just got hit and it threw us back and immediately floating like a balloon and we shifted sideways and began floating off the road northwards towards the railway line,' he said. The wave went straight over the top of the ute.

'All I could see was all this black, filthy water and that's when the ute snuffed out,' Fran said. 'It just picked us up like a cork, this big wave, and pushed us backwards up the road.' They both tried to open their doors but they could not push them open against the current. The cabin quickly filled with water. Soon it was up to their waists. Moments later it was up to their necks and they felt the vehicle sinking.

Danny had to get the children out of the truck before they reached Sandy Creek. They were floating past trees. Danny grabbed Zac, thrust him out the window and yelled, 'Climb, boy!' He turned to pick up Jocelyn but as he did the water swirled into the cabin, pushing Danny out of the truck and into the torrent. He grabbed a tree and climbed. Knowing his wife and two children in the truck had drowned, he yelled out for Zac and listened for the little boy's voice. 'I could just hear him over the rush of the water. Once I found he was alright I just kept telling him to stay safe, go higher if he had to and someone would be coming for us.'

Katherine ran up the stairs and got to safety just in time. From her front verandah she saw Danny McGuire, his wife Llync, and their children Garry, Zac, and Jocelyn in a fire truck being swept down the road by the 'tsunami wave'. She saw Zac thrown into a tree and Danny grab another one as the truck was swamped and disappeared beneath the floodwater.

In Brisbane, John and Kathy Mahon's daughter Rachelle closed her eyes and thought what to do. She didn't know how to contact helicopters. She didn't know whether to ask for the fire brigade or police but decided on police because they would know how to contact a helicopter. She dialled triple zero and asked for police. Her call was the first from Grantham.

'I told them my parents don't live in a flood area in Grantham, but they are flooded and cars are being washed away. You need to get helicopters there now or everybody in the town is going to be dead. They said, "Are you sure? How do you know?" I said, "I live there." They said, "Are you sure?" I said, "That's my home town. You need helicopters and you need them now." The operator asked again if she was sure. Rachelle gave the names and ages of the people in the house. She also gave the address, but told the operator they would not be able to use the address because everything was underwater. She described what the house looked like from the air – a large L-shaped house, second from the western end of town with a green roof, opposite farmland and surrounded by palm trees.

John Mahon, a solid man of over 130 kilograms, told the family to hold on to each other and stand behind him so he could protect them from the force of the water, which was already bowing the doors. Rachelle phoned her family. There was so much screaming at the house that Rachelle had to shout to them, 'The helicopters are coming, the helicopters are coming!' The phone cut out.

A few hundred metres to the west, Kenly and Fran needed to get out of the ute. Fast. Fran screamed at Kenly, 'Do something!' Kenly hit the electric window switch. His window went down. Fran was still on the phone to Kym. Both women were screaming. Fran hit her window switch. Her window started going down but stopped halfway. Fran told Kenly, 'Get out your window!' Fran squeezed with difficulty out of hers. As soon as they escaped, the ute sank immediately. From her vantage point across the creek, Kym saw the car go under and feared they were both dead.

Once in the water, Kenly and Fran tried to touch the ground but could not reach it. Fortunately they could both swim. The current was very strong and the surface was rough but they kept afloat as they were hit by submerged rubbish and logs. As they were carried along by the current, they managed to work their way towards a clump of spindly trees poking out of the water.

EMQ pilot Mark Kempton was flying a critically ill patient to Brisbane when he had a second call from police. 'We had a call, I think from the same police inspector, and this time he was really panicked and stressed saying, "Can you please come and help? The wall of water is going through Grantham now. People are being swept away. People are stuck on the roofs." He gave us a couple of street addresses and said there were people trapped in a fire truck.' Mark told the inspector he would get back to base, refuel, check the weather conditions, and fly there if they could but he could not guarantee it.

As John opened the doors water rushed in, hit the opposite wall, bounced back and propelled them all out of the house. Once outside it was obvious the current was too fast for them to get to higher ground on the railway – their only option was to climb on the roof.

The floodwater was higher than their pool fence. Jess and Andrea lifted the boys to the roof. John held a squatter's chair on top of the fence to help Kathy up. He could not lift his own weight. Looking across the pool yard, he considered climbing some bushes on the other side but a brown snake was rearing to strike. He decided instead to get a table that was floating around, and balanced it between the gutter and the pool fence, and held on tightly to the gutter.

He watched his life's possessions floating out of the house. When the white leather-bound family Bible floated past, Kathy shouted at him to let it go. John told her, 'I can't let the family Bible go,' so he jumped off and swam to it, threw it on the roof, and climbed back up onto the table. They heard a helicopter coming but it could not rescue them. It was a news helicopter, so they knew at least that someone would be alerting authorities to get help for the town.

Rob Wilkin saw that his wife, Lisa and all the children were climbing to safety on the railway line. He had a 90-horsepower boat on a trailer in his front yard – it could come in handy. He towed it on to the road. Gilbert Kilah walked past and stopped to talk to him. At that moment Rob looked across the top of his car and saw the first wave of floodwater come across Gatton Helidon Road, roll up the street and engulf an elderly man, Marcus Casalegno, who was walking towards the water trying to get home to his wife. Rob kicked off his shoes and ran with Gilbert to save him.

They grabbed Marcus and walked him out of the water. By then, the men were cut off from the railway line by swift-flowing water more than two metres deep, rushing down the table drain. They would not be able to walk the old man to safety. Rob recalls thinking, 'Shit, quick, let's jump in the boat.' Rob's brother Jim helped get the elderly man into the boat, which was still tied down to the trailer. When the next wave came through, the boat was surrounded by water and the current was too strong for Rob to stand up. He climbed in the boat, reached over the side under the water and undid the straps that held the boat on the trailer.

Gilbert left the Wilkin brothers and continued with his efforts to get his daughter's four-wheel-drive Prado car to higher ground along Railway Street. When he stopped he saw two teenage sisters, Holly and Emma De Longte, parked in their ute in front of him. Knowing the water was rising very quickly, Gilbert tried to run back to his own boat to get lifejackets for Holly and Emma but as he ran, he saw his boat and car already floating away down the street.

He ran back to the girls. By then, their ute was also floating and pushing up against the Prado. Gilbert called to the girls to climb onto the Prado, which was not yet floating. One girl climbed up. The other tried but slipped off and became trapped when their floating car squashed her legs against the Prado. Gilbert pushed the floating ute away to free her.

Holly and Emma climbed onto the car roof and hung onto the rails of the roof rack. Gilbert lay on the bonnet so he could hold himself on the car with his hands and use his feet to push other floating cars away from them. He could not swim and he was worried about the car tipping them into the torrent. He saw Rob Wilkin's house lift up and float along the road beside them. They passed a pig, trapped in a crate, that was squealing above the roar of the water and the sounds of destruction.

After floating about 500 metres along the street, they passed a power pole and the car hit a stay wire, which tipped the car on its side. Holly De Longte fell off, went under the car and came up the other side. Gilbert also fell in the water. Holly's sister Emma stayed on the car, and Gilbert saw her floating towards Sandy Creek. Gilbert was distraught, thinking she would be swept into Lockyer Creek and drown. He dog-paddled to keep his head above water and managed to avoid being swept onto a spiky date palm. He grabbed a power pole and hung on, forcing his fingers between the earth wire running down the power pole and the timber. He wedged his fingers in the gap and held on tightly.

His trousers were ripped down so he kicked them off. Debris around the bottom of the power pole was more than a metre high so even though the water was about three metres deep, he could stand on the debris and cling on to the pole with his knees to keep a better grip. 'I was worried about logs hitting the power pole and cutting my fingers off. That was terrifying,' he said. 'I realised I had to try to keep my hands above the water level so I had a chance to shift my hands to avoid being hit.' As Gilbert looked around he could see people in the houses, but he didn't know if they could see him. If they could, he knew no-one could rescue him because it was impossible to swim across the current.

Word from the shop about the highway being flooded at Helidon reached Matthew Keep and his brother Darren, a piggery manager, who were talking at Darren's house in Citrus Street. Matthew immediately rushed home. Darren's wife, Michelle, and their adult children, Brendan and Natasha, and Natasha's husband, Brad Long, were all at home. Their house had burnt down two years earlier and they'd had to rebuild. The new house was above the 1974 flood level. Michelle was worried she would have to rebuild her house again, but Brad and Natasha were not concerned. They were on holidays from university, watching a movie together. They thought Michelle was overreacting and continued watching the movie.

Darren called them all outside. They walked about 100 metres to the highway and suddenly saw the floodwater rolling rapidly across the paddock towards them. Darren asked Brad, Natasha, Michelle and Brendan to drive their cars to higher ground while he stayed at home to look after the family's dogs and to lift the fridge. As the four drivers turned from their home in Citrus Street on to Railway Street towards Matthew's house, they watched as the water hit his house from behind and engulf it.

As Matthew drove towards his home on Railway Street, he saw water coming from the south, over the paddock and across the highway. It began to pool around his house. 'I went into our home. My wife and mother were starting to place towels around the doorways.

The water soon reached the second brick on the side of the house, allowing water to enter into the frames of the house. I told my wife not to worry about the house,' he said.

'We got the children together and went into the lounge room. By the time we had done this, my mother's car was floating away. It was parked on the road at the front of the property.'

Matthew phoned the SES and told them that water was all around the house and still rising and that they would need to be rescued.

Matt and Stacy put their three young children on the kitchen bench. 'The windows could not take the pressure of the water and they starting smashing instantly and all the water came gushing in and the kids went flying off the kitchen bench,' Stacy said. 'We raced around to catch them.' Matt and Pauline quickly put Madison on the floating couch. 'While they were doing that, I was grabbing Jessica and I went looking for Jacob.' Stacy could not find him.

Matt and his mother-in-law, Dawn, went towards the garage, searching for Jacob. As Matt opened the door, the force of the water pushed him and Dawn into the garage and bent the roller door up.

Inside the house, Stacy held Jessica. Pauline was with Madison. The couch started floating and moving towards the front door. The water was still rising. Stacy needed to get Jessica up higher so she could help Pauline look after Madison. Stacy went to the garage and found a large sheet of plasterboard that had been ripped from a wall. It was floating but trapped in the garage. She put Jessica on it and tried to wade back to Pauline but she could not move forwards against the current. Stacy returned to Jessica and tried to get her onto the roof. She lifted Jessica on top of the buckled garage door and then tried to get herself up. She did not have the strength to lift herself up against the current. While Stacy was holding the door with one hand and Jessica with the other, a surge of water hit Stacy and she lost her grip on the door.

Jacob had recently begun swimming lessons. He swam to his parents' ensuite, held on to the shower screen and moved around it until he could grab the showerhead and stand on the taps.

Petrol station owner Marty Warburton joined a group of about 20 townspeople at the railway bridge watching Sandy Creek. At about 3.40 pm a friend phoned him to say the crossing higher up the catchment at Flagstone Creek was a metre over the bridge – higher than the 1974 record flood level – and urged him to get out of town. He shouted the information to the crowd and walked towards his service station to get his driver's licence, wallet and keys. As he walked in the door there was no water on the street. Two minutes later the flood was swirling waist-high through the shop and rising fast.

The front window exploded inwards, water gushed in, throwing goods around the shop. In a few minutes, the top of his hat was hitting the ceiling. He had to get out.

He took a breath and duck-dived out the front door of the shop. He could feel the current rushing down the road. He reached up and grabbed a rafter that held up the awning and heaved himself onto the roof. From there, he watched as cars and houses were swept past with people inside screaming at the windows for help. In the turbulent water he saw arms flailing. He reached out and grabbed someone's hand. He realised the person was dead. There was nothing he could do for them. A second body floated past, beyond his reach. A young couple sitting on the roof of their car floated past. The car sank. A man on top of another car floated past.

Bess Fraser was at the railway yard when she suddenly heard a roaring sound. 'I had no idea what it was. Then there was lots of water. I didn't know where it had come from. It wasn't coming from the creek. It was coming down the road. Every now and then I could hear people calling for help over the roar of the water.'

As word from the shop spread, Frank King heard from his neighbour in Railway Street that Lockyer Creek had reached 13 metres at Helidon bridge. He checked the Bureau of Meteorology website, saw the creek gauges, and ran with his son John to drive their cars to higher ground. Within minutes the water was around Frank's ankles. 'I looked up and the water was rushing over the bonnet of John's car and both cars got swept away,' he said.

John's car lodged against a tree. Frank tried to climb on it but he was trapped by a clump of weeds and sticks wrapped around his legs. The force of the water was dragging Frank under the car.

John grabbed his father's arm and held his head above the water. The speed of the current eventually dragged the weeds and debris from Frank's legs, and John lifted his father onto the car. He took out his phone and began filming cars, boats on trailers and horse floats being carried away down the road. Just then the tree cracked and gave way. The car was moving again. John told Frank to jump off the car and try to grab a tree. At that moment Frank fell from the car and into the water. He grabbed a branch and it broke. He grabbed another tree and it held. He clasped his fingers together around the tree and hung on.

John put his mobile phone in his mouth to try to keep it dry and jumped off the car. He grabbed a branch. It broke. He tried to swim to a tree but the current was so strong it had a bow wave that swept him around it. He had to get to a house before the current carried him 500 metres into Sandy Creek. 'I was trying to swim across the road to the houses, and I could feel the water going in my shoes and pulling me along by the shoes so I kicked them off. There were cars floating past so I had to dodge them. I grabbed a tree in the front of my parents' place, had a break for a couple of minutes, and swam across to the house.'

Once there, his thoughts turned to his mother and brother, who he had last seen downstairs. He called out to them. They were alive. John tried to phone triple zero but the power was down. He tried his mobile. He realised the operator could not hear him. Moisture in his phone from the swim home had damaged it.

As Frank King clung to the tree, the force of the water ripped his trousers and shoes off and sent mud up his nose. He could not turn his head to see what had happened to his son. He could only hope he had somehow stopped himself being swept into Sandy Creek. From his tree he heard a young woman he knew, screaming as she was swept away, tangled up in pumpkin vines. 'I could see her head bobbing up and down,' Mr King said. The woman pulled the vines away from her legs, struggled into a nearby front yard and managed to get up onto a verandah.

Further along Railway Street, Matthew Keep and Dawn Radke had been swept to the garage of his house. He saw Dawn clinging to a ride-on mower. He could feel himself being washed away and called to her, 'Sorry, Dawn, I can't help you.' Matthew was swept outside through the bent roller door but managed to grab an air-conditioning unit protruding from a neighbouring house. He heard voices inside screaming for help, but he was desperate to try to save his wife and children as he saw the furniture swept from his own house. Unable to help his own family, Matthew climbed into the house and lifted the neighbouring children and adults onto the roof.

Madison saw a lounge chair, also floating, but this one was wedged in the house, so she climbed across to the chair and stayed on it. She called for her little brother Jacob and he answered. He wanted to come to her but she told him, 'Jacob, stay there, Daddy's coming!'

Outside, Michelle, Brendan, Natasha and Brad realised they couldn't rescue their cars and that they must now focus on saving their lives and getting to Darren, who was still at the house. They started running back along Railway Street to try to alert him. As they ran, the water lifted all four of them from the road and swept them across a table drain filled with tall grass beside the railway line. As they were carried along by the torrent they managed to grab one of the few panels of chain-wire fence that was still standing along the railway line. Only about 30 centimetres of the 2.5-metre-high fence was sticking out of the water. They grabbed the fence and held on. From here they saw cars float past with people inside.

The noise was intense. A couple of houses floated past, with timber creaking and corrugated iron screeching as it gave way. Gas cylinders were slamming into the railway line and exploding. The houses started to break apart. Brad and Natasha could see media helicopters above but couldn't hear them over the roar of the water. Brad's phone had been in his pocket; it was soaked but it was their only hope. He pulled it out of his pocket and dialled triple zero. It connected. He told the automated answering service they were in a flood and needed help fast. The answering service asked if he wanted police, fire or ambulance. He said anyone would do – he swore in frustration and the line went dead. Brad gave the phone to Natasha, hoping she would be calm enough to ask for help without swearing.

On the railway line, Lisa Spierling tried to calm the children and keep them all together. She watched the shade houses of her flower farm collapse and dozens of boxes of hydroponic rose bushes float away. 'I saw 18 years of our hard work crumbling in front of me. The shade houses were crumbling like some papier-mâché. The water was so strong it was pushing the trays of rose bushes out of the shade houses. I saw a house tipping and the people were smashing the window and yelling for help. There was nothing we could do.'

Suddenly, her children and the Wilkin children began running. They didn't stop even though Lisa Spierling shouted at them to. All of a sudden, one of the adults looked west, saw what the children had seen, and yelled, 'Fuckin' run!'

'We all could see the railway line was disappearing and there was a wall of water coming over that, only about a foot high but running fast,' Lisa Spierling said. 'The only option then was to start running. We had to take our chances.'

A third wave of floodwater came through. It raised the water level at the Wilkins' place by at least two metres. Rob Wilkin started the engine and took the people in the boat to the railway line. There he saw Michelle Keep and her son Brendan clinging to a section of the railway fence. The two were pinned to the fence by the force of the water, and debris was pushing against them. Natasha and Brad Long were on the other side of the fence where the force of the water was pulling them off the fence. He saw that Michelle and Brendan were in the most dangerous situation, and used the bow of the boat to push between the debris and the people. Rob Wilkin's brother Jim pulled them into the boat. An alarm was going off in the boat because the mud was causing the engine to overheat. The boat was losing power. The engine cut out. The boat floated away. As it was swept away, the boat hit the railway embankment where Rob's wife and children were standing on the railway track. Rob, his brother Jim, Marcus Casalegno, Michelle Keep and her son Brendan were all able to climb out.

A fourth wave of water was now coming towards them from the west. This one flowed over the top of the train tracks. Rob saw it cover about half a kilometre of train track in about two minutes. 'From when we started running, knowing there was water coming up behind us, I realised our lives were all in danger,' Rob said. He screamed to everyone to run as fast as they could to get to the railway bridge across Sandy Creek and up to high ground near the Grantham Primary School. The adults who were able to run carried the little children in their arms. The older children ran. The elderly people were most at risk. When Marcus was not fast enough, Rob Wilkin carried him.

Brad and Natasha, who were still clinging to the fence, were holding on even though the fence was, by then, completely submerged. As more surges of floodwater hit them, it washed over their heads because they could not let go of the fence. Between waves, Natasha tried phoning triple zero. She answered the preliminary questions: 'What state are you in? Do you want police, fire or ambulance?' Just then the fence began to pull out from the ground. Natasha told the operator, 'Excuse me, I have to go. We're drowning now.' Something hit her in the water and she dropped the phone. It didn't matter any more.

Looking around, Natasha didn't think there was any way they would get out of this alive but she decided to fight for her life. Natasha told Brad, 'We have to let go.' They both let go of the fence and were swept along fast beside the railway line. Pushing floating railway sleepers, logs, tyres, tanks and other debris aside, they swam towards the railway embankment that was still above the water. They clutched at the long grass and weeds and Rob and Jim Wilkin grabbed them and pulled them up onto the railway line. Brad and

Natasha were out of the water. They looked to see why everyone was running and saw the water quickly covering the railway line. They got up and ran for their lives as well.

Back at his home, Darren Keep was swept down the hallway as water smashed through the back of the house. He managed to get far enough along the hall to get into a bedroom. From there he climbed from a window onto the roof. Looking across the unfolding disaster scene, he saw Brad's car floating along and he thought he saw Brad inside. If Brad had not survived, it did not look possible that any of his family could have survived, and he assumed his wife, his children and son-in-law were all dead.

Meanwhile Frank King saw his neighbour Gilbert Kilah on top of a car with two girls, floating down Railway Street. He watched as the car hit a telegraph pole stay wire, tipped, and threw Gilbert and Holly De Longte into the water. 'I heard them screaming, "Help!" and screaming in terror as they went past. I wished I could help them but there was nothing I could do,' Frank King said. Holly's sister Emma was clinging to the car's roof rack.

As the Prado was swept down Railway Street, local concreter Norrie Blume, who had been moving his cars to the railway yard, saw the teenager clinging on for dear life. He ran about 50 metres to the middle of the bridge, which by then was half a metre under water. Norrie had seen at least 30 cars smash into the bridge and sink.

He shouted to Emma to stand up and get ready to jump: she would have to jump over the bonnet of the car and over the railing of the railway bridge before the car sank. He didn't know if she would be able to leap that far but it was her only hope. 'As soon as the car hits, you have to jump!' he told her. The car hit the middle of the bridge and Emma jumped. She leapt over the bonnet of the car and over the railing. Norrie grabbed her. He helped her across the bridge to higher ground.

Kenly and Fran Arndt swam into the patch of spindly trees and each stood in the fork of a tree as high up as they dared. Once in the trees, they found that debris caught by the scrub formed a protective barrier shielding them from the worst of the current. But the water level was still rising. Kenly and Fran both climbed as high as they could. At its peak, the floodwater was almost five metres deep and came up to their necks. They could not climb any higher because the branches of the trees were too thin to hold their weight.

They looked around and saw a house. Fran called out, hoping for help. 'We're here! We're here!' she shouted. Someone called back. But they were stuck on the roof of their house and could not help.

Kenly looked around and suddenly became frightened. A green shipping container was coming towards them fast. 'It was only about 10 metres away and heading directly at us in the flow of the water and I reckon at least 20 kilometres an hour, maybe faster,' Kenly said. 'I knew that if it hit us it would smash and kill us. I said goodbye to my wife and I cringed and braced for it to hit us and wipe us out.' A few metres from them, the shipping container veered to the left, missing Kenly by less than the length of his outstretched arm.

From his tree, Frank could see people running along the railway line. 'I told them, "Keep running." They could not help me. There was a railway fence between us and the current was too dangerous for anyone to get into. There was no way any of them could have helped me unless they had a rope,' he said.

Once Norrie had taken Emma to safety, he looked back across the bridge and saw women with children and elderly people trying to wade across the bridge. He crossed over, tucked a small child under each arm and waded across. He returned again and helped Rob and Jim Wilkin carry all the children safely across.

Just as all the children had safely crossed, a shipping container floated down the street. Frank King saw it coming. 'It really frightened me. It was spinning around like a corkscrew. I was calculating where it might bang into the trees. Fortunately it went past my tree and hit a tree further down.' Frank was very relieved.

At the King's house in Railway Street, John King stood at the front door looking out at the devastation around him. He saw a girl in the water: it was Holly, who had fallen off the Prado. Immediately he jumped back in the water and swam to her. He helped her swim to an upturned car in the front yard and lifted her onto it so she could rest and catch her breath. They waited for a surge of floodwater to pass and then swam towards the house where, fortunately, wire mesh had been nailed to the wall. The two clawed their way up against the current to the front door and climbed inside. John then saw Gilbert Kilah clinging to a telegraph pole. He yelled out and Gilbert yelled back that he was okay. 'I told him to hang on. I thought about getting a rope but there was over two metres of water rushing through under the house and everything had been washed away. There was nothing I could do to get him and there were big logs coming past. He was at least 20 metres away. I couldn't have got to him. I had nothing to bring him back. I couldn't have helped him. I yelled a few times to him to hold on,' John said.

On the eastern side of the town, Harris Street resident Roy Abraham was moving equipment to higher ground with his neighbour Kelvin Woods when the two men got caught in the flood. They managed to wade to the Grantham Hotel. The record 1974 flood only came to the floorboards of the hotel but this flood kept rising. As the water rose more than a metre, the men stacked tables and chairs so they and the publican's family could climb on the roof. When they got up there they saw cars, trucks and houses floating past. They were terrified the pub would crumble; it was shaking as cars, tanks and pieces of buildings crashed into it.

Next door, the water was engulfing Brenda's house. Brenda phoned her sister Bess and told her she had rung emergency services. They were coming. But Bess had worked in emergency services and knew that the water was too dangerous for rescuers to reach her family. 'Water tanks and cars were shooting past. Brenda saw my shipping container go past the kitchen window. Then I saw it stop at the intersection. It sat there and then it just shot off like a bullet out of a gun.' Brenda told her sister the water was up to her knees. Bess told her to prepare to be evacuated by collecting her medications and putting them in a plastic bag. Brenda didn't want to leave her pets. Bess told her, 'It'll be okay. Stay calm. I love you, Possy. I'll see you in a couple of days.' Bess then spoke to Joshua. He sounded very scared. He told her, 'The lounge room's falling apart and the floor is moving.'

Bess told him, 'I love you so much. I am so proud of you. I want you to get on the bed and give your mum a hug. They're coming. They'll come as soon as they can to get you.'

Bess hung up.

But if they were going to die, Bess didn't want them to be alone. She phoned straight back. There was no answer. Bess knew in her heart that something terrible had happened. She just hoped someone at the pub might have been able to help them.

At the pub, everyone thought the building they were in would be swept away. They said goodbye to each other. They heard screams from next door and saw Brenda's brick house crumble and fall beneath the torrent. There was nothing they could do to help the people inside.

At Matthew and Stacy Keep's house, Stacy managed to grab a downpipe and held on for about five minutes and looked desperately around for somewhere she could get to out of the current. The house next door looked promising. She would try to get to that. As soon as Stacy let go, the current carried her and Jessica in a different direction, towards the railway line. She could not touch the bottom. Houses were floating past. She tried to get close enough to grab a house but she couldn't reach it. Stacy realised she had no option but to go with the current. Stacy held Jessica above her head, going underwater herself but keeping Jessica's head above the surface the whole time.

Stacy was swept to the railway line where the rocks and gravel had by this time been washed away, leaving the lines exposed. 'I got my legs stuck and then we went under water and I couldn't get them out,' Stacy said. 'The water was just so strong and Jessie got ripped out of my arms. After that I just gave up myself and I started to blank out at that stage because I was under water for too long. But then all of a sudden it felt like something lifted me out, just like a current of water or something.'

Once across the railway line, the current was not as strong. Stacy looked to her right and saw a big pile of sleepers. 'I managed to get myself over there and hop on top and I just sat there and thought that I was the only one left.'

All those who had just run a kilometre along the railway line had to then cross an open-slatted railway bridge to reach higher ground. As they were running, Ian Day took Ilsa from Lisa's back. Lisa then turned around and saw the slower adults behind her and the wave rushing up behind them faster than they were running. She yelled at them to run faster and saw the wave overtake them. But they kept on running through the water.

By this time, the huge volume of water flowing down Lockyer Creek was forcing Sandy Creek to flow backwards, sending water splashing and spraying up between the sleepers of the railway bridge. As the Spierling and Wilkin children crossed over, the water was up to their ankles. They had to step carefully from sleeper to sleeper to avoid falling between the gaps of the bridge.

As he crossed the bridge, Hahns Spierling recognised people he knew floating down the creek in cars and being sucked under the bridge. Other people on top of cars jumped before their vehicles hit the bridge, into the arms of men on the bridge who had been watching them and helping them get to safety. Once the children had crossed the bridge they then had to wade across an area of calm water that was up to their waists in order to finally reach higher ground.

The Spierling children looked back along the railway line searching for their mother. A shipping container was heading for the bridge but slowed down as it hit the walkway along the outside of the railway bridge. Two minutes later they saw Lisa, coming across the bridge with the other adults. The water was up to their knees by then and still rising. Hahns shouted at his mother to hurry up.

The group of people crossed the bridge and waded through the still water that had risen so high that a powerline was flashing and crackling on the surface of the water. The still water was up to the chests of the adults. When Brad and Natasha reached higher ground at the school, they fell exhausted on the grass. But the water crept up to them within moments and they had to get up again and move higher up the slope.

The Bureau of Meteorology issued a flood warning for moderate to severe flooding in Lockyer Creek at 4.16 pm.

The EMQ Rescue 500 helicopter was refuelled and equipped for winching. Senior pilot Mark Kempton made a flight plan. He took off at 4.24 pm with a rescue crew: a doctor, a paramedic, winch operator Darren 'Parso' Parsons and rescue crewman Mark Turner. There were patches of low cloud and very heavy rainfall. The panicked voice of the police inspector in Toowoomba played on Mark's mind as he flew, weaving north and south of his flight path to skirt around storm cells, knowing people were in danger. 'I did push the limits of what I was trained to do. I pushed the aircraft and the crew to the absolute limits to get us into that valley. We came round the hills near Amberley and could see an inland sea in the Lockyer Valley.'

At 5 pm the Bureau upgraded its 4.16 pm warning to a top priority flash flood warning, to be broadcast with the SEWS siren to warn of the extreme rises in Lockyer Creek, with very fast and dangerous rises possible downstream at Gatton. The siren had been sounded at least three and a half hours after witnesses reported the unfolding disaster. A weather forum member commented: 'About freakin' time!!! FINALLY!!!'

The Rescue 500 helicopter arrived in Grantham just after 5 pm. The weather had cleared slightly but the crew could not locate any street addresses because all the features on the ground were underwater. Their maps became useless and they had no GPS locations for the houses they were trying to find.

Mark Kempton decided to work from the western side of the town because he needed to be able to hover into the wind. They lowered rescue crew officer Mark Turner – nicknamed 'Teabag' – to the most westerly house with people on the roof. Amazingly, by chance, it was the Mahon's house. The children and women were all on the roof but John had not been able to pull himself up, so he was still lying on a table balanced on the pool fence and clinging to the gutter.

Mark Turner was suddenly on the roof. Lachlan put his arms up and the harness went over his head and tightened around his chest. In 15 seconds he was in the helicopter. A few minutes later Liam was also lifted to safety. From his table, John saw his grandsons whisked away and he burst into tears. 'I knew my grandsons were safe.' His wife, Kathy, and daughters, Jess and Andrea, were also lifted into the helicopter.

Stacy heard a helicopter. After a while she stood up, hoping she would be spotted. Looking around, she turned to her left and saw Matthew standing on a roof on the other side of the railway tracks. The helicopter hovered over her house. A rescue officer was winched down but did not go inside.

Seeing the disaster scene, Mark Kempton knew more help was needed but he also knew there were no other helicopters within range to fly in before nightfall, except a second EMQ helicopter Rescue 510 from Cairns that was in Brisbane for night-vision goggle training at 6 pm. They had to work as quickly as they could because there was no-one else who could help.

As Kathy was being winched up, she saw their neighbour Dave James clinging to the gutter in heavy-flowing water. Rescue 500 collected him but could not carry any more passengers. John was left clinging to the gutter. The helicopter crew signalled to John that they'd seen him and would be back. Pilot Mark Kempton looked for an area of high ground where they could drop the survivors and their doctor. He spotted a paddock, flew a circuit to scatter the cattle, and landed at Fullerton's farm, which became a base for the rescue operation. Farmers John and Betty Fullerton opened their home and provided food and clothing to the survivors, and beds for those who were ill.

Once on dry ground, Kathy Mahon borrowed a mobile phone to let her daughter in Brisbane know everyone except John had been airlifted to safety. They didn't think he would survive because the water was still rising when they left.

The helicopter crew was returning for John Mahon when they saw another neighbour of the Mahon's, Matthew Keep, on a roof waving wildly and pointing towards something in the water. They flew over John Mahon and signalled to him, indicating they had to get other people first who were in more danger.

They followed Matthew's hand signals and saw a tiny clump of trees on an island that was less than two metres wide and was being eroded away. Mark Turner was lowered on to what looked like a pile of debris. Stacy Keep was sitting slumped on a log.

'I'm glad we got to her when we did because the water was rising around her. Darren winched me down to put the rescue harness over her. She was really, really exhausted. She was very pale. We winched her in. She just looked like she wasn't there. Once we got her in the aircraft, she fell on the floor and the paramedic dragged her across into a seat,' he said.

Rescue 500 then collected Matthew and the people with him on the roof and flew them all to the Fullerton's farm. Matthew and Stacy were both exhausted and devastated. 'By then we thought that it was just us two and that we had lost all the kids,' Stacy said. But she had not given up hoping that Madison and Pauline might have survived. 'I told Matthew that Madison could still possibly be alive because Pauline was trying to save her before I left.'

Parso and Matthew carried Stacy from the aircraft. Matthew begged a doctor in the helicopter crew to ask the helicopter to go to his house to see if his children were there. Matthew was told the crew had no tools to get through the roof and explained it was too dangerous to go inside the house.

Kenly and Fran saw the helicopter flying overhead. No-one could see them in the trees. Fran stood further up her branch and shook it around to try to attract attention. The branch broke and she fell in the water. Fran climbed back up her tree.

For a second time the helicopter headed back towards John

Mahon, who was still lying on a table balanced on the pool fence and clinging to his gutter. They flew over, signalling to him again that there were other people who were in a more dire situation. Just as the EMQ helicopter had headed for John, pilot Mark Kempton saw people on another roof who were wildly gesticulating towards a group of trees in front of a house. 'As we hovered towards the trees the downdraft of the helicopter blew the trees apart and the winch operator saw a couple of heads poking out of the water. People were clinging to the trees,' he said.

Mark Turner was winched into the water so the current would sweep him into the trees. He found two elderly people there and clambered through the tree branches towards the woman, Fran Arndt. Kenly and Fran had been in the water for more than two hours and were very cold. The water had begun receding but it was still too dangerous to get out of the trees.

Mark put the harness sling over Fran's head. Once in the water, she began to panic and started pushing Mark under water. He desperately needed the winch operator to haul them up but he knew Parso could not see his hand signals. Mark was being forced under the water and could not hold his breath for much longer. He would have to press the emergency cable release button on his harness if he was not lifted in the next few seconds.

Inside the aircraft, Parso was getting very worried. He could not see Mark. He alerted the pilot: 'I've lost sight of him. I've lost sight of him. I might have to cut the cable.' Mark Kempton hovered his thumb over the cable cut button in the cockpit. They were all in danger now. Mark knew that if the cable was snagged there was a risk it could pull the aircraft into the water. If the cable suddenly came free, it could fly up into the rotor blades causing a crash. But losing the cable would mean the helicopter could not rescue any more people, and there were dozens more in grave danger.

Mark Kempton waited ten more seconds – hopefully Mark Turner would be ready by now. They could only hope so. He asked Darren to winch Mark up. In the water, Mark felt the cable begin to tighten.

Finally the winch started lifting them out of the torrent. As the cable tension increased, the pilot saw Mark Turner appear from among the trees with a person, Fran, in the harness. They had succeeded.

Mark Turner helped Fran into the helicopter. Once she was safely in the aircraft, he hastily asked Darren to give him 60 seconds only for the next rescue and then bring him up. Mark was lowered back into the trees. Again there was no way for them to communicate. Mark had to work quickly to get Kenly into the rescue harness. They had less than 60 seconds. Mark put the harness over Kenly's head and tightened the strap across his chest. They were ready. The cable tightened, they rose out of the water, through the trees and up into the air. In less than 30 seconds they reached the helicopter. Kenly's body was so cold he could not move his legs to climb into the aircraft. Parso grabbed his hand and heaved him in.

On the following sortie, the helicopter winched John Mahon to safety at last. As Rescue 500 landed back at the farm with John Mahon on board, one of his daughters saw him and shouted to let the others know he was alive. John's wife Kathy, their daughters and the two little boys all ran outside and gathered around John, hugging him and crying with relief.

After clinging to a telegraph pole in Railway Street for one and a half hours, Gilbert Kilah was exhausted. 'I knew I was all but cactus. I looked over my shoulder and thought I would try to get to the trees in my front yard, five houses down the street, with the plan of hopefully getting out of the water into a tree,' Gilbert said.

He managed to grab a branch of a tree in front of his yard, but then he got sucked under the water. 'I knew I had a weldmesh front fence, so I felt around with my feet. I don't know how long I was under there for. I found the fence with my toes and worked my way up the branch and got up in the tree. I was gasping for air,' he said. 'That was the worst – sitting in the tree and wondering where the girls had gone. They were my main concern. I remember seeing Holly on King's verandah so I thought she was okay, but I was worried about Emma.' Gilbert heard the following day that Emma was alive.

After being in the water clinging to a tree for almost two hours, Frank King was shivering uncontrollably. The sun was going down. Frank saw another tree nearby that had a branch. He let go of his tree and set out for it, and was able to grab it and pull himself up on the branch and out of the water. A rescue helicopter flew overhead, forcing beetles, spiders and ants onto him. The spiders and ants bit him and a beetle crawled into one of his ears. With no sign of help around he knew he had to try to get home, and started walking through the neck-deep water. Frank was overwhelmed with amazement and relief to see his son John emerge from his house and come to help him. He was alive. As John reached Frank the two clung to each other and then turned and waded home.

From the roof of his house, Darren Keep saw the helicopter coming to airlift his neighbour. They could take him but not his dog. The neighbour would not leave his dog, so he and Darren stayed until the water receded enough for them to climb down and walk the eight kilometres to Helidon.

As the water began receding, Johnathon Klaassen and his brother David went to see what was left of the town. Matthew Keep also decided to go back into the flood to try to find his children. He ran from the farm before anyone could stop him. Johnathon and David Klaassen saw the devastation and were on their way back when they saw Matthew Keep, wild with desperation, running along the railway line back towards his house. Matthew told them his daughter was in the house. He jumped in the water and was swept away, but managed to climb out and up onto the railway line again.

The EMQ crew had airlifted 28 people in just over two hours of intense concentration, repeatedly taking off, winching survivors and landing again. There were about 30 people still on roofs but the helicopter's fuel supply was critically low. Mark Kempton tried to phone his base but there was no reception. He saw a Channel 9 helicopter and asked the pilot to phone the EMQ base to see if the second helicopter could come.

Johnathon Klaassen ran 100 metres further along the railway line, got into the water, swam across the current, and floated down to the house. 'I went inside and saw his daughter on a lounge chair in the house that was wedged up against the wall. She told me her dolly was gone. I called back to Matthew, "There's a little girl in here."'

Madison, five, had stayed on a floating lounge chair as the water rose to almost two metres deep and waited for at least two hours to be rescued. Johnathon Klaassen went inside to pick her up and noticed there was another voice in the house. He asked her who it was and she told him it was her brother Jacob. 'I yelled out to Jacob that I'd be back to get him,' Johnathon said.

Jacob, four, had swum into his parents' ensuite and held on for about two hours. By the time the water was going down, Jacob was so cold that his fingers had frozen onto the showerhead. Johnathon Klaassen took Madison outside and told Matthew, 'Mate, there's another child in the house: Jacob.' Matthew burst into tears and rushed into the house where he found his son still hanging on to the showerhead, his little hands frozen and stiff.

Matthew carefully prised Jacob's icy fingers from the showerhead, gathered him into his arms and took him outside. The children were both shaking with cold. Matthew and Johnathon stood beside the house for more than 15 minutes, waving to attract the helicopter rescuers. They decided to climb on the roof and signal from there. Fortunately, an industrial bin had washed down the floodwater and landed on the patio. They climbed on it and lifted the children onto the roof and waved for a helicopter. At last they were seen and air-lifted to safety. Johnathon walked back to his brother's house and had a shower to warm up.

The New South Wales helicopter refuelled in Toowoomba and needed to lighten its load so it could airlift more survivors. They offloaded Andrew Neil and Brad Mills, the swift water rescue team from Brisbane's QFRS Special Operations Unit who had rescued Jenny Thorncraft at Helidon. Once on the ground, Andrew and Brad asked where they were and discovered they had been dropped off in

Grantham. The floodwater was still too deep and dangerous for them to safely take people from their roofs, so Andrew and Brad had to wait for the water to recede.

They began to think over what had happened during the day and the enormity of the disaster began to hit them. People on roofs had heard that another wave of floodwater was heading towards them. Andrew and Brad were not aware of the predicted second wave, and they assured the people on the roofs there wasn't one, even though they were not sure themselves.

In the paddock east of the town where Peter and Marie Van Straten had been swept away in their house, the couple had given up hope of being rescued. They had heard the last of the helicopters leave and said goodbye to each other, thinking they would not escape alive. Suddenly, the couple heard another helicopter approaching. Kendall Thompson and his rescue team had returned from having the aircraft refuelled.

Kendall had never been trained for winch rescues, and he was trying to do one of the most difficult rescues into water. The crew quickly made some plans and lowered him upstream of the house, so the winch line would not snag on the damaged house. As the helicopter descended low enough to winch Kendall down, loose corrugated iron began to flap wildly. Peter and Marie were terrified as sheets of iron pulled free and flew wildly around them. The helicopter ascended again.

In the house, Marie and Peter thought the rescue helicopter had decided it was too dangerous to try to rescue them. But a minute later the aircraft was descending again, this time about 30 metres from the house. Kendall was lowered on a winch cable into the water, and he swam towards the house. When he got there he climbed onto what was left of the floor. Above the noise of the engine, the rush of water and the downdraft of the helicopter, Peter shouted, 'Save my wife first. She can't swim.'

Kendall put the rescue harness over Marie's head and took her to the edge of the house. He would have to get her in the water so the helicopter could drag them both clear of the house wreckage. He tightened the harness around her chest and jumped with her into the murky water. They went under but quickly surfaced again and Kendall held her as the helicopter dragged them clear of the house. The winch line went slack and Marie went underwater again. She panicked momentarily but then the winch line tightened and she and Kendall rose to the surface and up into the air. Peter watched as his wife was raised to the helicopter. 'The biggest relief I got that day was seeing Marie get taken through that helicopter door,' he said. In the aircraft, Kendall released Marie from the strap and returned to get Peter. The dog, Chloe, was still clinging tightly to his shoulder. Kendall had nothing to secure her with, so she would just have to hold on as best she could.

Kendall wrapped the rescue strap around Peter and the two went into the water. The helicopter dragged them clear of the wreckage and lifted them into the aircraft. Chloe held on and would not let go of Peter's shoulder even when they were safely in the aircraft. Peter hugged Marie. Two crew members prised Chloe from Peter's shoulder and the little dog immediately began licking Marie's face. The helicopter dropped them at the school: they had more people to rescue.

The second helicopter airlifted another 15 people before it became too dark to continue. The pilots Ned Lee and Matt O'Brien had shared the workload of flying the helicopter for the difficult rescues and receiving urgent tasking instructions. Back at the Archerfield EMQ base, Mark Turner collapsed on the floor in exhaustion. A new crew came on duty, but the weather closed in and they could not continue the rescues even using night-vision goggles.

Peter and Marie went indoors and took off their wet clothes. Lisa Spierling gave them dry clothes and hot drinks. She had no medication for Peter's deep vein thrombosis or his diabetes and there was no doctor to attend to Marie's broken arm.

Once back at the Fullerton's farm, Matthew Keep took Madison and Jacob inside to see Stacy. It was hard to believe their two young children had survived. 'I was so happy but so sad at the same time because there was one missing,' Stacy said.

Matthew realised there still could be more people stuck in houses so he set off running back towards Railway Street. Johnathon and David saw him go and ran to catch up with him. The three men waded around the town, checking on people in houses where they could see lights, using their mobile phones to light their way. They found an elderly woman, Betty Charles, and helped her out of her house. They passed a house with several people on the roof but they had no ladder to get them down.

It was almost 7.30 pm when QFRS rescue team Nathan Chadwick and Phil Paff were heading back from Murphys Creek towards the fire station at Gatton. They decided to go through Grantham on the way, to check everything was alright there. 'We knew the creeks went that way but the country opened up a lot from there. Once you got to Helidon the floodplains were a lot broader so I thought the water would spread out a lot more.' Seeing the devastation, they shone a torch across the paddocks and some survivors started heading towards them. Johnathon and David Klaassen asked them to take Betty Charles to safety.

Once the water level was low enough, Andrew and Brad helped 22 people from the roofs of their houses in Harris Street. The rescuers then went to the railway bridge where cars were piled up amid tonnes of debris. Among the debris they saw something moving. It could be a survivor. On closer inspection, it was a pig. Andrew and Brad then searched each car. They found no bodies. They then searched trucks that had been swept away, and looked inside flooded houses. At the pub, they found a group of survivors, Roy Abraham and his neighbour Kelvin Woods, publican Lance Richardson, and his son and elderly mother.

On Gatton Helidon Road, near the bridge over Sandy Creek, Johnathon and David Klaassen heard a young boy crying in a tree. They walked towards the sound, looked up and saw seven-year-old Zac.

Zac made his way to the lowest branch of the tree. David Klaassen still could not reach him. He asked Zac to swing down from the branch. David caught the boy and passed him to his brother. David took off his shirt and wrapped it around the boy to warm him up. Zac told them his father was in another tree, and they went and helped Danny down to the road. A car came along and the driver asked for directions to Gatton and told them there had been a warning of another nine metres of water coming down the creek. Johnathon and David realised they needed to get everyone out.

They needed a ladder to help the group of people off the roof and Danny directed them to a ladder on the flooded fire truck that had been in his backyard from the night before. They used it to get the group off the roof and loaded all 12 people they had found, as well as dogs, cats and birds into the four-wheel drive. Danny and Zac, Katherine Godley and her brother Michael with their dogs and pet birds, and the family rescued from a house roof, were all crammed into the vehicle. They were all cold and shocked, but very relieved to be escaping the disaster zone. There was not enough room for Johnathon and David so the brothers walked back to the high side of Grantham, calling out as they went in case there was anyone else still in a house.

Nathan and Phil by this time had arrived at the Gatton bypass and handed Betty Charles over to be taken for medical care. They also met fresh emergency crews and guided them back to town. 'As we came to the bridge I flashed a big spotlight around. The township was blackened out and we couldn't see any sign of life but after a few sweeps with the spotlight suddenly we'd see lights appearing on the roofs,' Nathan said. The men waded through chest-deep water, towing their inflatable boat to Harris Street, checking on people to see if anyone needed immediate rescue. People on the roofs were frustrated and the rescuers felt powerless to help. 'They were waiting for some kind of government agency to come, but all that turned up was three blokes and a blow-up boat.'

At the school, Lisa Spierling acted as first aid officer, treating broken arms, a suspected broken leg, cuts and bruises, and a possible cardiac arrest. By evening, 50 people were at the school, all shocked, cold and hungry – but alive. Everyone that Hahns had seen sucked under the railway bridge or floating past in their houses came back during the night. Unless he had seen them himself, he wouldn't have thought it possible that they survived.

One of the women who had run along the railway line with them was looking very unwell. Lisa was called to check on Sharon McCray. Sharon stopped breathing. Lisa counted five seconds. She still wasn't breathing in. Lisa called to her. There was no response. She called again and again. Lisa prepared to begin resuscitation. Ten, twenty, twenty-five seconds. Thirty seconds has passed. Finally Sharon gasped . . . a quick, shallow breath. Then another and another. She was back, but breathing very quickly, too quickly. Relieved, Lisa breathed slowly with her for several minutes, helping her to calm down. More patients were waiting for her help so she needed someone to stay with Sharon to keep her breathing steady. She called her son Hahns, who knew Sharon well. Lisa told Hahns to speak gently but clearly to her, 'Breathe in . . . breathe out . . . in . . . out.' Hahns held Sharon's hand and sat with her for an hour helping her to breathe slowly and deeply, until Sharon's breathing stabilised.

Local residents who lived on the higher side of town brought food and clothing. One of Natasha's uncle's used the UHF radio in his truck to track down members of the family, and got his wife to phone Natasha at the school. Natasha's aunty told her, 'Your dad's fine, he's okay, he's made it. But your grandma didn't make it and Jessica didn't make it.' Natasha was shocked and devastated. She burst into tears and vomited. She and Brad wrapped themselves in blankets, lay on the floor and cried – for the lost members of their family and for the loss of all their possessions. There had been no information in the phone call about Stacy's mother, Dawn. Natasha remained hopeful. 'They haven't mentioned her; she must be okay.'

At about 1 am on 11 January, Marty Warburton was still on the roof of his service station. A thunderstorm came over and he was worried that lightning could electrocute him if he stayed on the roof. He started climbing down and was holding on to the gutter when it gave way. He fell in the water. He has no recollection of swimming against the flow of the floodwater, but somehow reached a verandah two houses upstream from his service station and knocked at the door of his friend Wayne. 'Wayne looked at me like he'd seen a ghost. He grabbed me and pulled me inside.' Wayne was amazed to see Marty and asked him, 'Where the hell did you come from? I thought you were dead.'

A swift water rescue team arrived at Wayne's house, linked arms with everyone in the house and waded with them to the railway line and up to the school. Once at the school they were given dry clothes, hot drinks and food. Looking back, Marty Warburton believes the phone call he received saved him and everyone at the railway bridge. 'Nearly every day I think how lucky I am. If we had been standing there looking up Sandy Creek we would not be here today,' he said.

Another band of storms brought more rain the next day. Floodwater inundated Grantham again. This time it rose slowly, backing up Sandy Creek and creeping into houses that had been devastated the day before. Sandy Creek peaked almost a metre above the major flood level of four metres, at 4.9 metres.

The aftermath

As darkness settled over the disaster zone, hundreds of people who had lost their homes – but escaped with their lives – gathered at local meeting points: schools and halls or neighbouring houses that had escaped unscathed. Local people who still had houses brought food. Power outages meant frozen food was defrosting, so it needed to be cooked and eaten because it could not be refrozen. Gas barbecues were kept busy cooking sausages and steak to feed the dozens of flood survivors in each township of the Lockyer Valley as survivors arrived cold, hungry, injured and shocked.

Dry clothes were brought by anyone who had them for the people who had no clothes except the soaked, muddy ones they wore. Blankets and mattresses came from nearby houses, so the survivors could give their children somewhere to sleep, or at least rest, on the floor, as comfortably as possible. The vision of the flood was still too fresh in their minds. Not knowing who had died and who had lived made it very difficult to sleep. Material goods, houses that had suddenly been destroyed, did not seem to matter any more. Rain still pounded on the roof. Life was what mattered now.

Many adults and children lay down that night with hearts heavy with grief – sobbing and keening with agony – for those they had seen swept away by the torrent. Some were family members, some neighbours, some friends, some strangers. Nothing would be the same. Inside the disaster zone, the few mobile phones still with battery power were shared among groups of shocked survivors who sparingly sent 'We're alive' text messages to the outside world. The messages were passed around families outside the disaster area who were waiting anxiously for news.

Truck drivers used UHF radios to get messages through where no phone lines or networks were working. In the outside world, where electricity existed, families and friends tried to find out if people inside the disaster zone were alive. Others used social networking sites to try to make contact. News media did not have the capacity to broadcast enough information about the disaster. Desperate for more information, people logged onto the Queensland Police Facebook page to get news faster, and searched online missing persons' registers. Videos were posted on YouTube and shared around, revealing that the disaster was not just centred on Toowoomba – it had extended to several townships and rural districts in the Lockyer Valley, a devastating display of the force of nature.

In each isolated township, injured and sick survivors were tended all night by volunteers with basic medical supplies – painkillers, antiseptic, borrowed prescription medications, bandages – whatever came to hand. With roads cut, communications disabled, and darkness preventing aerial evacuations, there was no possibility of getting medical help in or patients out.

During the night the flood continued relentlessly, moving both east and west of the mountains. To the west of Toowoomba it flowed towards the towns of Oakey and Dalby. To the east, the waters made their way to Gatton, peaking that night at 8 pm and continuing onward to Forest Hill, Laidley and Ipswich, towards the Brisbane River.

Next morning the survivors began to see the extent of the ravages wrought by the torrent. Timber houses had been lifted from their stumps while brick houses had been swiped off concrete slabs, leaving only tiles on the floor. Even the carpets had been ripped from the floors.

So many people had escaped with their lives. They were deeply shaken by how close they and their families had come to dying. The death toll could have been so much higher. In Toowoomba, firefighters were amazed that so many people had narrowly escaped from the unexpected torrent through the CBD. They were also astonished that those people stranded in cars on the range highway had all escaped despite their cars being partially buried by landslides. Paul Pepi realised he had had a very narrow escape as he drove up the mountain. 'If I hadn't backed back where I did, I probably would have died. I would have been pushed over the edge of the range. Where I got caught, there was no guardrail. If I had hesitated for another couple of seconds I wouldn't be here now.' The extra seconds he'd taken to think and to realise he had to slam his car into reverse had saved him. In Withcott, Postmans Ridge, Helidon and Grantham, hundreds of people had also escaped.

Many people in Grantham believe the death toll could have been far higher but for the quick thinking of people who climbed to roofs and scrambled to safety. The phone calls between sisters Sandy Halliday and Sue Turner were pivotal in informing the Grantham community of the disaster, giving them vital minutes to escape. Lisa Spierling believes 50 to 60 people came too close. 'I can't believe there were not more deaths,' she said. Brad Long was traumatised by the split-second decision he had made at his uncle's house to run back along the road to help his wife instead of going into Matthew and Stacy Keep's house where Dawn, Pauline and Jessica were lost. 'Why didn't I run inside? It still haunts me every minute of every day to think that I could have gone in there and saved the people who died,' he said. 'I don't know what I could have done. It's something that's going to haunt me for the rest of my life.'

Marty Warburton believes the phone call he received at the bridge, warning him of the flood, meant that he and dozens of other people moved away from Sandy Creek just in time. 'Nearly every day I think how lucky I am. I believe if we were still standing in those two locations looking up Sandy Creek, waiting for a normal flood to come, we wouldn't be here today, because where that water came from is 90 degrees to where the water normally comes from, so we wouldn't have stood a chance. The force of that water smashed double besser brick walls out of buildings. There were 50 to 70 people who were congregating in those areas that possibly wouldn't be here today if we hadn't got that warning and dispersed back to our properties.'

Despite the lack of warning of the severity of the disaster, the timing during daylight hours saved hundreds of people. At Murphys Creek, Susan Mouflih was grateful the flood had hit during the day. 'I'm truly thankful it happened in the afternoon and not at night. We would all be dead. It could have been a significantly worse disaster than it was.' In townships further down the creeks, the death toll could also have been far higher if the torrent had struck at night because most people would have been at home, asleep in bed, unable to see what was happening or where they could flee to escape. Frank King believes many more elderly people and children in Grantham would have drowned. 'Really, the only saving grace was that it did happen during the day because if it had happened at night time then very few elderly people or children would have survived. Our death toll would have been horrendous, really.'

Grantham resident Gilbert Kilah believes dozens, and possibly hundreds more people, would have died if all the creeks affecting Grantham had been flowing at the same time and at the same rate. He says simply, 'I wouldn't be here.'

The timing of the disaster during the school holidays also lessened the risk to dozens of children who would have been at 'ground zero' in Grantham and on the streets of Toowoomba, Withcott and Murphys Creek if the flood had struck on a school day. Had the intense storm struck a more populated area, such as Ipswich or Brisbane, the death toll could also have been significantly higher.

From his home south-west of Boonah, weather watcher Neil

Pennell was amazed that the death toll in Grantham was so low. 'It's testament to their tenacity. Frank King survived clinging to the tree by sheer bloody-minded determination.'

The morning after the disaster, Danny McGuire wanted to know if the bodies of his wife Llync, his son Garry, 12, and his daughter Jocelyn, five, who had drowned in the fire truck, had been swept away or if they were still in the truck. His colleague, rural firefighter Stuart Damrow, phoned to find out. The answer came back within a few minutes. 'Yes. They were recovered in the truck.'

Danny was relieved. 'At least I knew they were there. Some other people will never be found and I couldn't live with that.' Their deaths were reported by police media: 'CLARKE, Llync-Chiann, 31, and two children, boy, 12, and girl, 5. 10/01/2011: Rural Fire Brigade Truck became inundated while on Gatton Helidon Road. Two occupants escaped to safety. Three occupants, mother and two children, were trapped inside and were later found deceased in the vehicle.'

As Danny contemplates the failure of authorities to order an evacuation the night before the flood, he is understandably devastated. 'I'm not real good in the gut. We shouldn't have waited for answers from up above. We should have just evacuated the place and got a kick up the arse later on.'

As news filtered to the outside world, the magnitude of the disaster shocked a state already reeling from the most widespread flooding in history. Grantham vegetable farmer Derek Schultz reported the paddocks of his 300-acre farm were covered in debris, including the wreckages of two houses. The violence of the torrent and the toll of dead and missing were terrible. Emergency relief agencies and individuals responded to the urgent need for food, clothes and shelter for hundreds of flood victims. Social networking pages were hastily established to coordinate the needs of people in each community, with donations of goods, equipment and labour to help in the clean-up. The Australian Defence Force (ADF) was called in to assist with the search for survivors and victims. They began the enormous job, which would continue for months, of removing the debris from the destroyed houses, roads and bridges. First there was the task of removing the sticky, stinking mud that lay a metre deep over much of the disaster zone.

Widespread, heavy rain continued falling, threatening to extend the disaster to the east and to the west. As the torrent flowed to the east, through Gatton, the creek gauge peaked at 15.38 metres – 0.75 metres higher than the record set in 1974. The only higher recorded flood was the great flood of 1893, when Lockyer Creek at Gatton registered 16.33 metres. Authorities in Brisbane began warning people in low-lying areas of the state's capital to prepare to evacuate. Anyone in Brisbane who hadn't been worried until then realised they were now at risk. But their distress at the coming flood was tempered by the deaths the previous day. Even as they packed and evacuated, they were grateful for the warning: they and their children would survive. Damage to houses and the loss of possessions was already put into perspective after witnessing the horror of the deadly torrent that swept away an unknown number of lives less than 24 hours earlier.

By 11 am, helicopters began evacuating people from the towns east of Gatton at Forest Hill and Laidley. Further east, residents in the city of Ipswich were warned to expect flash flooding that night. By midday, the lowest banks of the Brisbane River were already breaking from the heavy rainfall the day before, and the CBD and low-lying suburbs were being evacuated. Brisbane Mayor Campbell Newman warned 6,500 homes would be flooded. The Bureau of Meteorology predicted the biggest floods since 1974 would reach Brisbane in two days. The warnings were underlined by the identification of the first of the flood victims who had died the previous day: Steve and Sandy Matthews of Spring Bluff, who had been swept from their house after telling their children to climb to safety in the ceiling of their house. In Toowoomba and the Lockyer Valley, eight people had been confirmed dead and 70 had been reported missing. Fears that the hundreds of cars swept away in Toowoomba may have had people inside were allayed when police completed searching the cars and found no bodies inside.

In surviving families, parents gave their children extra hugs. Almost everyone could clearly identify the terrifying moment their priorities instantaneously changed when the flood engulfed them, from trying to save possessions – cars, photos, electrical goods, computers – to realising they had to abandon material goods and save the lives of their family or friends. Grantham survivor Lisa Spierling, and many other people, reassessed the importance of material goods after losing their homes. 'Losing everything means nothing,' Lisa said. 'You spend half your life collecting stuff and the other half trying to work out what to do with it. I don't have anything to worry about what to do with it – it's all gone. We are still waking up every morning. Having all those things doesn't change who you are.'

North of Brisbane, police issued an emergency evacuation order for residents of Caboolture to move to higher ground. Caboolture was isolated and all roads to the town were cut. People in towns ahead of the westerly moving flood were now in danger. The whole town of Condamine was evacuated. South of Toowoomba, the New England Highway was cut north and south of the town of Warwick.

By 12 January the number of missing people in the Lockyer Valley and Toowoomba had risen to 78 and would top 500 before long. Andrew Gurr's hopes that his mother Jean had survived were fading. He tried again to get to Grantham but no-one was allowed into the town. He went once more to the evacuation centre in Helidon. Church ministers and counsellors had arrived. A missing person register had been set up. Andrew gave his mother's name and address.

That evening, police contacted Andrew and told him his mother's body had been found on Monday night, in her house. The force of the torrent had smashed her front door off its hinges. There was not much consolation but Andrew clung on to small mercies: his mother had spent happy years with her grandchildren, and her death, when it came, would have been very quick.

On Wednesday evening, police also found the body of Bruce Marshall, 66, at his home in Grantham, and informed his family.

Bruce had chosen to stay at home on the day of the flood because of the severe arthritis in his knees and degenerating discs in his back after a hard-working life as a welder and fruit picker. His son Aaron had asked him to accompany him to Toowoomba to collect some enrolment forms from the TAFE college but Bruce had declined, suggesting his wife Shirley go instead.

When they left home, Bruce was in his favourite chair watching television. As Aaron reversed out the driveway he paused and told his mother, 'Look, Mum, I don't know. I feel we should take Dad.' As they drove towards Toowoomba, Aaron noticed an eerie silence. 'No birds are singing, Mum. Everything's so quiet.'

Bruce was not aware of the impending danger until the power went out and he looked outside to see if there was any obvious cause. He saw floodwater up to his top step, phoned his daughter in Oakey and spoke to her about the flood before hanging up so he could call the SES. That was the last his family heard from him. They had been phoning schools and evacuation centres trying to find him for two days when police delivered the news they had most feared.

Heroic stories of rescue and sacrifice were also emerging. Jordan Rice, who had died in Toowoomba, was honoured as a hero for asking his rescuer Chris Skehan to take his brother Blake first, a decision that was to cost him his life moments later. Frightening stories emerged of people being saved by mere seconds, as the torrent roared down Murphys Creek and Gatton Creek.

Food and clothing donations from the public began to arrive by the truckload to the Lockyer Valley towns that had been hardest hit. Bottled water, milk, nappies and baby food, tinned food, toothbrushes, soap and medical supplies were delivered to the make-shift evacuation centres in each town. As roads were repaired enough to be passable, survivors returned to what was left of their homes and properties to look for signs of life – dogs, cats, birds, fish, horses, cows – anything that might have survived. In Grantham, police sealed the whole town declaring it a crime scene.

At Carpendale, Tom Friend's cows that had been released by his neighbour when the floodwater overtopped the quarry had swum in the flood, survived, and walked home. They stood in their muddy paddock, now fenceless, but preferring the security of their old pastures. One of Tom's sows was also found ten kilometres downstream in Gatton. They brought her home and a fortnight later she delivered six healthy piglets.

Two of the Warhursts' dogs had swum in the floodwater and survived at Postmans Ridge when the family home was swept away and destroyed. The dogs were found making their way home.

And at Grantham, Brenda Ross's German shepherd kelpie cross Penny had somehow escaped as the brick house collapsed and disintegrated into the torrent. Penny swam for three days among the debris and was helped ashore a few kilometres away at Placid Hills by a man who saw her and waded into the water. He moved debris aside so she could swim through. Once she stepped from the water, Penny fell exhausted onto the ground.

Wendy Hodda's kelpie labrador cross Stevie was found, alive, four days after the flood, still guarding the house. She was taken to a refuge where a neighbour recognised her. Almost all of Stevie's coat had fallen out but it was already beginning to grow back.

Australia's Defence Force and a volunteer army helped survivors begin the enormous clean-up job. Friends, neighbours, strangers – anyone with willing hands pitched in. Hundreds of soldiers and civilians helped clean up houses, properties and roads, shovelling mud and combing paddocks for anything that could be salvaged. Searchers found sections of roofs and walls, furniture, kitchenware, clothing, books, tools and dead animals. When they found personal items like wedding photos still in their frames and photo albums, they gathered them and handed them in so the families of the owners could be traced.

Amazing discoveries were made. The old butcher's block John Mahon had used for 38 years in his butcher shop in Grantham had floated from his garden shed where he had stored it, all the way back to his butcher shop in town and was lying in the mud beside the back door. A wallet swept away from Murphys Creek washed up in the Brisbane suburb of Jindalee, 130 kilometres downstream.

The continuing rain was unnerving. Many survivors had frightening flashbacks to their video memory-loop of the flood that haunted them in the night. Parents comforted children who had nightmares about the raging waters, of being lifted to rooftops where the expanse of the flood lay before their eyes. The haunting imagery would not go away. Some parents felt guilty that they had not evacuated their children to safety earlier – but no-one had told them of any danger to flee.

As days turned to weeks after the disaster, the survivors gradually left the evacuation centres and moved to live with relatives or in rental houses. Surviving families were scattered from Brisbane to Toowoomba, still not knowing the fate of many of their friends and neighbours. As they contacted their insurers, many were told they were not covered under their 'flood' policies because the disaster was 'not a flood'. Some were lucky. Insurers told them they were fully insured and everything would be replaced. But months of uncertainty followed for many families as they waited for flood hydrologists to examine the cause of destruction for their homes and report back to insurance companies. The definitions of 'flood', 'flash flood', 'deluge' and 'storm' that were irrelevant to those whose homes had been destroyed were to become of vital importance. Frustration welled up as survivors in the worst-hit areas were unable to access emergency government payments because they had no identification – they had escaped with only their lives.

Generous donations of houses, cars, money and volunteer labour buoyed the spirits of survivors. Musicians staged fundraising concerts and bushfire victims from the Black Saturday fires in Victoria arrived with convoys of trucks loaded with donated goods. Federal and state political leaders visited the disaster zone. A week after the disaster, Queensland Premier Anna Bligh announced that an independent Commission of Inquiry would examine the impact of the flooding, which by then had affected 70 per cent of the state. Soldiers and police were still discovering bodies inside houses. A Grantham house searched three times was searched once more. This time, the body of a victim was found.

Survivors who had been saved from the floodwaters began to publicly thank their rescuers. Stories of sacrifice and heroism emerged. People who had risked their lives to save members of their family, or strangers, were reluctant to call themselves heroes. They invariably avoided the clichéd media tag: they told reporters they were just doing what anybody else would do. But the many people who owed their survival to the courage of others bonded strongly with their rescuers.

The Grantham community, where so many people escaped with their lives because of the close-knit family and friendship networks, drew much closer to each other. The identity of the Perry family, filmed on the roof of their car floating down Lockyer Creek, was finally solved eight days after the flood. As police worked as quickly as they could to identify flood victims, they issued an appeal for public help to confirm the fate of a young woman photographed in floodwater in Dent Street in Toowoomba. The survival of Hannah Reardon-Smith and her mother Kathryn was confirmed by rescuers at the scene. The nation breathed a sigh of relief.

The new school year was about to begin and families with school-aged children needed to buy schoolbooks and uniforms – many for a second time – before school started. Some people were able to salvage uniforms from flooded houses because waterproof schoolbags had floated, preserving the clothing inside.

As army, police and SES searchers found bodies, and forensic teams formally identified them, families organised funerals. In ones and twos and threes, grandparents, parents, husbands, wives and children were laid to rest, after moving services during which their lives and the tragic circumstances of their deaths were remembered. The first funerals were held under the glare of a national and international media contingent.

Families who had the bodies of their loved ones to bury were relieved they had been found. Some felt guilty that they should be so lucky. Other families had no body to bury and maybe never would. How would the family ever come to terms with the reality of death when they had no body to bid farewell? Not knowing seemed infinitely harder than knowing, caring, grieving and having a burial place. Three people remain missing: James Perry, who was swept from the roof of his car at Helidon, and Dawn Radke and Christopher Face, who were both swept from their houses in Grantham.

Many people who had survived wondered why they had escaped. Some battled with survivor guilt, while others saw their survival as an amazing coincidence or the hand of God. Grantham retiree Frank King was heartbroken for the loss of life in the town. 'Initially you're almost embarrassed that you've survived, when you hear of the death toll. After that you're embarrassed that it didn't go in your house. You wonder why you should be left, unscathed. Someone was looking after us, I think.'

As weeks passed, families and friends of the people who were still missing lost hope that they could have survived and realised the best outcome then would be for searchers to find a body for them to bury. Bess Fraser was relieved when the bodies of her nephew Joshua and her sister Brenda were identified. She didn't want to continue to wonder, 'Where are they? Did they go out to sea? What happened to their bodies?' She found relief in knowing. 'If I didn't find them I would be looking every day until I could find them.' A few belongings were also found in nearby paddocks – Josh's red pyjama pants with penguins on them, which he often wore to the pub next door, and a work shirt that has been dry-cleaned and framed and hangs at the childcare centre where he worked. Knowing many young children would be at Josh's funeral, Bess provided lots of coloured balloons, bubble blowers and butterflies. Josh's mates wore pyjamas to the wake held on what was left of the deck at the Grantham pub, and at the childcare centre, a shelf of teddy bears dubbed 'Joshy bears' has been provided for the children to cuddle and to take home to comfort them. Sometimes, even staff take home a Joshy bear.

Meanwhile Bess held on to any consolation she could find. 'People are going to find this very strange but I find it a blessing that the house collapsed down on top of them, because they would have been knocked out and wouldn't have known anything else that would have happened.' She is grateful to her partner Chris Barrett for asking her to go with him to move vehicles. 'I am blessed and grateful that Chris knew the area. He knew how water flowed through that area and he saved me. I'll never ever forget that.'

As the huge body of floodwaters moved south through New South Wales, a new natural disaster threat was already looming. In the Coral Sea, Cyclone Yasi was forming and heading for the north Queensland coast. Media focus shifted from the devastated Lockyer Valley and the Brisbane floods to the new peril. Cyclone Yasi intensified into a Category 5 cyclone, the most severe cyclone since 1918, and crossed the coast near Mission Beach, 1,500 kilometres north of Brisbane, at midnight on 2 February, destroying hundreds of houses.

A few days later, another natural disaster on the west coast of Australia was looming, as dangerously hot, dry, windy weather sparked bushfires. On 5 February the bushfires began raging out of control in the Darling Ranges in the western suburbs of Perth, destroying 72 houses. Just over two weeks later, a 6.3 magnitude earthquake struck the city of Christchurch in New Zealand, killing at least 182 people on 22 February. The public was becoming fatigued with the succession of natural disasters, but there was one more to come in what became known as the 'summer of disasters'. An 8.9 magnitude earthquake and a ten-metre tsunami struck Japan on 12 March, killing an estimated 7,653 people and causing a nuclear reactor to melt down.

As disasters struck successively in north Queensland, Western Australia, New Zealand and Japan, the media spotlight on the Lockyer Valley dimmed as families struggled to provide for the basic needs of their families, with returning to work, dealing with insurance companies, and filling out seemingly endless flood relief application forms without having the 'evidence' they needed because it had been washed down the creek. Some relationships and marriages were strained, while others were cemented by the disaster. Wives who had been aggravated by aspects of their husband's personalities now revered them for their calmness under pressure to rescue them and their children. The trauma of the flood triggered a wide range of mental health conditions, from depression and anxiety to post-traumatic stress and suicidal ideations.

Bess Fraser reached a low ebb when she spiralled into depression in the months after the flood. Intent on ending her life, she took the keys of her caravan and her shipping container of furniture to Grantham and handed them to a friend telling her, 'I can't do this any more.' Bess got in her car and drove home. Bess's friend told her husband late that evening and he recognised the risk of suicide and phoned a police officer working on the flood recovery in Grantham. The officer phoned another police officer close to where Bess was living, to check that she was alright. He turned up at her house at 10.30 pm that night and called an ambulance.

The paramedic diagnosed that Bess was hypothermic and had very high blood pressure. Bess was unwilling to be taken to hospital because she needed to feed her pets. The police officer looked at the ambulance officer. They nodded knowingly to each other and the police officer sectioned Bess, committing her for involuntary medical care. Bess was taken to hospital. When she was released she returned home, realising only in retrospect how much she had needed medical help. 'Looking from the inside out, all I could see was the mud.' Bess doesn't know who the police officer was but she knows she owes her life to the caring concern of both officers. 'When I find him I will thank him for saving my life.' Bess has a new grip on life: 'Now I have to help make sure that the mistakes that have been made are fixed.'

In March, Britain's Prince William visited Grantham during a tour of communities affected by the floods and Cyclone Yasi. On the day of his visit, a tour organiser phoned Bess Fraser and told her the prince had asked to meet her. Bess and her daughter TaNaỳa were already on the way to Grantham for a lunch reception, and Bess was not ready to face any reporters or television cameras. She warned her daughter she would stay in the car rather than be confronted by the media. Her fears were allayed as she walked into a marquee without being hounded by any reporters. Then Prince William approached her and hugged her. She told him simply, 'I'm Bess.' The three sat down and Bess was soon at ease. 'We forgot the protocol of calling him "sir". I called him "love" and "darling",' she said.

'He is what you see – a very natural young man. We were talking about how to cope with loss – to talk to the people you have lost. When we were talking I got a bit emotional and he held my hand on my knee or on his knee. He was a young man when he lost his mum. It hasn't made him bitter. He's gone forward in every possible way. That gave me hope that if a young man can do that, I can do that and help others too. He's full of compassion. He understood where I have come from. I constantly talk to Brenda and Joshua every day. I learned that from him.' The visit from the prince gave Bess strength. 'I walked away with a filled heart, thinking, "I could do this." It's incredible knowing he came from the other side of the world and he wanted to meet people in Grantham.'

Bess finds solace in knowing that Brenda and Josh are together and knowing they can't be hurt. 'If Brenda was here without Joshua she would will herself to death. I know that. If Joshy was here without his mum, I don't think the love and comfort I have for him would be enough to fill that hole of missing his mum.' Bess is also conscious of living for Josh to make up the years that he missed out on. 'Josh was a thrill-seeker. He would go on the fastest rides, sliding through the world. I've always been a bit reserved. Now I'm taking risks and doing things I've never done. I'm going on a plane. That's a massive step for me – way out of my comfort zone. I've never been on a plane. I've got to do all this for Josh.'

In the first round of hearings of the Queensland Floods Commission of Inquiry, sittings were held in Toowoomba for two days on 18 and 19 April, and another three days from 27 to 29 April 2011. Many of the survivors in the Lockyer Valley didn't have computers and didn't know when or how to contribute to the inquiry. Most survivors did not give statements or submissions. For some of those who did know, the grief was still too raw to speak in public about what had happened.

Almost four months after the flood, Stacy Keep gave birth to a baby girl, Sienna Lily-Ann, on 4 May 2011. Sienna's middle name was given to her in memory of Jessica, whose middle name was also Lily-Ann.

As summer gave way to autumn and winter, flood survivors needed warm clothes. The clothes that had been donated immediately after the disaster had been summer clothes. Word went out via Facebook support sites and bags and boxes of jumpers, blankets and heaters arrived at flood relief centres.

Sam Matthews was rebuilding his life: he bought a block of land in Murphys Creek and was setting up temporary housing for himself. The death of his father meant he needed to find a new job – they had worked together in the family business. He was planning to return to TAFE and pursue his preferred career, but he was also giving himself time to grieve for his parents, Steve and Sandy. The day of the flood still haunted him. While he knew he had done his best, he felt guilty that he had not achieved a 'perfect result'. He had saved himself and his sister but not their parents.

As Sam worked on his property he also returned to his hobby of working on cars. He and his father had spent many hours together under the bonnets of cars. One of them, a Jaguar, had been retrieved after the flood and Sam began restoring it. He was working on the car on 27 July when the car caught fire. Sam dialled triple zero for help. He tried to put out the fire as it spread across the grass and phoned triple zero again.

Firefighters arrived and extinguished the blaze, which by then had destroyed two cars and a shipping container. They found Sam's body on the ground near the shipping container. He was due to turn 21 on 7 August.

Sam's death was a cruel blow to his family and the local community. Sam's siblings released a brief statement: 'This year we have suffered so much tragedy in such a short period of time and our grief for our family is extremely overwhelming. We are aware of the intense media interest in Sam's tragic accident but at this stage our focus is on our family and young children, and therefore we will not be participating in any media interviews.' At his funeral a fortnight later, Pastor Bob Crockford articulated what so many other people were thinking: 'Why Sam? Why now?' Sarah and Victoria told the congregation they wished Sam had just run from the fire, but they knew it was in his nature to fight to save his beloved motorbikes. Sam's elder brother Dan told the congregation the flood tragedy had resulted in the brothers mending their strained relationship. They'd had six months to get to know each other again. 'It was a second chance and I'm so thankful,' he told the congregation.

Attention began turning at the end of winter to a new La Niña climate pattern that was beginning to develop in the central Pacific Ocean. Many houses damaged in the disaster remain in vulnerable areas, because insurance cover provided enough money for owners to repair the houses but not to remove them to a higher location, or to build a new house and demolish the damaged house.

There is a wide variation in attitude to the risk of another flash flood disaster among the residents. Some people are fearful of a similar event some time in the future and are moving away from the flood zone; others hold on to a self-assurance that 'it will never happen again' because it hasn't happened in living memory. Others believe it can happen again but hope it won't in their lifetime. Time will tell.

Rebuilding

'If people don't tell people what happened, the next time it happens there will be just the same awful consequences.'

Many survivors have shared their survival stories publicly as a way to begin raising community awareness of the risks of flash flooding locally, nationally and even internationally. They recognised the significance of the disaster and the importance of documenting what happened.

For some people, telling the story was therapeutic, while for others the retelling was very difficult. Some people told their story for inclusion in this book having not previously spoken to anyone else about their experiences. These people had a strong desire that the event be recorded as accurately as possible, so that if similar floods occur here or elsewhere in future, people are prepared, timely warnings are given and the death toll is minimised.

There is a sense that history is being written. Murphys Creek resident Nelly Gitsham said people would want to know what happened in years to come.

> They will want to look back and go, 'Wow. That really happened.' People around here are struggling. They don't talk to Red Cross, community services or any of those people. They'll

talk to friends and have a few beers and have a cry on your shoulder. Just to talk about it sometimes helps. I've got no problem with talking because if my story is out there then maybe the authorities can look back and say, 'There's a person who didn't get warning, like everyone in Murphys Creek and all the poor people in Grantham who lost their lives.'

Nelly's neighbour Sue Patterson also saw benefit in the sharing of personal stories of survival. 'I like the idea of people's real stories being told: not what people think happened but the actual story from that person's point of view. I think it's very beneficial to be able to talk it out. I think that as you talk it helps you sift through things in your own mind. It's very healing.'

Pilot Brian Willmett recounted what happened during the flood to contribute to an accurate record of the event. 'I think history is history and it's got to be told, hasn't it? I think if history is going to be recorded it's got to be accurate as well. I've told you what I believe happened.' Brian's grief at the death of Sylvia was also a factor. 'Talking to you helps me honour Sylvia. To get emotional about Sylvia honours her.'

Helidon resident Angela Emmerson volunteered to talk about what happened in the hope other people will learn from her experience. 'If someone else can learn just one lesson from what I've said then that might save someone's life. It was horrible for me but I survived. If I can save someone else's life from them hearing this, then that's great.'

Future safety was also the motivation for Withcott publican Neil Simpson. 'I think it's so important that we look at ways of preventing this horrible thing happening ever again. If I can give one little bit of information that helps a bit, that would be great,' he said.

Helidon resident Jean Warr would like to see changes to security screens to ensure people can escape their houses through windows. 'If we don't tell people what happened, people don't learn. Insurance companies insist that people put security screens on their houses.

Had we had those on we would have died. They need to rethink these policies. Safety screens need to be able to be opened from the inside. It should be mandatory. Whether it's a flood or a fire, people can be trapped.'

Some survivors saw the opportunity to relate their experiences as an integral part of their own recovery. Grantham resident John Mahon said talking over events has been therapeutic for him. 'You relive it again but I think it helps you get over it. Talking has got me through it. I do get a bit emotional but that's just part of being a human being. Talking to reporters and other people has helped. Plus, I'd like to try and get the story out there to people about what happened.'

Grantham survivor Marie Van Straten saw telling her story as a way to encourage other survivors that positive changes could emerge from painful experiences.

> I hope with all my heart that my story is going to help somebody. I need people to know that out of horrible things, good things can come. You can help people more when you've been through something like that, but if you withdraw into yourself and don't talk about it, you don't help yourself and you don't help anybody else either. People did die. For a long time I wouldn't laugh or even smile because I felt, what gives me the right to enjoy life when people around us died? I need people to hear my story and know that you can be a better person by having something really horrible happen. I wouldn't wish it on my worst enemy, much less someone that is close to me. That's why I want to tell the story now.

As months went by, and surviving families set up home in rented houses, caravans, sheds, shipping containers and mobile homes, they could look forward strongly enough to dare to also look back – and see more clearly what they had escaped. The lack of warning, the failure of communications, everything that jeopardised their survival on that day now needed to be fixed before the next wet season. Lessons needed to be learned.

For many years, Australians have been more focused on risks associated with drought than flood. Yet on a global scale, flash flooding is a major cause of deaths in natural disasters. The World Meteorological Organisation (WMO) reported in 2007 that flash floods kill more people worldwide than any other type of natural disaster. The WMO has developed an international flash flood warning system to improve warning lead-times. Queensland's 'summer of disasters' was a wake-up call to individuals, organisations, and governments of all levels to better understand the risks and to be better prepared. The recommendations of the Queensland Floods Commission of Inquiry will contribute substantially to focusing the efforts of local, state and federal governments to respond.

Australia's climate patterns are among the most variable in the world, often oscillating relatively quickly from drought to flood and back again. The relatively short climate record since European settlement means it's difficult to estimate recurrence rates for what appear to be extreme weather events. Truck driver Paul Pepi says the disaster is a wake-up call for all Australians about the potential for flash flooding. 'This is the first time we've had a flood like this in white man history. It must have happened hundreds of times before – we just haven't been around to see it.'

Preventing loss of life in the future is important for Helidon resident Jean Warr, whose husband saved her by helping her climb to the roof of their house. 'If people don't tell people what happened, the next time it happens there will be just the same awful consequences. We will be in the position again where too many people will die for stupid reasons.'

Grantham father Gilbert Kilah, who was lifted from Railway Street as the tsunami wave engulfed his car, volunteered to speak about what happened, despite his personal distress at reliving the event, because of his sense of duty to the community that every lesson that can be learned is learned. He wants to ensure an early warning system is put in place in Grantham before the next wet season arrives.

Some families have battled with grief and the disturbing knowledge that no official warnings of the severity of the disaster had been given in time for people to escape. Their trust in government authorities, which they had previously believed would warn them of any imminent danger, was shaken. Matthew Keep was wracked with grief: 'There has to be a level of accountability for local governments to adhere to frameworks that are determined at a state level. To say that they will get it right for the future holds little comfort for my family; they should have had it right to start with. This was one of the biggest floods to take place in Queensland's history and yet no-one knew about it.'

Grantham families knew the flood could not have been stopped, but they wanted to know why they had not been given any official warning of the severity of the approaching calamity. 'That day, [from the time] the first raindrop hit the ground, our fate was sealed. Nobody can stop Mother Nature. It was what happened that we weren't given any kind of warning at all, that's what I find really hard. I know I can't expect the police or SES to build a huge wall and to stop that water. There was nothing we could do. But someone could have done something to tell us that we needed to get to higher ground, to get people and loved ones out of that,' Lisa Spierling said.

Johnathon Klaassen believes that less than an hour would have been enough time to get everyone safely out of town. 'A police car with a bull horn going down the street and telling people to get out, or ten people knocking on doors would have done it easily. It would have been nice to have some warning for the people.'

Weather watcher Neil Pennell was devastated by the loss of life. 'There's no excuse in this day and age for Matthew Keep's family to be sitting in their house and get washed away by a massive flood from rain that occurred three hours earlier. It shouldn't happen. We've got the tools to warn them appropriately, we've had them for a long time. There are a lot of reasons why that didn't happen.' He sees a larger network of rain gauges and a siren in Grantham as key elements of an improved counter-disaster plan. 'Upstream rainfall and river gauges are capable of giving two and a half to three hours' warning for Grantham. If the Bureau has a river gauge at Postmans Ridge and the height is near what it was in this flood, then they can say to the people of Grantham, "You need to get out of your house right now."'

Some flood survivors are sceptical that their local councils and state and federal governments are able to adequately fund the recommendations made by the Queensland Floods Commission of Inquiry's Interim Report. Others are disappointed that the inquiry has recommended councils remain the sole agency for warning of flash flooding.

Neil says the Bureau of Meteorology is better equipped than councils to warn of flash flooding because, in small rainfall catchment areas like Toowoomba city, council warnings based on rainfall data will be too late to allow people to move themselves and their cars to safety. 'Rainfall data is only available half an hour after the rainfall started or half an hour after the rainfall is finished. That's too late. The only people who are in a position to say "You need to evacuate near the creeks" is the Bureau,' he said.

For flash flood warnings in locations high in catchments to be effective, Neil says the only way is to forecast them based on radar images.

> It would have to be forecast by the Bureau on the basis of approaching rain to have any useful effect. I understand there are plenty of occasions where farmers phone each other about creek flows and roads or bridges being cut, but the only way the January disaster was going to be managed in any sort of way was for someone to have identified that there was a big storm indicated by the radar. As far as I can see, the only way that a flash flooding warning is going to be effective is if it gets to people half an hour to an hour before it is required. The only way that's going to happen is if the Bureau issues the warning. The Bureau needs to have enough resources and capacity

> to ring Toowoomba Regional Council when they see the rain approaching and say, 'You need to evacuate the centre of town now,' not wait for the storm to get there and start measuring rainfalls – that's way too late.

After the flood, several families moved away from the disaster zone, but most people repaired their houses, outbuildings and fences and remained in the same location. Most of the houses in the district are built along the creek. Many houses and outbuildings sustained damage or were totally destroyed. Families who had insurance cover were able to rebuild, but many are uneasy returning to homes that were engulfed by the flood. Financially, their options are limited because the flood has greatly reduced the market value of their homes. Sue Patterson and her husband Colin have rebuilt their home but are staying in the same location. Sue says, 'I still love my position on the creek. But what option do you have? No-one is going to buy it.'

High in the catchment at Spring Bluff, lack of lead time will remain an obstacle to effective warnings for people, because the rain-to-flood time is very short. At the railway station, Craig Ritchie has added flood evacuation plans to his fire evacuation plans. While forecasts of expected extreme rainfall will provide useful warnings, being prepared for isolation is a priority for families who will need to deal with extended power cuts and failed communications systems in future. Many residents have bought generators, battery-operated radios and UHF radios to cope with that reality.

Ean Stewart, who spent several months helping the community recover from the disaster, would like to see improved disaster plans for every community. 'It's not something you just apply like slapping on a coat of whitewash on a building. There need to be disaster management plans in place for every community, from the community level to the council, state and federal governments, and it needs to be coordinated.' He said EMQ needed to be able to accept local offers of help in the immediate aftermath of a disaster.

In Murphys Creek, the failure of power and communications

systems and road closures were major problems. The communication black spot, which had been an inconvenience before the flood, became a life-threatening failure on the day of the flood. The ten-day power blackout after the flood has also led local people to actively establish their own means of communication if they are cut off from radio and television news. Some residents have established informal telephone chains to enable people upstream to warn them of sudden creek rises further up the catchment.

Susan Mouflih, who was swept away twice and both times rescued by her brother, has bought a UHF radio to be able to communicate with friends higher up the creek who can give her warning. Susan will also extend her monitoring of the BOM website to include monitoring creek gauges once they are installed upstream of the town.

National media attention was drawn to the lack of mobile reception in the town a few days after the flood, and two mobile phone companies delivered mobile towers the following day. Resident Nelly Gitsham welcomes the improvement in mobile phone coverage but laments the personal cost to herself and other residents. 'It's really pathetic to think that to get some action around here, there's got to be a natural disaster and all this loss of lives and all these people scarred for life. Nobody needed to go through this. The picture will never go away. It was just so real, so close, just there – the vision of the flood.'

The isolation of the Spring Bluff and Murphys Creek communities during the disaster, due to landslides and flooded roads, has reinforced to many residents the need for them to be self-reliant, especially when they most need medical or emergency help. Rick Luchich said the death toll had given a lot of people a wake-up call about appreciating family and friends and being prepared to protect them. 'Take care of yourself and your family and use your own initiative; don't expect someone else to do it for you. If you think it's too wet to go to work, stay home.'

In Toowoomba, Queensland Fire and Rescue inspector Steve McInerney debriefed all his staff and has implemented several improvements for rescue preparedness and operations. He has developed a disaster plan that can be activated if similar weather conditions to the January 2011 floods threaten, which includes boosting the numbers of swift water rescue crews. Extra crews will be brought to the city on stand-by, providing three crews and appliances in each of three sectors of the city, one east of East Creek, one west of West Creek and one in the CBD between the creeks.

Truckie Greg Twidale, who rescued a woman in James Street, Toowoomba, by anchoring her to his truck with a load restraint strap, now keeps the load restraint strap in his truck cabin in case of future emergencies. He has also added a rope to his emergency kit. Many Toowoomba residents believe the city's constrained creek system needs to be upgraded to cope with much larger flows of water. Eddie Spark, who clung to a tree in Dent Street during the flood, said East Creek and West Creek need much larger underground pipes to reduce the risk of high-velocity water flowing across inner city streets.

While there were no deaths in the town of Withcott at the base of the Toowoomba Range, many homes and businesses were destroyed. Businessman Norm Head and his son Chris closed the service station and both had to find different jobs. Norm would like to see better warning systems to reduce the risk to lives. 'It's amazing everyone survived. The flood changed our whole life. Our job, our business, everything is gone. It makes you stop and think how quickly your life can change.'

At Postmans Ridge, where the violence of the flash flooding was most severe, survivors have learned a new appreciation for life. Gayle Teal is deeply grateful her family survived. 'I take from the flood how fortunate I really am. We had two businesses underwater but no family members were lost. We've been very fortunate.'

Rod Alford, who spent 20 years working in counter-disaster planning, doesn't lay blame for the lack of warning but he wants to see changes to reduce risks in the future.

> Looking back, I don't know how authorities could have warned anybody because the phones fell over. There was no power, therefore there was no television. There was no radio. There was no way to let anybody know. Having sirens would not have worked because the rain was so heavy you wouldn't have heard a siren anyway. In hindsight it's been a very good lesson; however, councils need to look at where they're letting people build. It's easy to say in hindsight that Sylvia's house should never have been where it is.

For the future, Rod Alford says, awareness of what can happen will help, but he wants creek maintenance to be improved. 'The creek upstream from me now is clogged with thousands of tonnes of trees, parts of houses, and cars. If it floods again it's going to flood badly because the water can't flow.'

Jeff Neumann has taken from the disaster a resolve to spend more time with his family. 'Life's too short. We've decided we're going to have holidays and go travelling.' For many flood survivors, family connections were reinforced and the generosity of volunteers and donors lifted their spirits. Helidon student Angela Emmerson learned a new appreciation for her family. 'It teaches you that you really do love your family and that's all that matters. Now we make sure we say, "I love you" before we go to bed or before we leave the house.' Angela was thankful for the generous support of her family in the clean-up. 'People drove down to help at our house from Townsville and Tamworth. People sent us money, food and clothes. It makes you stop and think there really are good people in this world,' she said.

Life-threatening experiences during the flood have changed people's views on materialism. Grantham survivor Peter Van Straten has less attachment to goods and chattels. 'I have put aside any feelings for personal possessions because I've found they can be taken off you in a very short time.' His wife Marie's close escape has made her re-evaluate her priorities too. 'I don't sweat the small stuff any more. I ask, "In a month's time is this really going to matter?" I live the day.

I used to think: if we get to this point, things will be better. Now I think, "This is it. This is the moment."' The Van Straten's relationship with each other has also changed. 'We were in the water together. I'm extremely grateful it was Peter who was in the water with me. I don't think anyone else could have been there for me like Peter was.'

The largest structural change to be made as a result of the flood is a land swap being offered by the local council to landholders. The council has bought and developed land on a hill behind Grantham in exchange for house blocks that were flooded in the Lockyer Valley Regional Council area. Grantham residents Natasha and Brad Long were among the first flood victims to suggest the lower section of Grantham should be moved from the floodplain. 'Now that the flood has happened, we know it can happen again,' Brad Long said. 'The town needs to be moved to higher ground, even though some houses are repairable.' The development was fast-tracked, and 80 blocks were selected by ballot seven months after the flood.

The decision to move the lower-lying section of Grantham to higher ground was vindicated by the findings of a hydrology study conducted for the Queensland Floods Commission of Inquiry by Sinclair Knight Merz hydrologist, Dr Phillip Jordan. Hydraulic modelling compared how the flood would have behaved if the quarry had not been built with how the flood behaved including the existence of the quarry. A model of the flood event downstream of the quarry, which assumed the quarry had not been built, found that the amount of floodwater was so great that the area between Lockyer Creek and the railway line (including the houses on the southern side of the town of Grantham) would have been engulfed. The study also revealed that the effect of the quarry on the flooding downstream was to reduce the flood peak in Grantham township by five to ten centimetres. There was no measurable change caused by the existence of the quarry in the velocity of the torrent at the peak of the flood through the town.

However, upstream of the quarry, the modelling showed the 380-metre earthen wall along the western side of the quarry increased the height of the flood by a maximum of half a metre for about two kilometres upstream. Here the water level rose three metres in half an hour and continued rising very slowly for another fifteen minutes before beginning to fall over the following two hours, Dr Jordan said. Landholders at Carpendale believed the quarry wall would pose an ongoing threat if it was rebuilt and they were relieved that in the months after the flood, bulldozers removed remnants of the wall that had not completely collapsed during the flood.

More rain gauges and creek gauges in the upper reaches of the catchment will provide important early warning for future floods. Postmans Ridge resident Brian Willmett and others want to see more automated rain gauges connected to the Bureau of Meteorology and an automatic warning system to mobile phones, especially in rural areas where sirens would be ineffective. In Helidon, warning systems are also a priority to alert local residents and people downstream.

Farmer Gavin Zischke says more rain gauges are needed and should be linked to the Bureau. He would also like to see gauges where creeks cross roads, linked to warning lights for drivers to notify them if water is over the road.

Bess Fraser believes new rainfall and creek gauges need to be linked to an alert system that can be heard outdoors, rather than relying on the mass media to deliver warnings. 'Media isn't going to do it. Radio is not going to do it. We need sirens outside. This is a farming area. Everyone is outside.'

Emergency services authorities developed improved helicopter rescue techniques during the disaster, and have since bought new rescue equipment. Kendall Thompson and the New South Wales helicopter crew developed a technique for quickly rescuing large numbers of people from roofs. 'Instead of going up and down with one person at a time we could just hover and put four people straight into the helicopter while it was hovering about a foot above the roof,' he said. EMQ helicopters have adopted a helmet communications system so winch operators can speak to their rescue crewman by radio, instead of having to rely on hand signals requiring line-of-sight. Rescue straps for babies and children will also be added to EMQ helicopters.

Many survivors of the disaster, including those most affected, realise their best protection from possible future flash flood disasters is awareness of their environment and early activation of personal safety plans. Matthew Keep has publicly urged people to make plans for the safety of their own family. He realises that assurances his house was above the record 1974 flood gave him a false sense of security: 'I was complacent and thought we were safe. I thought there would never be a bigger flood.'

Matthew Keep hopes other people will learn from his experience: 'Don't be complacent about the risk of natural disasters which strike suddenly. Don't expect warning. Don't rely on anyone to save you. Be prepared to protect your own family.' Living through the grief he has borne, he is compelled to spare other people the risk of the same fate. Complacency that 'it will never happen' is no longer an option.

Controversy

~

In the months after the flood, Carpendale residents raised their fears about the possible effect of the Grantham sand quarry in the disaster. University of Southern Queensland academic fluvial geomorphologist Dr Jerry Maroulis was asked for his expert opinion within the first few months after the flood. He visited the neighbouring properties and the location of the quarry. From Dr Maroulis's observation of the remains of the quarry wall, he was able to say that the structures were not part of the natural landscape but were layered deposits of soil. 'It is unconsolidated material – just a mass of reddy sandy clay material loosely deposited. It had no ability to withstand the force of the water. It wasn't a natural structure. It was a deposit. It wasn't serving any purpose,' he said. Dr Maroulis estimated the material had built up within the previous ten years because he could see grass layers and sand layers but no tree seedlings.

The Wagner family sold the quarry site soon after the flood to Boral, which sold it in turn to Zanows' quarries. The new owners plan to fill in the mined section of land and graze cattle on the property. Dr Maroulis left Toowoomba and moved to the Netherlands where he now lectures at Wageningen University.

Residents hoped that forensic investigations into the state's summer of disasters would clarify what had happened at Grantham and why. It was not until the findings of the inquiry and inquest were released that the need for a separate inquiry into the unprecedented severity and deadly nature of the flood in Grantham became obvious. The findings of the state-wide commission of inquiry were delivered in March 2012 and the coronial inquest findings were released in June 2012. The commission of inquiry findings dedicated little of its 653 page report to what happened in the town of Grantham. State Coroner Michael Barnes registered his unease at restrictions on his investigation due to the terms of reference of the inquiry.

Michael Barnes initially briefed Police Taskforce Galaxy to capture all potential available evidence regarding anything that could have been seen to have contributed to the cause of death of people during the flood event. However, the scope of the investigation was narrowed due to the legislative framework of the commission. Taskforce Galaxy therefore did not investigate natural or artificial features of the landscape. There was no investigation by Taskforce Galaxy on behalf of the coroner relating to whether the existence or breach of the Grantham quarry had a material impact on the damage caused by the flooding at Grantham or whether the breach of the quarry had implications for the evacuation of Grantham. The coronial inquest in November 2011 spanned less than two days of hearing evidence into the cause of death of 23 people, breaking early on the second day in time for the live broadcast of the Melbourne Cup.

More than half of the people who died in Toowoomba and the Lockyer Valley had perished in one town where none of the many triple zero calls from those in peril could be responded to, except by helicopter. The inquest did not call for live evidence from the many residents who were eye witnesses of the disaster in Grantham about what they saw and experienced. The Queensland Floods Commission of Inquiry (QFCI) also did not call for live witness evidence from Grantham residents but relied primarily upon written statements, some of which contained significant errors of fact.

A statement by a volunteer member of the State Emergency Service claimed officers set out on the five-minute drive from Gatton to warn the people of Grantham at 2.30 pm but that they could not reach the town because it was already flooded. This timing was accepted as correct, when it was not. Acceptance of the statement caused great distress because had that warning in fact been given, as alleged, there would have been time for everyone to be moved to safety and those who perished would possibly have been saved.

To residents of Grantham this was a painful denial of their reality. 'When I found out how many hours earlier people had been ringing to warn the authorities – if we had known earlier – nobody needed to die,' Lisa Spierling said. 'We would have always lost material things but people didn't need to die.' Several Grantham residents challenged the incorrect finding but their protests were to no avail.

Timed photographs and telephone records proved the flooding in Grantham did not strike, as alleged, shortly after 2.30 pm. The sudden onset of swift water flooding at Grantham occurred shortly after 4 pm. However, a faulty handwritten note in an SES log was accepted as correct. Findings of the coronial inquest verified that triple zero calls from Grantham residents were not made until about 4 pm or later. Bruce Marshall had phoned triple zero at 4.11 pm, Danny McGuire at 4.21 pm, and Brenda Ross at 4.27 pm.

Acceptance by the commission of evidence that was obviously incorrect undermined community trust in the commission. It also led to distrust of the authorities by residents. Many residents were furious that highly paid legal professionals had evidence from timed photographs and telephone records that the flood struck the town after 4 pm yet the authorities accepted one single piece of evidence that was in error and discounted the weight of evidence.

Local businesswoman Lisa Spierling swung into action, gathering evidence to challenge the QFCI findings. Her desperate search for information distracted her from her family responsibilities of rebuilding her home and business. Her mind and emotions remained trapped in the trauma of the flood, unable to let it be in the past until the truth, as she knew it to be, was accepted by the authorities. 'When I should have been concentrating on my family and rebuilding, I spent months and years to get the truth about why they took an hour away from us,' Lisa said. 'The Queensland Flood Inquiry got it so wrong. They said the SES came into town at ten to three. We knew that was ten to four. Sometimes I wish I'd never started delving into it because the deeper I looked into it, the more I realised how many hours we had – and it was never given to us. That was probably one of the hardest things for me, being told that they didn't believe us. Even though we had phone records and photographic evidence but they just still stuck by some SES volunteers who couldn't tell the time,' she said. 'That put me through many years of mental anguish. They wouldn't believe a whole town of people saying that it hit us later than what they said. For me that was very hard.'

Lockyer Valley Regional Council and many individuals began lobbying for a separate and thorough inquiry into the flooding specifically in Grantham. This was necessary because if residents believed the quarry wall had been somehow to blame for the sudden and severe onset of the flood – and the wall was removed – then they would be safe in the event of a similar weather event. If, however, the quarry wall was not a material factor, then the location of their homes remained potentially deadly if a similar weather event occurred again.

In February 2014 Dr Maroulis returned briefly to Australia and I was able to interview him again. This time he was able to examine and comment on satellite imagery, aerial photographs and field photographs that had not previously been available. A satellite photograph on the Queensland Reconstruction Authority website clearly showed a large area of sedimentation west of the quarry. The sedimentation in that location indicated the flow of the water across the landscape had stopped for long enough for a huge amount of sediment to drop from the flow. However, only a few hundred metres to the east, there was evidence of very fast destructive easterly flows that had shifted brick houses and bent steel farm sheds and sheared off steel bolts.

The direction of the main force of the current was indicated by trees on the western side of the quarry wall that had been plucked out by a fast destructive easterly flow. Dr Maroulis said the location and position of physical flood debris downstream of the quarry provided additional evidence that modelling to that point had not picked up – that the direction of the main destructive current had flowed east across the quarry, along Gatton Helidon Road and towards the town.

Based on his observation of the satellite photographs, aerial photographs and on-ground evidence of flood damage, Dr Maroulis was convinced that the hydrology studies to that point had not provided sufficient explanation for the ferocity of the event in Grantham. 'Models are great and they do a great job with known variables and known relationships,' he said. 'But in this particular case, we have a flood that has never happened in this part of the world in recorded history.'

Dr Maroulis believed at that point that further scientific study was needed to explain the event. 'Effectively you do have a wall of water coming through. The speed and rate of vertical rise were phenomenal.' The frequency interval estimated to be somewhere between one-in-300 and one-in-1000 years is in question, he believes. 'We can't talk about recurrence intervals because this goes beyond any historical records that we have. We may need to research these river banks to find out the age of these things and see if there is evidence of past river banks being formed under such extreme events,' he said.

In May 2014, Lockyer Valley Regional Council mayor Steve Jones asked Premier Campbell Newman to instigate an inquiry specifically into the Grantham flood. The mayor's request in May 2014 was refused by Premier Newman. In March 2015, Steve Jones wrote again – this time to Independent Peter Wellington 'as a matter of urgency' – and again he requested a full and independent investigation into flooding issues between Helidon and Grantham.

The incoming Premier Annastacia Palaszczuk announced in Parliament in May 2015 that the government would hold an inquiry, acknowledging that the Grantham community needed closure.

Walter Sofronoff QC was appointed and the inquiry was hastily staffed. Investigators collected witness statements from flood survivors, many of whom had not been able to make statements about the flood. Public hearings began two months later. Residents filled the public gallery to hear the evidence of those who had been in danger or who had rescued or tried to rescue their family, friends and neighbours from the torrent. When each witness stood down, people in the public gallery clapped and cheered their courage as they recounted the terror of their ordeal. At last the community was being heard and knew they were being heard.

One of the most distressing topics investigated by the Grantham Floods Commission of Inquiry was the lack of warning for the residents of the town and the alleged timing of the attempted warning by the SES crew. An elderly SES volunteer gave evidence that she did not clearly understand 24 hour time. She admitted she had made a mistake. Thus it was not until October 2015, when Walter Sofronoff made his findings, that the public record was finally corrected to reflect the truth that Grantham residents had had no warning of the impending sudden onslaught of floodwater.

The large number of witnesses who gave evidence at the public hearings of the Grantham Inquiry meant the allotted hearings had to be extended. In early August, the premier announced the hearings would continue until 21 August and the Final Report would be extended until 30 September 2015.

Media coverage of the findings focused on the exoneration of the quarry from being implicated in the ferocity of the flood and in the deaths in Grantham. However, for many residents in Carpendale and Grantham, the more important finding was that those residents who had claimed to have seen large mounds of dirt and gravel building up around the quarry over almost a decade were finally vindicated. The area was not 'natural ground level' as had been repeatedly claimed. In closing submissions, Wagners' counsel conceded the bunds were human-made. Importantly, Walter Sofronoff validated the residents' calls for an inquiry. 'I discovered at the beginning of my job, people there were extremely upset, some of them were extremely angry about what had happened, they had deep suspicions about what had caused it and, they were rightly very angry that no investigation had been undertaken into some aspects of the matter,' Mr Sofronoff said. 'I really hate it when people say it's time to move on. A thing like this will affect you for your whole life – there are people there who will never recover.'

Handing down his report, Walter Sofronoff also commented that some sections of the media had 'unfairly and viciously blamed' the Wagner family for the severity of the flooding.

Within weeks of the release of the findings of the Grantham Floods Commission of Inquiry, in October 2015, Sydney-based solicitors for the Wagner brothers filed a statement of claim in the Queensland Supreme Court. Four brothers, Denis, John, Neill and Joe Wagner, each sought $376,500 in damages and aggravated damages of $250,000 each, plus interest, from media outlets 2GB (Harbour Radio), Radio 4BC, broadcaster Alan Jones and journalist Nick Cater for alleged defamation in relation to the Grantham quarry and its possible implication in the flood deaths in Grantham and other allegations. The plaintiffs claimed their reputations were injured on 34 occasions in broadcasts from October 2014 until August 2015 and caused embarrassment and distress.

In addition, the plaintiffs claimed that the radio stations and broadcaster Alan Jones had not apologised for his 'relentless campaign of vilification' even after the findings of the Sofronoff Inquiry found the Wagners had been 'unfairly and viciously blamed' for the flooding by some media outlets. Aggravated damages were claimed on the basis that the defendants allegedly knew the information to be untrue at the time of broadcast.

The four defendants, all represented by veteran defamation lawyer Bruce Burke of Sydney firm Banki Haddock Fiora, signalled their intention to defend the allegations on the basis that the meanings of the words were not defamatory of the plaintiffs. The action was yet to be heard at the time of publication of this book.

In a separate action, the four Wagner brothers also sued *The Spectator Australia* and journalist Nick Cater, claiming damages of $376,500 each and aggravated damages of $100,000 each plus interest, and sought an injunction to restrain the magazine from further publication.

The Channel 9 television network was also sued by the four Wagner brothers over alleged defamation in a segment on its *60 Minutes* current affairs program. Two of the main claims were that each of the plaintiffs 'was responsible for the catastrophic flood which devastated the town of Grantham and killed 12 people' and 'tried to hide his responsibility' and that each of the plaintiffs 'was responsible . . . in that the enormous wall at his quarry burst, unleashing the flood'. The case was heard in February 2016 and Justice Boddice ruled in April 2016 that both of these claims should be struck out but he allowed the plaintiffs to reword the pleading because he found that the word 'responsible' in the original statement of claim was ambiguous.

At the time of going to press the cases were continuing.

Five years on

Just more than five years after the flood I revisited as many of the flood survivors as possible to document their recovery from the disaster. Not everyone could be contacted but those who have participated in follow-up interviews provide insightful examples of how different people in different circumstances have coped in the years since. Almost everyone who was approached was willing to be interviewed again in the interests of documenting and recording their post-flood experiences. I am grateful for their trust in me and their generosity in allowing readers to understand what has been for some people a very difficult and confronting part of their lives.

For some people recovery from the disaster has been relatively quick. Those who lost possessions but who were not traumatised by the disaster, who remained healthy and had insurance with companies that promptly paid their claims, were able to resume their work, repair or replace their homes and return to a relatively normal life within months or a few years. However, for those people who were bereaved of one or more family members during or after the flood, who were traumatised on the day, who lost their ability to work or whose insurance claims were slow and difficult, the journey has generally been far more challenging. Some residents whose homes were damaged or destroyed struggled for months or years for their insurance claims to be paid – some ultimately without success. There were many cases in which insurance companies chose to pay for the repair of houses in flooded areas because this was a cheaper option than paying for a replacement house and land above the flood zone.

These decisions by insurers resulted in such low payouts that it did not enable owners of flooded homes to move to higher ground. Even when the house was repaired, the land value remained depressed and the owners could not afford to sell and rebuy above the flood zone. Some people have therefore been trapped in a location where they experienced distressing events on the day of the flood and are still enduring daily triggers of the trauma. Some families freely chose to remain in the worst-hit area in the lower part of Grantham – because the soil there is better, they had a larger area of land or access to bore water – but others remain there simply because they could not afford to move to the new estate established on the hill above the town.

Rumours of a higher death toll than reported in Grantham still persist. Some residents believe unregistered farm workers from overseas who were working in paddocks perished, but no firm evidence for this has yet emerged. Authorities deny the rumours.

Grantham couple Marie and Peter Van Straten, whose house was ripped from its stumps and carried out of town, have sustained a series of economic losses as well as damage to their health and working capacities. After the flood they moved to a rented house in Gatton. The destruction of their rented home in Grantham and the loss of all their possessions meant they needed emergency clothing and shelter. They were deeply grateful for public donations of food, clothes, furniture, household appliances and kitchenware to enable them to re-establish a home. St Vincent de Paul provided them with a car, to replace the one that had also been destroyed in the flood. They were desperately dependent upon donations because despite losing all their possessions they qualified for only $4,000 from the Premier's Appeal fund. Their house contents in Grantham had not been insured because, as pensioners, they could not afford the premium. Marie's broken wrist, which had been re-broken during the flood when she grabbed her husband Peter's hand to save him from being swept away, did not mend well. A metal plate was inserted in her wrist but her arm and hand have been left too weak for her to be able to return to work as a nursing sister.

Despite their personal losses, the couple returned regularly to Grantham in the months after the flood, drawing strength from the strong community spirit in the town. They felt understood by others who knew what they had experienced and who also relived the terrifying sights and sounds of the roaring water, which intruded upon their minds day and night.

At the end of 2011, Peter noticed an itchy, inflamed sore on his chest. He was diagnosed with an aggressive form of melanoma and had urgent surgery. In 2012, Marie was diagnosed with breast cancer on her birthday, 4 October, and had a mastectomy the following month. Marie takes consolation in the fact that their scars were both in the same location on their chests. In 2014, Peter was diagnosed with an aggressive metastasised cancer in his stomach and was given the confronting prognosis of a six-month life expectancy that might be extended to 18 months if his disease responded well to a newly available treatment.

Peter began the treatment with confidence and held onto high hopes of a recovery. Marie's nursing experience meant her expectations were more realistic. The couple moved to Ipswich so they were close to Ipswich Hospital where he was being treated. Sadly, the medication was not successful and Peter lasted less than a year. He died in mid-2015 during the second week of the public hearings of the Grantham Floods Commission of Inquiry. At the same time, their dog Chloe, which had been winched to safety clinging desperately to Peter's shoulder, was also very ill. Reluctantly, Marie took Chloe to the vet to have her euthanised. Marie then went to the hospital that afternoon to see Peter. He had already died, on the same day, within three hours of their beloved dog.

Following Peter's death, Marie's carer allowance ceased and she could no longer afford the rent on their house. She moved in with one of her married daughters. She also had to sell the car to help pay for her husband's funeral. Her goals now are to finish paying off the funeral, save up for a headstone for Peter's grave and find a job so she can become financially independent again. 'It's very confronting to be looking for a job at 61, but I am lucky my family is able to let me live with them at the moment,' she said.

Returning to Grantham in 2015 without her husband for the flood memorial, Marie went early to avoid the public ceremony. She wanted instead to quietly honour Peter alone – to remember the six months they had lived in Grantham, by themselves for the first time in their married life, to remember the day he had saved her by standing on one leg to get her head above the surface of the water and to remember that she had saved him.

Despite Marie's optimistic outlook on life, she has been challenged by the losses she has endured. However, she still is able to find consolation in speaking about her life in the hope that she will persuade other people, especially men, to share their feelings rather than bottle up their fears and anxieties. 'I have a lot to be thankful for,' she says. 'My daughters have not abandoned me.' Marie's experience exemplifies how people can sometimes possess extraordinary emotional resilience despite being financially and physically vulnerable. To her, the losses endured in the flood seem as if they are continuing still. She now recoils when she meets other flood survivors who have repaired their homes, returned to work and whose lives continue much as before. If they urge her to 'get over the flood, it was five years ago', she feels misunderstood.

The New South Wales volunteer rural firefighter Kendall Thompson, who rescued Peter and Marie Van Straten, received several individual awards for his daring rescues of Teddy Perry, eight, at Carpendale, and Peter and Marie in Grantham, as well as another two men he airlifted from house roofs downstream of Grantham. The highest honour he received was the prestigious Benjamin Franklin

Award for valour – an honour that is only awarded to one person in the world each year – by the International Association of Fire Chiefs. The award was presented to Kendall at a ceremony in the USA. NSW Rural Fire Service nominated Kendall for the award because he conducted all three technically difficult rescues without any training. Kendall also received awards for valour from the NSW Rural Fire Service and the Life Saving Society. He and the helicopter crew also received a group citation for the rescues from the Queensland Royal Humane Society.

Kendall's swift water rescues led to substantial operational changes and upgrading of the NSW Rural Fire Service. Some officers are now routinely trained and equipped for swift water helicopter rescues and night winching operations for use in firefighting and swift water rescue situations.

Kendall did not experience post-trauma reactions after the rescues although he believes this is because the three rescues he attempted were all successful. 'There are a lot of things that could go wrong but you know you could also get hit by a bus tomorrow too, so it doesn't really matter what you do, there is always a danger,' he said. Kendall met Peter and Marie Van Straten in 2014 in a surprise reunion at the State Library of Queensland, during the launch of the flood archive. They have kept in touch since then. Kendall was sad to hear of Peter's death in 2015.

Spring Bluff

The railway line at Spring Bluff was repaired within months of the flood and coal trains resumed their slow descent of the range on their way to the Port of Brisbane. The winding road leading from Murphys Creek Road to Spring Bluff railway station was also repaired. Kirsop Bridge was rebuilt.

Many people in the picturesque rural community sold their properties and left. The 18 residents who had lived in McCormack Drive, where Steven and Sandy Matthews were swept from their home and drowned, were reduced to three. The coronial inquest confirmed that the bodies of Steven Matthews, 56, and his wife Sandra, 46, had been located 2.1 kilometres and 2.3 kilometres downstream from their house. The Matthews' house, which had safely sheltered their children Sam and Victoria in the ceiling during the worst of the disaster, was demolished after the flood.

The bereaved children received generous public donations. Their insurance claim was initially denied by the insurer, which argued the event was 'not a flood'. This decision was soon overturned and their claim was given prompt attention by the insurer. The Matthews' neighbour Sharon Powlesland observed that the swift processing of their claim appeared to lead to jealousy and ostracism by some local residents who believed the family was given special treatment because they had been in the media spotlight. Victoria lived for a time with her older sister Sarah, who later moved to Brisbane with her children.

The land where the Matthews' house had stood was quickly overgrown with vegetation. A small group of Spring Bluff residents now plans to make the vacant block into a memorial park in honour of Steve and Sandy Matthews, but this has not yet eventuated.

Across McCormack Drive, Sharon Powlesland and her daughter have remained in their home, even though the floor slab is only marginally higher than the Matthews' house slab. Two and a half years after the flood, Sharon began experiencing survivor guilt – that she and her house survived unscathed when her neighbours suffered deaths and material loss. Her own house had been for sale when the flood struck and became unsaleable afterwards. Real estate values in Spring Bluff dropped substantially and many of the people who left took significant price discounts to sell their properties. Five years on, Sharon Powlesland is still torn between her desire to get away from the location of the disaster and her desire to stay because of her love for the beautiful environment and the stability her home provides for herself and her daughter. However, realignment of the creek by the flood means the main creek channel now flows directly towards her backyard, gouging soil from behind the house when there is heavy rain.

Despite feeling more connected to the community than she was before the flood, Sharon Powlesland has become increasingly concerned about the dozens of cracks that have appeared in the structure of her house. Her insurance claim was referred to the ombudsman and more than five years after the flood is still not settled. Sharon recognises the trauma cycles of approach and avoidance in herself. She vacillates between feeling unable to address the engineering issues in the structure of her house and trying to do so but being re-traumatised when she does. Filling in forms for her insurance company is such a strong reminder of the flood that it takes her back into the trauma of the event. Although she knows she needs to make decisions about what to do for the future, she recoils from making decisions that might lead to an uncertain time to come. She does not know whether her home will eventually need to be demolished and replaced with a house on stumps to make it more resilient in case of a future flood. In another five years, she hopes to have moved away.

Murphys Creek

The township of Murphys Creek has been rebuilt and has a new community centre with sporting facilities and two monuments, one to Australian servicemen and one to the flood victims. Funds for the community centre and memorial were donated by Rotary Clubs in Tasmania, Toowoomba and Brisbane. The coronial inquest found Murphys Creek residents Selwyn Schefe, 52, and his daughter Katie, six, were swept from the tray of their utility in their front yard beside Murphys Creek. Selwyn's body was found more than 49 kilometres downstream at Tarampa. Katie's body was found 3.4 kilometres downstream from her home.

The disaster recovery operation in Murphys Creek was the only community recovery operation in the Lockyer Valley in which a local resident became the coordinator of the recovery. Former ADF officer Peter Souter stepped in when he realised there was a leadership vacuum in the town in the days after the flood. He had been at home with his family at their adventure tourism property, Murphys Creek

Escape, on the day of the disaster and was not aware for some time of the severity of the devastation in the district. In the days before the flood his property had been isolated by floodwater and he had already strung a rope across the creek to use with a dinghy to reach a car on the town side of the water. When the heavy rain began on 10 January, the creek rose about ten metres in ten minutes, ripping the steps from their office building, undermining a large retaining wall, shearing off a concrete driveway and sweeping away their entire campground on the creek flat. The family watched in amazement as parts of houses and appliances such as washing machines swept past.

Four days after the flood, Peter Souter ventured across the creek and used his car, which was above the flood level, to drive into the township with one of his staff. Arriving at the Murphys Creek Tavern, which had become a makeshift evacuation centre, he could see there was a need for leadership. Even after four days, no-one knew how many people were missing. No-one knew how many were dead. But the people looked exhausted. Peter's army training taught him to recognise the signs of collective exhaustion in military terms. 'They were not dead but they were neutralised as a fighting force,' he said. From his experience in war-torn countries, he assessed that the level of interruption to normal life was more akin to war than peace. He conducted a military appreciation process, assessing immediate vulnerabilities such as the number of displaced people, the lack of communication with the outside world and a lack of any reporting process.

Peter returned home. Knowing that his own business was not operational because the entire campground had been stripped to bedrock, he decided to collect his army command bag that he had used to train soldiers at Duntroon, got his swag, kissed his wife and daughter goodbye and returned to Murphys Creek township. Local residents remember the day he stood in the grounds of the tavern, raised his arms and commanded everybody to stop. The stature of the man and the authority in his voice were enough to capture attention from everyone at the evacuation centre. 'Can everyone just stop? Everyone just be quiet? Just take a deep breath,' he said. Peter explained that they were all exhausted and had only about 24 hours left before they, as a community, would be completely ineffective. He told the curious but relieved crowd that he had a background in the army and assured them that they would be able to repair the town if they worked together.

He asked the woman who was coordinating the truckloads of donated goods that were pouring in to raise her hand. He asked her how many people she would need to provide a 24-hour roster. 'Six people,' came the reply. Peter called for six volunteers. From those who raised a hand in response, he selected six. Then he explained that the community needed situational awareness to verify who was alive, who was missing and if any others had perished. Leaders were appointed for various tasks and volunteers were assigned, allowing those who were not on duty to sleep. Within half an hour the evacuation centre had become functional.

Essential services were the next priority. Most properties depended upon an electric pump for their water supply. Authorities had turned off power supplies as a precaution. For people to be able to return to their homes, electricity supplies needed to be restored. Questionnaires were created that allowed residents to quantify their storm damage so that power could be restored as soon as possible where it was safe to do so.

Peter Souter made a large map and allocated areas to local service groups, including the rural fire brigade and the State Emergency Service. They began to work collaboratively. Even though the local fire brigade engines were both unusable, members brought quad bikes from their properties and within a day they were able to check on the occupants of every house in the district.

Peter also addressed the town's lack of communication with the outside world. Landlines and mobile towers had been destroyed. He spoke to the Lockyer Valley Regional Council to let them know what he was doing and spoke on ABC radio about what had happened in the township. Peter asked the public in his radio interview for large earthmoving machinery so that the many driveways that had been washed away could be restored, enabling residents who were isolated to access their properties. Hardware retailer Bunnings sent 50 staff to Murphys Creek to help doorknock every household to check that no-one was lost. Within a couple of days, power was restored to properties and the residents sheltering at the tavern were able to return home and begin cleaning up.

After six weeks, the town was functional and substantially repaired and Peter stepped down from his coordinating role. Returning to his property, he assessed the damage and realised his insurance was not going to cover his losses. 'Our greatest problem was that we lost dirt and you can't insure dirt,' he said. Using the small amount of insurance payout he did receive, he arranged for residents at an at-risk youth centre, BoysTown (now known as yourtown), to repair his house and office. The project was the first works program in which the centre worked for a private business. In three months, the foreman and seven workers replaced the retaining wall and put the house back together.

Murphys Creek Escape's business plan was brought forward. Damaged infrastructure was upgraded rather than just replaced. Lockyer Valley Regional Council was still reeling from the disaster and the Souters were advised to repair as best they could to get their business functional without worrying about council approvals. By 2015, the campground was able to cater for 28,000 camper visitors in a year, making it one of the largest tourist attractions in the Lockyer Valley. But the lack of council approvals for the infrastructure work eventually led to a court case brought by the council.

Despite his work for the community, Peter Souter was not recognised beyond the community for his leadership. He is recognised by local residents who invite him to speak at the town's annual Anzac memorial service.

In 2013, Peter was diagnosed with post-traumatic stress disorder (PTSD), not as a result of the flood but as a result of his army service in Iraq in 2007. Since that time he had not slept through the night due to intrusive memories of being in an Iraqi army barracks when a

Katyusha rocket landed five metres from him and he feared the compound was about to be overrun by enemy forces. 'The one time in my life that I can clearly remember thinking that my number is up, I am going to die here, was after the rocket went off next to my stretcher. I didn't want to turn over because I thought the hordes were coming over the mud brick wall behind me and I was about to get a bullet in the back of the head,' he said. Memories of the incident and the fear he felt can be triggered by noises. 'The worst spook I had was a screen door falling off its roller and falling onto concrete,' he said. 'That triggered the same sensation as the rocket going off.' He understands now that his army officer training to be hypervigilant when on active service, combined with his memory of the rocket attacks, led to his condition. He is being treated and is recovering.

Murphys Creek cleaning contractor Angie Pohl, whose car was swept from a causeway at Murphys Creek, is still recovering from her near-drowning ordeal, and her rescuers are still affected by the risks they took to save her. A few days after the rescue Mrs Pohl went to Toowoomba for the first time and vividly recalls walking into a newsagency to buy a newspaper and seeing photographs of flood damage. 'I broke down. I just had to walk out. I cried all the way home. I didn't even stop to shop. I just went straight home,' she recalls. Angie can pinpoint that her depression began on that day. However, over the following months, despite her depression continuing, she also felt a desperate need to know what happened. 'I watched everything to try to make sense of what happened. You watch and you look at every show to try to understand, how did this happen? Why?' After a year her depression gradually began to lift but she still prefers to stay at home and calls herself a hermit.

Amazingly, despite Angie Pohl's distress and her exhaustion as she clung to the tree in the raging floodwater, she was able to clearly assess the risk to her rescuer as he plunged into the torrent to try to save her. 'I didn't want him to get in the creek and get washed away,' she said. 'I would always try to look after someone else first. I could see what they were doing. I was hesitant in letting go of that tree.'

Looking back, Angie is grateful that the person who happened to be at the causeway was capable of getting help and saving her. 'It was just sheer luck that everybody was in the right place at the right time,' she said. Angie doesn't dwell on what happened but sometimes her thoughts go back to her memory of hanging desperately onto a thin tree in the torrent, unable to get any higher even though the water was rising and rising. 'My mind does play out what was going to happen if they didn't turn up,' she said. 'That's when I go back to thinking about Matthew and Ian not turning up and where I was going to be in a few minutes' time. I just saw where I was, the big logs that were floating by me and going over the edge of that dam – and that was not far from where I was – and I knew I had no chance. If they didn't come, I knew there was nowhere I could go.'

In hindsight, Angie believes she should have agreed to undergo the counselling that was offered to flood survivors. 'I did not go to counselling even though I nearly drowned because I thought I was tough.' Angie has not spoken to anyone who was in the creek like her and still wonders if speaking to someone who could identify with her experience would help. Even though she was so close to drowning, she remembers how peaceful she felt. 'If I had to die, I would choose to drown. I was calm,' she said.

One of her rescuers, Matthew Eddison, did have counselling after the flood but he is still traumatised by the danger he put himself in even though the rescue was successful. He feels challenged when some close to him ask if he thought about his family before taking the risk of going into the torrent to rescue Angie. 'I couldn't answer them. Someone was in danger. I was there, I had to respond,' he says simply. He is only now able to acknowledge how dangerous his actions were in the circumstances. 'I risked my life to save Angie. I was thinking so strongly about getting her out of there. I didn't hesitate at all,' he admits. Not many people know about the rescue and Matthew is reluctant to talk about it because of the people who have been critical of his courageous actions. He feels isolated from the community because his experiences during the flood are known only by those close to him.

Even when Angie told him to get out of the water, his response was, 'I'm still going to do it.' But he justifies that decision on the basis that the rescue was successful, saying, 'She's alive today. I must think of the results.' However, other scenarios also play out and haunt his thoughts and dreams. If Ian Hoddinott had not stopped at the causeway and had not sought his help, Angie would have been listed in the newspapers among the casualties, he said. If Matthew had been there alone, he would have grabbed her and floated away with her. He tells himself that they would have had a chance of getting out alive. There were a few gumtrees and he thinks he could have swum and pulled her towards the trees. He believes that wider recognition and understanding of what he did would help him feel more connected to the community.

Matthew recognises the trauma cycles of approach and avoidance, resilience and vulnerability, and integration and fragmentation in the stages of his own recovery as well as in the community recovery. 'Murphys Creek has been changed but has not recovered. Life with the memories is not that normal – it's challenging,' he said. Matthew sees the irony of the flood memorial in Murphys Creek being built below the flood level. And he is very disturbed that a housing subdivision was allowed to be completed after the flood with new houses being built where they would have been inundated on that day in 2011. There are still no flood height indicators at the causeway where Angie's car was swept away. 'There are flashing lights in James Street in Toowoomba. Here, two women were almost killed and there's nothing here.' Matthew feels compelled to warn one new resident that they need a solid one-metre-high curved besser block wall in front of their house to protect them from a similar flood in future. He wonders if they know the risk they are taking by living there.

Angie Pohl's other rescuer, Ian Hoddinott, is not haunted by visions or memories of the rescue. Despite seeing Angie's car sink below the surface of the water at the causeway, Ian is more disturbed now by the circumstances of other people who were in worse situations that day. Nevertheless, seeing Angie's car sink is still vivid in his memory. 'The last thing I saw was about a square foot of white car roof and the two ladies going down sitting on the window sill of the car, holding on. From memory, just the tops of their hair. Their eyes had gone. They were under. I remember looking away to race off to Matthew's place, thinking, "I've just seen two people drown."' Ian did not go in the water despite preparing to do so. He had ripped off his trousers and shirt and kicked his shoes off. He was a confident swimmer but when he saw the concrete pipes going down the creek with branches and logs in a pea soup torrent thick with mud, he told himself he would be foolish to go in. 'I don't think I was scared. I tend to think it was a rational decision at the time,' he said.

The day after the flood, ABC reporter Paul Lockyer landed in a helicopter at Murphys Creek opposite Hoddinott's house. Ian drove him around to show him the devastation at Murphys Creek but directed him to Grantham because it had become obvious by then that the town further downstream was the epicentre of the disaster. After the flood, Ian received a letter from a member of the public who had seen him on television and had sent $500 for him to distribute directly to flood victims as he saw fit. 'It made me feel privileged to be an Australian,' he said. When he passed the money on, Ian told the recipients about the anonymous donor in Ayr, south of Townsville. Even after the cyclone struck north Queensland, the generous donor sent more funds for Ian to distribute in Murphys Creek.

Ian's most compassionate thoughts turn to Catherine Schefe, who lived a few kilometres up the creek and who was a teaching colleague of his at Murphys Creek Primary School. Ian feels broken-hearted for her. 'Catherine lost her husband, her only child, her house, every possession and even the clothes off her back. She was naked in a tree with everything swept away. I don't know of any story that comes close to the sheer tragedy that that suggests. I have not seen her since that time but I can only imagine the pain in her heart and the struggle to rebuild a life that has just been ripped out of her grasp with no warning, no precedent – nothing but a swollen creek in times past, every couple of years.'

In the weeks after the flood, a storm had washed some of the mud from the debris. Ian had been walking along the creek when he saw something he thought might be human remains among tonnes of debris. Police confirmed he had found the body of Catherine's daughter, Katie. Rather than feel morbid about the find, he realises that the recovery of her body was potentially a great consolation to her grieving mother. 'It was a million-to-one find – an amazing moment in my life that provided comfort for the mother of the little girl in a most tragic event when she lost everything.' A second staff member at the school, the groundsman Bruce Warhurst, was also killed at Postmans Ridge.

Ian also keenly felt the loss of Steve and Sandy Matthews at Spring Bluff. He had visited their home many times and knew them, as well as their children. Ian's close association with so much human tragedy meant his own losses of material possessions paled into insignificance. With the life-changing events he saw others experience, he resolved to hold his own loved ones and possessions more lightly, more aware of the frailty of human existence. He was relieved that the floor level of the house he built in Jesse Lane beside Murphys Creek was 2.5 centimetres above the flood level. His property lost no more than fences and topsoil, and he and his wife decided to remain in their house. Compared with the tragic human toll that was so obvious to him, Ian sees the shredding of black plastic ground sheeting from his plant nursery as a mere nuisance. 'For the rest of my life, I will be picking up bits of black plastic that are sticking out of the ground. That's how the flood affects me. As I walk around, that is the lasting memory of it.'

A few hundred metres downstream of the Hoddinotts, Sue and Colin Patterson also remain in their home despite the house sustaining significant damage. The building was not finished when the flood struck and they could not afford to walk away, so they stayed to clean up and finish the building before deciding what to do next. Before buying the land to build their house, they had asked local residents about the risk of flooding and found the area had not been flooded for a considerable time. Despite the negligible risk, they had a small flood insurance policy. After the flood, their claim was paid promptly without dispute. Friends and family helped them clean up and gave them gifts of money and goods to re-establish their home. However, their decision to stay also meant they remained vulnerable in their location beside the creek and became anxious during rain or thunderstorms. When the creek rose rapidly the following summer, Sue realised she really wanted to leave. She had not taken up the offer of counselling after the flood because she had a strong personal support network, but in retrospect she realised she should have engaged with a professional counsellor earlier and should have encouraged her teenage daughter, Sarah, to do so too.

Sue sought medical help and was diagnosed with severe anxiety related to her knowledge that her daughter's life had been in jeopardy and that she had been powerless to help her. 'On the day of the floods I had no recollection that my daughter's life was in danger and that I really could do little about it,' Sue said. 'And at the time, I wasn't recognising that at all. I was more in control mode thinking, "Let's make smart decisions. This is what we are doing." It wasn't until quite some time after that, that the reality of that situation became apparent to me,' she said.

Sue is still uneasy that the council has changed the flood risk for land along Murphys Creek to a one-in-ten-year risk and has restricted building on land beside the creek. Despite the revision in flood rating, the couple are not planning to sell their property because they like the location and don't think a major flood is going to happen again. But they are not in denial about the possibility and are better prepared. If another flood of similar severity struck, Sue believes they would leave rather than take any further risk. For now, she is planning new gardens and projects rather than allowing fear to steal their enjoyment of their natural environment.

Community spirit in Murphys Creek has remained strong with a monthly farmers' market being established.

Toowoomba

Toowoomba City Council made extensive repairs and improvements to the city's waterways, roads and bridges to mitigate future flooding. Stormwater drainage systems were upgraded to cope with a one-in-100-year storm event by widening the creek channels and increasing the capacity of underground drains. A flood warning system for Toowoomba including automatic and manual river gauges was installed to enable authorities to monitor fast rises in East and West Creeks and to close roads and warn residents and businesses of flood threats via email and SMS messages. Downstream of the city, a warning system was installed to notify Oakey residents of flooding in Gowrie Creek. At the intersection of James and Kitchener Streets, where Donna Rice and her sons were suddenly overtaken by the rapidly rising floodwater, a board is inscribed with the simple message 'RIP Donna and Jordan Rice'. Bunches of flowers are taped to the protective steel rings around the base of the telegraph pole.

John Tyson's sudden loss of his wife Donna and son Jordan left him desolate and inconsolable. He was angry about perceived emergency services failures that he blamed for their deaths. He and his son Blake left Toowoomba, leaving John's business and income. John has worked tirelessly on inventions related to disaster preparedness and recovery, helping to develop a mobile phone emergency communication application and a modular building system to quickly rehouse people displaced by disasters. John set up the Jordan Rice Foundation to honour his son's name. The goal of the foundation is to open a retreat – Jordan Rice House – 'where families who've suffered loss are able to recharge, reminisce and restore'. In April 2011, the Toowoomba RSL presented Jordan posthumously with the Spirit of Anzac Award in recognition of his self-sacrifice.

At the end of 2011, John Tyson was notified that the police had reported to the coroner that his wife had driven into floodwaters, resulting in her death and the death of their son Jordan. With very little time before the inquest, he and other next of kin were going to need legal representation that few could afford. The premier's office provided legal representation for all the families so that everyone who wanted to was able to brief a lawyer to represent them. At the inquest, in November 2011, a Toowoomba police officer conceded under cross-examination that the police report to the coroner could have incorrectly stated what had happened. He admitted a comment made by Jordan Rice near their home at Vanity Street for his mother to drive through some water had been wrongly attributed to a location in Kitchener Street, near where the vehicle was inundated and swept from the road. For John, this concession vindicated his wife because she had not driven into floodwater. She had stopped at a red traffic light where her vehicle was struck by very fast-flowing water that had broken the banks of East Creek and gushed down Kitchener Street. This was confirmed by CCTV footage of the intersection.

In addition to the police report error, John was also greatly distressed at the inquest to see a video held by police – but that had not been shown to him until the inquest – of his son Jordan disappearing beneath the floodwater in East Creek. The video had been taken by a bystander who only noticed he had inadvertently captured vision of a person in the water after replaying the footage at home and seeing it on a larger screen. Distressing as the vision was, it was the apparent withholding of the video by police for several months until a public hearing – during which John Tyson saw it for the first time from the public gallery – that added greatly to his distress and his distrust of authorities.

At the same intersection of James Street and Kitchener Street, truck driver Greg Twidale had thrown a snatch strap to secure a woman from being swept away. The two have maintained contact and Greg now knows that Sue, a local medical practitioner, had prayed as she sat on her car roof. She was confident that she would be alright, despite the precariousness of her situation. Greg, also a Christian, was aware that even though his truck would be damaged by driving it into the water, he knew he had to attempt to save the woman. 'I had to do it because, if I didn't, I never would have forgiven myself,' he said. 'I didn't know if it was going to save a life or not at that stage but I had to get the truck in there and try and do something for her. His actions were recorded and made public by several bystanders who took video footage and still photographs of the rescue that were subsequently posted in online news reports.

Greg has not been distressed by his memories of the flood except for one occasion on the first anniversary of the flood in 2012, when he happened by chance to be in the same place at the same time of day. 'I was driving along through that intersection at virtually exactly the same time as I did the 12 months before and it gave me an uneasy feeling. It was eerie that it was 12 months to the day, to the hour, that I was there.' Although Greg had driven frequently through the same intersection the location had not distressed him previously. However, the timing of driving through on the anniversary, at the same time of day, triggered the emotions he had felt during the rescue and his fear for the woman's safety. Greg knew his own life was not in danger because his truck was carrying a heavy load and it would not have been swept away, but he realises that if the woman had not survived he could have been far more affected. He realises that her car would have been washed away by the force of the water if he had not protected her because it had already spun 90 degrees before he arrived.

Greg was a finalist in the Australian Trucking Association's Highway Guardian Awards for his rescue of Sue. Fellow truckie Michael Munchow, who rescued a mother and daughter from their blue Honda Jazz in Withcott, won the award.

Despite several promises from senior Australian politicians that Jordan Rice would be recognised for his bravery, years rolled by with no award being offered. John applied directly to the Australian Bravery Awards Council but his application was rejected. In disgust, John started a change.org petition to mobilise public opinion to have Jordan's bravery honoured. 'My son died saving his little brother. It would mean the world to us to have his bravery acknowledged,' the petition said. John noted that despite his son's bravery, Jordan must have been petrified because he could not swim. More than 300,000 Australians signed the petition. Five years after the disaster and two years after the petition began, the Bravery Award was finally bestowed posthumously on Jordan Rice on 6 May 2016 at Government House in Brisbane by Governor Paul de Jersey. Speaking to the media, John said his son, whom he had thought of as a shy teenager, was actually tough. 'He was the toughest fella I'll ever meet in my life,' he told reporters.

Withcott

At the foot of the Toowoomba Range, the town of Withcott lost some businesses from the main street, destroyed by the very fast-flowing water coming down the range highway. However, most of the businesses have been rebuilt. Publican Neil Simpson and his wife decided to stay at their hotel despite their business having water lapping the floorboards on the day of the flood. They don't believe it is likely to ever happen again – and if it does, he hopes the rebuilding of the range highway will divert floodwater around the town. Surprisingly, businesspeople in Withcott have not been told if protection of Withcott's CBD was a consideration in the engineering of the new highway. Neil has had no anxiety about rain since the event or over the rescues of the two women on the highway; however, he agrees he would have been far more affected if the women had not been saved.

In the months and years after the flood, Withcott Hotel was a social hub for locals and visitors to swap stories. Hotel staff and management heard more than their fair share of accounts of the damage to homes, the clean-up and the protracted struggles to make insurance claims and to receive compensation for their losses. 'There were a lot of houses damaged around the area so that made it really hard with lack of workmen and it took a fair while for the insurance companies to get mobilised,' Neil Simpson said. Some companies denied that the event was a flood and disputed or rejected claims. The economic impact on local residents had a flow-on effect for the hotel, severely reducing its income. The major road works to repair the range highway also severely reduced the hotel's passing customer base. Fortunately, the Simpsons were able to cope with the drop in trade by drawing on savings to manage the downturn in business. They were not eligible for government support but their insurance company promptly paid their claim for external damage to the hotel, carpark, gardens and fences. The force of the water had lifted the carpark bitumen, transported it several hundred metres, and dropped it beside the highway.

Norm Head and his son Chris did not rebuild their service station Heady's Pitstop, where they had been trapped in 2011. The site is now a bakery. Norm experienced depression after the flood and was prescribed antidepressant medication for six months. Chris retrained as a carpenter and works as a handyman for a real estate business. They sold the service station in its flood-damaged state at a discounted price because they were told buyers would be required by the council to remove the underground fuel tanks to rehabilitate the property. To their surprise, the council allowed the new owners to leave the fuel tanks in the ground and to establish a food outlet on the site. Norm, now 64, and his wife retained their other Withcott property, Tomatoland, and live on the lease income, supplemented by their earnings from supervising university exams in Toowoomba for three months of the year. The couple have bought a caravan and plan to see Australia during their retirement.

Other business owners have left town. Withcott Antiques owners Ben and Anthea Burton reopened their antique shop three months after the flood but sold it in 2013, retired and moved to Victoria. The insurers of their home and shop both honoured their claims, not for flood but for storm run-off. Considering his situation from the vantage point of Victoria, Ben Burton believes he would not be alive today if he had not moved when he did. The stress affected his heart, which required an operation after the flood. His wife Anthea was more seriously affected on the day of the torrent when she was trapped in fast-flowing water that was carrying broken glass and china. Anthea was distressed for several months after the flood by the sight of a cloud in the sky, worrying there could be another disaster.

Ben found a website about post-traumatic stress disorder and his wife answered a quiz that indicated she might have the condition. Both had counselling but Anthea took much longer to recover.

Ben Burton was amazed that friends and family they spoke to about the flood did not respond to their accounts of what was a terrifying experience. 'They just don't know what to say, so they say nothing,' he said. But later in Victoria they spoke about their experience and found it beneficial because the people were interested and were able to ask questions.

Despite the loss of some businesses from Withcott, many new ones have opened and there are now more local businesses than before the flood. In addition, a new housing estate is being built, so the town's population is also growing.

Postmans Ridge

The greatest ferocity of the inland tsunami in January 2011 struck the rural community of Postmans Ridge. At this location, two creeks that rise high above the escarpment converge. Despite the onslaught, former workplace health and safety inspector Rod Alford and his wife Wendy decided to remain in their house. Almost all their neighbours have left or died, but the couple have stayed because they love their five-acre block and home beside the creek. They also had few other options because the flood destroyed real estate values. The site next door, where Silvia Baillie's house once stood, has been left vacant. A bare concrete slab surrounded by a few hardy rose bushes and fruit trees are all that remain of the cottage and garden. The coronial inquest found that Sylvia, 72, was inside her house backing onto Rocky Creek when the house was washed away. Her body was found 14 kilometres downstream, in Harris Street, Grantham, a week after the flood.

It is difficult to imagine the amount of force required to cause the complete destruction of Sylvia's lowset brick house so quickly. Rod Alford was better able to describe what happened in the moments before Sylvia and her house disappeared. 'The first wall of water came down the back of our place from a north-north-westerly direction down Rocky Creek. Across the road is Gatton Creek and it comes from the township of Withcott. The second wall of water came down from a completely different direction – from a south-westerly direction. So we were hit by two different walls of floodwater. Both came from the range but from different directions of the range, within five minutes of each other.' Sylvia's house is at the intersection where the two creeks meet. It was the second surge that destroyed Sylvia's house. 'It came crashing like a wave at the ocean and it rolled down to Sylvie's place and it was so high that it literally broke over her house. Within seconds the whole house disappeared. It exploded under the weight and the actual speed of the water and within no time at all there was nothing left – just this ocean of water flowing where her house had been. After that initial wave went the water level stayed that deep for probably half an hour to an hour,' he said.

Rod still mows the grass at Sylvia's place to keep the yard looking tidy. He doubts the council will allow another house to be built but no-one has spoken to him about changes to the zoning or the introduction of any building restrictions. Rod would like the block to become a memorial community park.

Gayle Teal was injured while struggling to rescue her racehorses during the flood. She tore ligaments in her shoulder and sustained a prolapsed disc in her back. She and her husband separated after the flood, but Gayle stayed at the property and helped with the clean-up, cared for the horses and dealt with their insurance claims. In addition to her physical injuries, Gayle was diagnosed with post-traumatic stress disorder in June 2011. 'There'd be times when I would walk across the road to feed the brood mares and I would get halfway across the road and I would get a flashback of the height of the water and I'd think, "I'm going to drown again,"' she said. In 2016 she finally left the property and moved to Murphys Creek to live with her father.

Helicopter pilot Brian Willmett, who helped to rescue Kevin and Eileen Lees, has moved away. Kevin Lees and his family accepted a land swap and moved to the new development at Grantham. Further along the road, Bruce and Wendy Warhurst's house was not rebuilt. The inquest found that Bruce was last seen in his yard walking towards his house backing onto Gatton Creek. A short time later the Queenslander house was broken apart and washed away. His body was found six kilometres downstream near Helidon Spa.

Insurance payouts in the district were generally slow because there was indecision about the cause of the damage. After several months, hydrologists confirmed the event at the Alford's place was a flood, so their insurance claim was honoured. Since the flood, Rod Alford was unable to continue in his work as an inspector of workplace accidents because he could no longer cope with being at accident scenes. He was surprised that after many years working as a counter disaster planner, he was not prepared for the emotional toll of being in a disaster himself. 'I hate to use the word "victim" but when you're involved in the disaster – not as a responder – it is a totally different concept. I found that I thought I could be very professional and cope and it wouldn't worry me but I was totally wrong. I don't consider myself to be a weak person at all – just the exact opposite – but I am surprised at how it has stayed with me. I thought I would simply move on but I haven't moved on. I am a totally different person now compared with who I was five years ago. That will stay with me. The horror of it will stay with me forever,' he said. When Rod was interviewed in 2016, he had not spoken to anyone in detail about the flood between then and my first interview with him in 2011.

Soon after the flood, doctors thought Rod may have PTSD but his current diagnosis is an anxiety condition that is triggered by thunderstorms. Even when he occasionally stays in a city high-rise building he is so distressed by heavy rain, thunder and lightning that he gets out of bed and puts on the lights to look at the rain. He has become aware that he is not triggered by living at the location but by storms. He believes that moving house would not resolve his symptoms. Although he was willing to be interviewed by phone for the book update, he found speaking about the flood was still stressful.

'I am presently walking from one end of the house to the other, staring out my windows at the creek, talking about it and reliving the horror of it all. I will probably spend a couple of days now just winding down from it, but I find that I just simply do not ever relax.' Although he was not able to return to his previous job after the flood because of his anxiety, his workplace was willing and able to redeploy him as a workplace health and safety inspector. He and a colleague have written a new syllabus, which is being widely adopted in Australia.

Helidon

The coronial inquest answered questions about most of those who died in the flood but no trace has been found of some of the victims, including Toowoomba racing steward James Perry, who was in his car at Helidon when it was swept from the highway on the western side of the bridge. Mr Perry was captured in helicopter vision sitting on top of his car roof with his wife and son at Helidon. The heroism of James Perry, 39, was described during the inquest. In a statement to the inquest, it was revealed that James had carried his son Teddy on his back in floodwaters from Helidon to Carpendale and almost to Grantham – a distance of more than six kilometres. At Carpendale, the father and son were propelled from Lockyer Creek across farm paddocks, where a large steel cattle feeder was just visible above the surface. James was able to lift his son onto the cattle feeder, where Teddy was spotted by a NSW Rural Fire Service helicopter and winched to safety by volunteer firefighter Kendall Thompson. Detective Sergeant Paul McCusker gave evidence at the inquest that, despite James' heroic effort to save his son, James was not able to lift himself onto the cattle feeder and he disappeared under the water. His body remains missing.

Civilian and professional rescuers risked their lives to save others in 2011. Full-time emergency workers found that the rescues they carried out were very confronting. Despite their training and their ability to cope with daily rescue operations, their resilience was challenged by the suddenness and riskiness of the rescue operations they undertook in the Lockyer Valley. Brad Mills, a Queensland Fire and Rescue officer, experienced more distress following his rescue of Jenny Thorncraft in Helidon than he had in the recovery operation in the aftermath of the earthquake in Christchurch, New Zealand, also in 2011. The body recovery operation in New Zealand was not so distressing to Brad as seeing James Perry and his wife and son on the roof of their car, needing help but having no equipped helicopter to save them. 'We could see them sitting on the car and we could see the distress they were in. Also, at the time the boy was a similar age to my youngest daughter, so you can relate to their family situation. That makes it a little bit harder as well,' he said.

Despite knowing that the rescue team did everything they could for the family, the loss of Jenny's husband left the rescue team with unanswered questions about what had happened to him and feeling like their mission had not been completed. Brad Mills is surprised that even five years after the rescue he still remembers what happened minute by minute. 'It is that vivid – what we did and how we went about it – it is one of those jobs where you can remember every moment,' he said. The frustration of the rescue team at seeing the family in peril but not being to reach them was eclipsed minutes later by their desperation to find the trio when the car suddenly vanished. 'We organised the Channel 7 helicopter that was flying around and by the time they picked us up and we got in the air, the car and the people had disappeared. That was a bloody stressful time and then we had to obviously search for them,' he said.

Brad's training, which taught him not to put his own life in danger during a rescue, was set aside that day. Brad and Andrew did risk their lives but they succeeded in their difficult mission to save Jenny. 'We evaluate everything. We do a risk assessment, however, when you are swimming across a body of water and you have got light poles and bits of houses and everything and you are dodging that, and you don't know what is under you either – barbed wire fences and things like that – you certainly are at risk,' he said. Their decision to attempt the rescue was made under time pressure because of radio reports that another wave of water was coming through. They realised that if another surge came through, Jenny Thorncraft was not going to be able to hold on much longer.

The rescue pilot, winch operator and swift water rescuers have maintained contact with each other but they have not met Jenny Thorncraft or her son since the flood. Brad went back to Grantham for the first time on the fifth anniversary of the flood in 2016 and met local rural fire brigade volunteers he had worked with during the rescues and the recovery operation. Brad realises that Jenny meeting him would bring back difficult memories for her and he understands why she has not made contact. 'If we had got all three, I think there wouldn't be so much of an issue with it, but this is about James and that makes it very difficult for her and for the rescuers.'

Brad and his colleagues received awards from organisations including the National Humane Society, the Australian government and the fire service. Accepting awards is uncomfortable for many officers when they perceive they were just doing their job. But in this case Brad was happy to accept the award in recognition of the risks he took on the day. 'That is something I do wear with pride, particularly because I know what we did together,' he said.

Staff debriefings by emergency services led to the adoption of new equipment by helicopter rescue services – harnesses for airlifting children, life vests for water rescues of children, multitasking of fire crews to conduct winch rescues and a change to coloured wetsuits for the swift water officers to improve their visibility at night. The fire service has also added powerboats to their rescue vehicle fleet.

Medical sonographer Neil Pennell, who most accurately predicted the timing and severity of the flood in Helidon and Grantham, has remained emotionally connected to the flood survivors, following their stories of recovery in the media, sympathising with their losses and admiring their resilience. 'I have incredible respect for those people,' he said.

Neil remains critical of the failure of the Bureau of Meteorology to provide accurate warning of the impending disaster. 'In Australia in 2011, people should not have been sitting in their houses and all of a sudden they are fighting for their lives from rain that happened three hours' earlier.' He recognises that the flood was always going to happen but the lack of warning added a human-made element of trauma to the event. 'No-one has ever gone to that community and said, "We're sorry. We left you in the lurch,"' he said. In 2012, at the launch of the first edition of this book in Grantham, Neil himself made an apology on behalf of the authorities. The reaction of the audience was immediate and heartfelt. 'Their response was incredibly healing for me, incredibly generous,' he said. 'Marie Van Straten made a beeline across the room and just wrapped me in her arms and gave me a big hug. She cried and said, "You don't need to apologise to us." I felt like someone had just taken a brick off my shoulders,' he said.

The installation of stream gauges higher up the Lockyer Valley catchments now enable the Bureau of Meteorology to monitor stream rises and to verify any sudden rises lower down the catchment rather than dismiss them as erroneous readings. For this reason, Neil believes it is unlikely that communities in the Lockyer Valley could be struck by a similar disaster without warning. 'The key thing that has changed is that everyone knows that it's possible now. If it happens in the next 20 or 30 years it's hard to imagine a single soul losing their life because there would be people upstream who would let them know.' Evacuation of residents would also be planned and rehearsed. 'If there was a flood like that in Helidon they would be getting the people in Grantham off that flat,' he said. 'It's very clear that that community on the flat is as exposed as any community in Queensland at least. They need to know what the plan is. There needs to be a definite plan in place which is a condition of living there.'

However, Neil remains concerned that over time, memories will fade and preparedness may languish. 'Everybody in that community should know what to do the next time it happens. They should know what the plan is. They should know how it's going to happen. They should know who is going to warn them. They should know where they're going to go and how it's going to all work out. There should never be any uncertainty. They should never have to deal with that uncertainty again.'

The flood has changed Neil's love of weather-watching and rain. 'Every now and then there is a similar radar pattern and I get a feeling of dread,' he admits. 'I used to love the rain before. Now, when it starts to pour off the hills, I don't like it any more. I feel the same dread in the stomach.'

Helidon sisters Angela and Rebecca Emmerson, who climbed to the roof of their house to escape the torrent, taking their cat and a supply of crackers and water with them, have both prospered despite their ordeal. They returned to university and school soon after the flood. The girls moved with their parents to a rental house in Toowoomba for nine months until their house was repaired. Angela continued at university and completed her commerce degree. She then undertook postgraduate study, completing a Master's degree in accounting. Angela works in a bank in Gatton as a senior personal banker and is second-in-charge in the branch. She has bought a house in Gatton that she shares with her sister. Her younger sister Rebecca completed Year 12 in 2011, achieving the highest possible result with an Overall Position (OP) 1 and was dux of her grade. Rebecca intends to go to university, but is working for the time being. Mr Emmerson was transferred with work three years after the flood and he and his wife moved away from the district. The couple tried to sell their house in Helidon but when it didn't sell they decided to rent it out instead.

In her new role as a banker, Angela meets customers who are still affected daily by the floods. She has learned more about the legal definitions of terms used by insurers when referring to floods and storm surges. 'A flood rises and falls slowly over days. There is a slow rise, then the water sits around for a couple of days.' In Helidon, the event was ruled a storm surge by some insurers because it came up and down again in only four hours. The insurer of the Emmerson's house assessed the event as a storm surge and paid out their claim.

Angela counts herself and her family lucky to have escaped relatively unscathed. 'We survived it. We didn't lose our pets or anything. We lost stuff. We didn't lose life.' However, she recognises that she and her sister were in danger. Although her parents lost all their possessions, their consolation is that their daughters are both alive and well. 'We were all just grateful that we got out of it. We've been very lucky,' Angela said. Her own experience has been one of accepting that the flood happened and talking about her experience with her family. No-one in the family attended counselling after the flood and none of them has any psychological distress as a result of it. Looking to the future, Angela's family is not concerned about a repeat flood of the same magnitude. 'We don't think it will happen again, or if it does, we don't think it will happen in our lifetime,' Angela said.

The Emmersons' neighbours, Lloyd and Jean Warr, repaired their house and returned there to live. A few hundred metres downstream of the Emmersons' house, the Zischkes have remained at their farm. Kelly and Gavin's farm shed, where Gavin was trapped by the rapidly rising floodwater, was damaged. Their insurer accepted that their damage was caused by a flood and honoured their policy. The Zischkes used their insurance payout to demolish the shed and rebuild it higher up on their property. It is now on the same level as the house and hopefully beyond the reach of any future flood event. Kelly still feels uneasy when it rains heavily. Minor floods have occurred again but Lockyer Creek at Helidon has not had such a major flood since 2011.

Kelly is surprised that the local council has not contacted residents at all to see how they are faring since the flood. She realises the council was very busy for the first two years after the flood, rebuilding roads and other infrastructure, but she wonders why no-one has written to them or other local residents who live beside the creek to acknowledge the magnitude of the disaster. Kelly is concerned that a lot of people were not insured and the disaster has taken a heavy financial toll on many families who have had to repair and rebuild their properties beside the creek. She would like the council at least to have written to residents to express an interest in their welfare.

Carpendale

The farming district of Carpendale, about six kilometres downstream of Helidon, became a focus for intense research and hydrological study because of the existence of a sand quarry that local residents believed could be implicated in the extraordinary amount of flood damage and might account for the unusually high death toll from the flood.

It is also the location where volunteer New South Wales rural fire fighter Kendall Thompson found and rescued Teddy Perry. Kendall is self-effacing about his role in the rescue. 'We just worked with what we had and just did what we needed to do,' he said. But the rescue was a courageous attempt by an officer who had never been trained in helicopter winching or swift water rescue. In addition, the helicopter was only equipped with a harness to fit adults. 'When I went to get Teddy – when I went to put the harness on him – it was too big for him, so I ended up having to wrap it right around him twice so it would hold him,' he said. Kendall was grateful to hear from Jenny Thorncraft via a letter she wrote to Queensland Fire and Rescue Service, thanking everyone involved in the rescues of herself and her son and to know they were recovering.

Tom Friend and his wife Sandra moved to a small farm at Carpendale in the early 1990s, keeping cows, pigs, chickens and geese, and growing lucerne on their smallholding. Sandra's elderly father lived with them. Despite their house having been destroyed, Tom and Sandra were thankful when they returned from a holiday at Hervey Bay that they had five changes of clothes each and their caravan to live in, at a time when other flood victims were left homeless and without any possessions. Sandra phoned their insurer from Hervey Bay and was told their house was covered.

When the Friends returned home they found their house in ruins with half a metre of mud inside. The concrete slab on which the house was built had shifted so the structure had to be demolished. Their water tanks, bores and fences were all gone. But most of their animals that had been swept away were gradually walking home. Friends and relatives appeared and camped in Grantham. They spent a week shovelling mud from the house and sieving through every barrow load for possessions that might be cleaned and preserved. Sandra cooked each day that week for up to 30 volunteers. Most of their possessions were gone but from the mud emerged surprises, such as still-intact crystal glasses that had belonged to Sandra's mother. They were found in a china cabinet that had fallen forward, protecting its contents.

A large farm shed had withstood the force of the water. Tom parked their caravan in the shed to use as a bedroom and he and Sandra accepted donated carpet and furniture to create a temporary home. 'It was thanks to the public we got all our bits and pieces – carpet for the floor, cane chairs to sit on, heaters and a double bed,' Sandra said. They were comfortable except in the depth of winter when it was so cold they wore beanies to bed.

Six weeks after the flood, the insurance assessor arrived and arranged for their claim to be paid out. They were not entitled to public funds from the first two rounds of the Premier's Appeal because they owned a small farm, but in the third round they received $30,000. They were eligible for the land swap. Had they accepted, they would not have been able to keep their animals and their land area would have been reduced to one acre. They decided to stay put and build a new house in the same location. Tom believes a similar flood will never happen again.

While the house was being built, Sandra visited her elderly father, who was in an aged care home because he was too frail to live in the shed. He died before the new house was completed. Tom and Sandra found the psychological battles more difficult than the physical challenges. 'Nobody would think you would be this far down the track and have visions of everything still. I don't think it ever leaves,' Sandra said. The hardest thing was losing their baby photos, wedding photos and representative sporting gear their children had left at home. A small trophy won by their son Nathan, a professional footballer, that was washed from the house floated to the Grantham railway bridge and was later returned to them.

Neither Tom nor Sandra engaged in counselling, thinking they would just focus on rebuilding their home and farm. Tom did not sleep well for years. The couple were aggrieved that the owners of the quarry opposite their farm had denied publicly that substantial earthen mounds had been built around the sand quarry. The couple had witnessed the changing landscape over years. The finding by the Grantham Floods Commission of Inquiry that the mounds were human-made brought a measure of relief.

The house across the road from the Friends' farm was unliveable. Graeme and Helen Besley did not return. The force of the current was indicated by the large tree trunk that had speared through the western wall of the house and lodged in the hallway. The couple initially moved to Toowoomba and then settled on Bribie Island. Although they miss the solitude of the farm, they like living near the beach. For two years after the flood, Helen nursed a painful artificial hip that she had broken during the flood without realising. Her hip was X-rayed in 2013, revealing the ball socket was broken in three pieces. The broken joint was replaced and she was finally relieved of pain. In a bid to understand the disaster, the Besleys attended the inquiry in Gatton in 2015, but they found it too distressing to hear the evidence. 'I came out a jabbering wreck,' Helen said. For a long time after the flood, Helen questioned whether it had really happened. It seemed surreal. After five years she has at last come to grips with the reality of the event and the effect it has had on their lives.

Grantham

Grantham was the most severely affected town in the disaster zone. The name of the town has become synonymous both locally and around the world with the flash flood disaster. Twelve people died and dozens more narrowly escaped with their lives when the deadly torrent struck. People who were fit and strong survived when others who were frail or elderly perished. Many women and children survived because their husbands were at home and were able to help them climb to safety in their ceilings or on their roofs. Understandably, many of the survivors have been diagnosed with PTSD and other psychological disorders. In addition, the social dynamics of the community have been severely affected by the large number of deaths in a town with a small population.

The most deadly force and speed of the onset of the flood occurred along Gatton Helidon Road, a kilometre north of Lockyer Creek. Here, residents who were at home on a fine day had no reasonable expectation they were in danger of a potential disaster.

Video evidence taken by teenager Katherine Godley shows floodwater rising from Sandy Creek and flowing towards the west – but not flowing fast or dangerously – filling the table drain along the highway. The camera then records fast-flowing water from Lockyer Creek moving north with visible waves covering a dry paddock. The time between when Katherine noticed this wave and when the wave struck her house was 56 seconds. All the houses to the west of her house – where people died – were lowset houses. Within moments of Katherine sprinting up the front steps of her highset house, she saw a third wave from the west, bigger and faster by far than the other two. She saw it strike Danny McGuire's fire truck, pick it up and swirl it down the road and then sink outside her house.

By the time the people in the houses realised their lives were at risk, all roads to the town were cut and there was no means of escape. People in four households from 1346 to 1420 Gatton Helidon Road died. These included Llync Clarke and her children, Garry, 12, and Jocelyn, five, at 1346, and three elderly residents: Jean Gurr at 1362, Regina van der Werrf at 1380, and Bruce Marshall at 1420. The bodies of Llync and her children were found in the fire truck. The bodies of the three elderly people were all found in their homes. Residents who survived in this location did so because they were away on school holidays or at work, or because they were given direct individual warnings or help to escape. Bruce Marshall's wife and son survived because they had gone to Toowoomba that day. Lisa Spierling and her children, Hahns, Klaus and Ilsa, survived because a former employee, Rob Wilkin, took them in his utility to the railway line moments before their home was engulfed. Lisa's neighbour Wendy Hodda survived because a farmer phoned her and told her to urgently get a ladder and put his children and her son on the roof of her house.

Some people in this location were unwittingly exposed to greater danger by acting on warnings when they did not know that there was no safe escape route. Kenly and Fran Arndt and their neighbour Danny McGuire and his family all left the relative safety of their houses in their efforts to escape.

Some people in this location survived because they acted on urgent warnings from friends or family who told them clearly what to do. On the western side of town, Kathy and John Mahon and their daughters and grandsons were urged to climb to their roof. Their daughter successfully secured a Rescue 500 helicopter crew, which found their house and airlifted them to safety. Some people survived in this location because other people alerted rescue crews to their precarious predicament. Mahon's neighbour Dave was rescued when Kathy Mahon, who knew he was at home, spotted him from the helicopter, clinging to the gutter of his house and alerted the crew.

The house blocks backing on to the houses on Gatton Helidon Road faced Railway Street. Here, the Keep family was suddenly in peril. The two elderly members of the family both died, as did the youngest, Jessica, 23 months. Amazingly, Matthew, Stacy and their young children Madison and Jacob all survived. The inquest confirmed that Matthew's mother Pauline Magner had drowned. Her body was located eight kilometres away in Gatton. The body of Jessica was found at Mount Tarampa, 35 kilometres downstream of the family home. The body of Stacy's mother Dawn remains missing. Matt and Stacy built a house on the new estate in Grantham and live there with their children, Jacob, Madison and Sienna.

Only a few hundred metres to the east, on the other side of Sandy Creek, the direction of the main force of the torrent struck from behind the Grantham Hotel and neighbouring houses and businesses. The inquest found that invalid pensioner Brenda Ross, her son Joshua and her carer Christopher Face all died when their house exploded due to the force of the water and collapsed. The body of Brenda was found in a farm paddock at Phillips Street in Grantham, 1.8 kilometres away from where her house had stood. The body of her son Joshua was found in a farm paddock on Gatton Helidon Road at Grantham, 1.7 kilometres away from where the house had stood. The body of Christopher Face remains missing.

Brenda's sister Bess Fraser lived in rented accommodation in Grantham after the flood. Even though her house was destroyed, Bess did not qualify for Premier's Appeal funding because the house was owned in her nephew's name. She therefore had to sell her property in Newcastle to buy a removal house, which was brought to the new estate in Grantham and refurbished. The house was not properly finished, leading to a legal dispute.

In retrospect, Bess believes Grantham flood survivors should have been offered the option of moving away from the disaster zone. Her anxiety about future floods has been heightened since road authorities changed their plans to link the new estate with the Gatton bypass. Now that the new estate will not have an escape route in times of flood, she feels at risk of being trapped again.

Bess was diagnosed with thyroid cancer in 2012, had her thyroid removed and undertook radium treatment. She was also diagnosed with post-traumatic stress disorder and is receiving specialist trauma therapy for her condition. Now that she is more emotionally stable, Bess is planning to scatter the ashes of Brenda and Joshua in the ocean at Wynnum in Brisbane, their childhood home.

Bess has a pet dog Asoka, a mini fox terrier, that is her constant companion. Asoka has learned to press a key on Bess's phone that dials the Brisbane ambulance communications centre in case of a medical emergency. Asoka has successfully called for emergency help three times. Bess plans to leave Grantham to escape the memories and to buy a motorhome so she can travel around Australia.

The crew of the Rescue 500 helicopter airlifted 28 people from roofs and trees in Grantham. The people who were airlifted from roofs were not in deadly peril but they and the rescue teams did not know that because they saw some houses swept away. The people who were airlifted from trees, such as Kenly and Fran Arndt, were rescued in daring circumstances.

Helicopter crew rescue officer Mark Turner conducted all the winch rescues by Rescue 500 with support from his winch operator Darren Parson and pilot Mark Kempton. The crew received several awards in recognition of their courage. Mark Turner returned to work after the flood and continued for four years without any apparent emotional distress. The year after the flood, the helicopter crew read *The Torrent.* Mark found this helpful in putting the pieces of the puzzle together and realising that many civilian rescuers did not receive recognition for extraordinary rescues. 'There are quite a few people who didn't get the praise they deserved. They did an extraordinary job,' he said. Mark had access to peer support and psychological support.

At work, the Rescue 500 crew used their experience from executing multiple swift water rescues of children and adults to make suggestions for equipment and training that needed to be changed or added to their existing capabilities. Winch-rated child rescue capsules have become part of their rescue helicopters' equipment. Improved communication between the helicopter pilot, winch operator and rescuer officer are now possible thanks to waterproof radios in the rescuer's wetsuit pocket. Mark passes on his knowledge and experience of winch rescues by sharing his expertise with colleagues in the field. 'It was a positive experience for the industry as a whole, especially our aircraft type – the AW139 – the rescues really highlighted its capabilities and its reliability. It is a really good winching platform. A lot of helicopter providers in Australia will start in 2017 to use the type of aircraft we use here in Queensland.'

It was only in 2015, when Mark conducted a rescue from a plane crash off Stradbroke Island, that his unresolved memories of the Grantham rescues were triggered and he sought medical help. He had six months' sick leave and fortunately has been able to return to work in the same job. In retrospect, Mark realised that being the focus of community recognition and some public criticism had distracted him in 2011 from being able to work through the emotional burden of the rescues and find his own resolution. 'We are not superheroes,' he said. Mark realises that being put on a pedestal for his rescue work meant he was not processing the underlying trauma and the emotions of the mission. The crew had felt overwhelmed by the magnitude of the whole event and the number of people who were needing immediate help. 'We were just trying to save as many people as we could,' Mark said. Flying back to Brisbane, the crew had been almost silent. Despite his exhaustion, Mark wondered if they had reached everyone. 'We were unaware of who we didn't get to.' It was only in the 2016 interview that Mark came to understand that no-one had died because Rescue 500 had to leave the town on nightfall.

Once he was on the road to recovery, Mark and his colleague Darren Parsons both attended the fifth anniversary memorial of the Grantham disaster and visited the farm where they had dropped the survivors. They spent time with many of the people they had rescued, including the Mahon family and elderly couple Kenly and Fran Arndt. The families stay in touch with their rescuers via Facebook and the rescuers have a strong bond of friendship with them. Mark Turner has not spoken to his New South Wales counterpart, volunteer firefighter Kendall Thompson, despite both men conducting winch rescues in Grantham. However, Mark is amazed that Kendall was able to successfully conduct swift water rescues without any specific training. 'He has done an extraordinary job,' he said.

Businesses in Grantham fared worse than those in other locations because many were damaged or destroyed. The local council did not allow the business owners to move their businesses to land above flood level in the new estate. Several of the town's largest employers closed or moved away. Only a few rebuilt in the same location, leaving the town with a greatly reduced local economy and fewer job opportunities. The pub that had been the social centre of the town was not rebuilt. The general store was still in a demountable building in a park next to the public toilets in mid-2016.

The five years post-flood have been particularly difficult for Grantham residents whose lives were at risk during the event and for those who were suddenly bereaved of family and friends. Many residents knew several people who died. The local florist, Lisa Spierling, for example, knew several of the victims. By the evening of the disaster, Lisa was adamant that her family would be leaving the town that had been their home for 18 years.

Despite her grief for those who died and her psychological struggles, Lisa was able to suppress her emotions enough to run her business and continue as a busy mother of five children. Her family moved into a rented house and later relocated to their farm at Mount Sylvia. She and her husband set up makeshift accommodation in a farm shed for themselves and their children and she yearned for the day she would be able to go to a place that felt like home. The Spierlings used the proceeds of their insurance payouts to build a pole house at Mount Sylvia. It has spectacular rural views and is well beyond the reach of flooding. They also expanded their flower farm operation.

The Spierlings joined the land ballot and swapped their house and business blocks in Grantham for land in the new estate. The flooded house was cleaned and moved to the new land where it was repaired and sold. Outwardly, their lives were recovering. 'We're trying get back to "normal", but normal is never normal. Life as you know it changed on that day,' Lisa said. Their lives have changed for the better in some ways but there is a legacy of intrusive fears of danger. 'You know that one second your life is normal and then how quickly things can change. I scan all the time. I scan rooms for the exit. I scan terrain in case something happens – which is the quickest way to escape?' she said.

Lisa is shocked that she made split-second decisions to blindly trust someone with her life and her children's lives. If Rob Wilkin had headed west, driving away from the flooded Sandy Creek into the front of the flood wave, she knows she and her children could have all drowned. Time was of the essence. 'Only a matter of seconds either way and we could have all drowned in that vehicle,' she said.

At other times, the 'what ifs' include scenarios that would have resulted in saving the lives of those she knew who had perished. 'I think about running the other way and that I might have been able to find Stacy and the baby on the railway line. We might have been able to save them.'

Lack of warning for the community is still keenly felt and Lisa has spent countless hours piecing together the sequence of events that led to the authorities' failure to warn the whole community about the imminent disaster. Knowledge of the intense rainfall at midday was known by various authorities for four hours before the wave struck with deadly force in Grantham. Lisa remains angry that families were not given the information they needed to get to safety. 'We could have saved our neighbour if we had had a little bit of time,' she said.

As the local florist who supplies flowers for funerals, Lisa knows the impact of a death in a town like Grantham. The ripple effect of 12 deaths in a small community was devastating, she says, and authorities did not recognise the profound psychological impact of the death toll on people who had lost their homes and possessions, narrowly escaped with their lives and were confronted by so many deaths.

A team of counsellors was sent in a week after the disaster. A second, different team arrived the following week and a third, different team came the third week. 'People who had been in the previous weeks did not come back. The counselling service was stopped because no-one wanted to see them. The service was totally inadequate for what was needed,' she said. The cancellation of the service meant deeply affected survivors became reluctant to seek help and felt stigmatised if they sought psychological care.

Lisa recognises the cycles of trauma that makes her thoughts oscillate from avoidance to a desperate need to know; from vulnerability, thinking they could have died, to resilience, knowing they survived; from thinking the event was a nightmare from which she will one day awaken to integrating it as something that really happened and is now part of her life. Everyone who was in the water on that day travels a similar road. 'Some weeks we will look at each other if we see someone in the street and you know they are having a really bad time of it. But you are doing okay, so you are there for them. Then other times you can look at each other and realise you're the one who needs the help.'

Five years on, Lisa has lost hope that the remaining questions she has will ever be satisfactorily answered. 'It will always be there. There are days I can now go through Grantham when I don't think about it. There are days I can drive through and get to the other end without picturing it with water. Other days I can be driving through it and just be right back there like it was yesterday.'

Some Grantham survivors still live in the same location but are not severely traumatised, despite their lives having been at risk on the day. Retired farmer Frank King, in his early 70s, often drives past the trees across the road where he clung on for more than two hours in the torrent. 'When I go past the tree I say, "Thank you very much."' He chuckles, not worried at all that he's talking to a tree. 'Well, if it wasn't there I would have been in serious trouble.' His attitude is down to earth. 'Thank God I'm alive. I just have to get on with it,' he says.

Frank King survived the flood because his son John pulled him on top of his car and because Frank was able to grab a tree to prevent himself being swept away. Frank nursed a sore shoulder and could not swing a hammer for several months but eventually his shoulder recovered. He used proceeds of his insurance payout to buy building materials to close in the upstairs verandahs of his house. He also rebuilt his backyard hydroponic strawberry-growing operation, although he redesigned the steel-framed tables to fold up rather than float away, if they are ever hit again by fast-moving water.

The Kings were encouraged to move to the new estate, but when Frank did his sums he realised that as pensioners they could not afford to move. 'I chose to stay here because I had no alternative.' He believes the initial media coverage of the disaster was enough evidence that the council and the state government should have immediately determined that the location was not safe and compensated residents to leave and choose where they wanted to go. 'They missed a golden opportunity.' Frank thinks that even those people on the new estate would have preferred to be able to live somewhere else. 'If they had an option, there would be fewer people on the hill,' he said. 'There was no community consultation.'

Frank, who is related to the Wagner family, has never blamed the quarry for the ferocity of the flood in Grantham. 'I never really blamed the Wagners because when you look at some of that video footage of the Perrys and you see the amount of water that was going past the Helidon bridge, whether the Grantham quarry was there or not was just immaterial. When you look at that amount of water, that was just a horrendous amount of water. You realise there was no hope for Grantham anyway.'

Frank's farm irrigation experience meant he was able to calculate the amount of water that would fill the Grantham floodplain and found it would have filled within a few minutes. 'And it did,' he said. 'It was a bit surprising when I worked it out. It is not safe for anyone to be in this area. We are here at our own risk now.' Despite the inquiry findings, there has been no renewal of effort to relocate people from 'ground zero'. Frank believes nothing short of another similar event and the political pressure that would follow will persuade the federal and state governments to buy out everyone who is still living on the floodplain. 'I was disappointed that they did not take a step back and say, "We need to get everybody out of this area." Blind Freddy could see it was a dangerous place to live in that couple of weeks after the event.'

Frank has noticed a big difference in the attitudes of people who have stayed in the lower section of Grantham compared with those who have moved. 'The community is divided now. There was a small division before but they might as well be living in another town now as far as us down here are concerned. People who have moved have psychologically removed themselves from the scene of the disaster. Some of them have also gained a bit of altitude, not only in a physical sense, but in a social sense – that's the feeling you get,' he said.

Fran and Kenly Arndt, like Frank King, are stoic bush battlers. They did not have counselling after the flood. Fran went to a doctor and was prescribed antidepressants but she did not take them for long. 'I was not depressed. I was upset because I had gone through trauma,' she said. 'The pills didn't agree with me so I threw them down the sink.' Their way of coming to terms with the event is to watch the video footage occasionally. 'I can't even believe it really happened – it was so surreal,' she said.

After the flood, Kenly made a resolution never to chop down another tree. He saw the irony of spending his life as a timber cutter and then being saved by a tree. Fran and Kenly chose to remain in the lower section of Grantham because if they had moved to the new estate they would not have had access to bore water for their vegetable garden or to the volcanic soil of their current location.

The couple rebuilt their house and moved back to the same location. The flooded house was condemned because it had been lifted up on one side by the flood and fell back down, landing out of alignment with the stumps. Joists and bearers were broken, the structure was warped and the walls were cracked. Fran is glad they were not in their house during the flood because she would not have wanted to see it destroyed. 'I preferred that it happened that we were not at home to see it because your house is your castle,' she said.

Young couple Brad and Natasha Long, who survived by clinging to a span of railway fence, cope with the memories of the disaster by not talking about it. They both returned to university, where they had been studying education. After the flood they both changed courses to study human services.

Marnell Fuels owner Marty Warburton became the town's spokesperson for Grantham in the weeks and months after the disaster. His face appeared frequently in the media. Marty took on the role because local residents chose him to represent them. He volunteered to do so because he had lost only his business when so many others had lost their homes. Marty's home, a few kilometres from town, remained intact and he had his own bed and his own pillow on which to lay his head at night. Five years on, Marty wishes now that he had cut his losses and moved away immediately.

Staying to rebuild his business meant he remained vulnerable to a subsequent flood in 2013 that destroyed his service station a second time. Marty rebuilt again only to have his business destroyed a third time, this time by a freak powerful tornado in January 2014. It has taken two years to rebuild a third time. This time he has put up a 'for sale' sign. The destruction and rebuilding of his business were not as personally depressing as the reaction he received from residents of nearby towns who are angry that his advocacy for Grantham 'stole' media limelight from other townships. 'I don't feel welcome in the wider community any more,' he said.

Although Marty decided to remain in Grantham immediately after the flood, he realises now that his hope that the town would return to the way it had been before the flood was not realistic. Although he had felt accepted in the small community and had developed a sense of belonging, he now believes acceptance and belonging will be impossible to regain. His feelings of rejection by the community triggered childhood feelings of rejection stemming from being adopted and from having an Aboriginal heritage. 'I've always wanted to belong. To be part of something,' he said. Now that his sense of belonging is gone, Marty has become a hermit, rarely leaving his home in a peaceful valley south of Grantham.

Marty also struggles with intrusive memories of being trapped in his service station and scrambling to the roof. These distressing feelings of being trapped and at risk of drowning are triggered by running water, rain and being in a room from which he can't see out.

'I could not have imagined it would be like this. I always thought depression and anxiety were things people got because they wanted to get it,' he said. 'It wasn't until this experience I have seen firsthand what depression and anxiety and PTSD is all about.' His condition has left him feeling suicidal at times and that his wife, despite her diagnosis with breast cancer and subsequent mastectomy operation, would be better off without him.

Financial struggles have also been difficult to manage because of the complex rules for welfare support. Marty needed to care for his ill wife but he did not qualify for a Centrelink carer's allowance. Owning a business, even though he only had $3000 in the bank to meet expected bills, precluded him from financial support. At his lowest ebb, it has only been his perception that his son, eight, needs a father, imperfect as he believes he is, that has stopped him from committing suicide. 'An eight-year-old boy needs his dad, whether he is functioning or not. A dad is better than no dad.'

Marty was surprised that an inquiry was eventually called into the Grantham disaster. He knew many people had lobbied for an inquiry but as the years rolled by, he lost hope that there would be one specifically into the circumstances of so many deaths in a small town. 'I thought we had more chance of hell freezing over. I was very surprised how many people pushed in the background to get the inquiry to happen. I'm pleased it happened,' he said.

Marty is determined now to return to study and qualify as a psychologist in trauma and loss. In another five years he hopes to be qualified. 'I would not wish that day or the last five years on anyone. I hope the next five years are better.' Marty would like to see mental health become a recognised issue in connection with disaster recovery. 'Medicare, post-disaster, should fund unlimited mental health support,' he said.

John and Kathy Mahon moved to Toowoomba after the flood and then back to Grantham once the new estate was opened. They lived in a council house while they waited for their insurance claim to be paid out. They wanted their damaged house to be written off but their insurer would only pay for repairs. A team from Legal Aid New South Wales took on their case and successfully argued that the house should be written off by their insurer. The write-off was ordered on two grounds: firstly, the ongoing trauma to the Mahons' children and grandchildren who felt very distressed returning to the location of their brush with death; secondly, even if the old house were repaired, its asset value would have remained depressed for a long time. Once the court's decision was made, other Grantham flood victims insured by Suncorp or their subsidiaries received additional payouts to equal a write-off value.

The higher payout meant John and Kathy Mahon were then able to build a new house on the land ballot block they had been given in the new estate. After two years, they were finally able to move into their new home just before Christmas in 2012. They have very few possessions to remind them of their previous home. Two pieces of furniture were all that remained – the solid timber family dining table and the outdoor pool table. They could not bring themselves to part with the table that had saved them. They had used it to climb onto the roof. 'We can't get rid of it yet,' Kathy said.

QFRS swift water rescuers Brad Mills and Andrew Neil, who rescued Jenny Thorncraft in Helidon, were both sent to Grantham on the evening of the disaster. Brad still recalls his feelings of distress at seeing people on roofs calling for help but being unable to help them. Despite his almost 20 years of experience, the conditions meant he could not help everyone who was in danger. 'We got 14 people out of houses and a couple of them were in hairy situations but then there were other people where we just couldn't do anything,' he said.

In the years since the disaster, he has repeatedly questioned himself about whether he could have done more for anyone. His sense of helplessness was exacerbated by the departure of the rescue helicopters at dusk. 'We had people on roofs across from us. We were telling them that it was going to be okay because we have air support and then all of a sudden all the air support left because it was dark. There was noise from the helicopters – then all of a sudden they just left – and it was quiet, with people yelling and screaming at us. But you couldn't do anything. It was a terrible feeling. There was nothing we could do to help. We just told them to sit tight and wait. The worst part of that is, you think on your roof you are pretty safe but when you see the house next door get ripped off its footings and get washed down the river, you don't feel as comfortable as you were before.'

Brad and Neil spent three days in Grantham and returned after a few weeks to help with police searches of waterways. Seeing the town in daylight helped them to realise that if they had entered the water that night they might not have survived. The realisation helped them accept that their decisions had been sound. 'There were certain areas that were just 100 per cent "no go" – you just were not going in there,' he said. 'There were other areas that we went in and it wasn't too much of a drama. And there were other areas where we were taking people out and the water flow was right on that borderline where you know if it was any stronger, we would have been having to do something different.'

Legacy

Thousands of individuals and families from the top of the Great Dividing Range in Toowoomba to the towns and rural districts of the Lockyer Valley were mildly to severely affected by the 2011 flash flood disaster. The people who lived there and who still live there will forever refer to the flood as a turning point in history. Their lives will be divided into the years that were 'before the flood' and those that were 'after the flood'. Likewise their home, employment, relationships and assets will also be described in terms of 'before' or 'after' the flood.

The flood survivors and rescuers who have generously spoken so candidly about their post-flood experience have given new insights into the wide range of human reactions to the experience of a natural disaster. The complexity of recovery for individuals, families, businesses and the wider community deserves far more attention from non-government and government organisations. The need for dedicated psychological support for individuals and families for as long as required is obvious. People whose lives were interrupted and suddenly threatened are understandably affected by feelings of loss, vulnerability and uncertainty. Those who suddenly feared imminent death for themselves or others may require long-term nurturing care. Those who suddenly were bereaved of one or more family members are likely to require long-term financial assistance, medical care and psychological support for themselves and their families.

The need for strong multidisciplinary support in locations where a population has experienced collective trauma is clear. This disaster highlights the need for appropriate mental health services for people affected by the disaster and that a lack of suitable services appears to delay or prevent optimal recovery. Provision of these services for people who need to leave the location of the disaster, at least in the short term, to reduce their trauma triggers is also necessary.

A greater understanding is needed by the community and the media of the important role of communication in prevention and harm minimisation in the face of the extremes of the natural environment. Clear, accurate and timely warnings are necessary. Careful, factual and forthright reporting in the aftermath is necessary. The accounts here indicate that it is also necessary for authorities to remain engaged with communities and for the media to stay with the story until the short-, medium- and long-term effects of the disaster are all resolved as far as is possible.

The lack of sufficient consultation with affected communities by government and non-government organisations about infrastructure repairs, replacements and upgrades post-disaster has left communities and individuals unsure about the risk of future extreme weather events.

Given the scope of the disaster, it is not surprising that some people have not yet fully recovered. What is remarkable is the degree to which so many people have been able to rebuild their homes, businesses, farms and communities. Most people have also been able to repair their sense of peace, calm and safety. Families have returned to work, school, sport and recreation. Gardens have been replanted. Farm paddocks are being sowed and harvested. Interestingly, some people have experienced post-traumatic growth. They have a new or deeper appreciation for life itself. They keenly sense the preciousness of their spouse, children and grandchildren. They choose to focus more on family relationships and nurturing friendships rather than pursuing material possessions. Many people are more community-minded – contributing to local groups and social activities. It is these social connections being forged between people, families and groups that have the potential to make their communities more resilient in the future.

Appendix I

Flash flood precautions

The risks posed by flash flooding can be reduced substantially by early preparation, gaining local knowledge and making plans early about what to do in case of emergency. Families with young children or babies, elderly, ill or infirm family members should prepare to evacuate early to reduce the risk of being trapped by flash flooding.

Emergency Management Queensland provides information on flood preparedness, but not specific information for flash flood preparedness.

The following flash flood precautions have been prepared using the accounts of survivors in this book.

Useful equipment

- Battery-powered radio in a waterproof plastic bag (e.g. Ziploc bag)
- Internet-linked mobile phone in a waterproof plastic bag
- Waterproof plastic bag for personal items in case of emergency evacuation – food, water, medication, mobile phone, radio, warm clothes, waterproof list of emergency phone numbers

- Waterproof torch with spare batteries
- Ladder to reach the house roof
- Lifejackets for all members of the family
- Coil of rope
- Bottled water
- Unperishable food in a waterproof container.

Local knowledge

- Know the location of the nearest gullies, creeks and rivers, and the minor, moderate and major flood heights at local gauges
- Know the Bureau of Meteorology district in which you are located
- Know how to monitor the Bureau of Meteorology website radar, rainfall and creek gauges
- Know weatherproof roads to reach higher ground
- Know the location of your nearest council evacuation point.

Precautions and preparations to protect life

- Identify high ground and the safest available route
- Work out and agree on 'stay or go' conditions appropriate for your family, e.g. non-swimmers, risk of isolation by road or creek, children/elderly/ill etc.
- Evacuate early as a precaution if you have children, babies, elderly, ill or infirm family members
- Prepare to evacuate to the roof if necessary (e.g. via a ladder)
- Keep mobile phones charged
- Ensure vehicles have fuel
- Ensure family and neighbours are aware of potential risks
- Ensure you can leave the house via a window/s in an emergency to climb to the roof
- If evacuating, turn off power, water and gas
- Let others know where you are or where you intend to go
- Plan what you will do with your pets – they cannot be carried in rescue helicopters

- Avoid entering floodwaters. If you must, wear solid shoes and check depth and current with a stick.

Precautions to protect property

- Ensure local gullies and creeks are clear of debris
- Ensure important documents are stored well above the potential flood zone
- Ensure vehicles are stored well above the potential flood zone – do not attempt to move vehicles through floodwater
- Store all loose items – outdoors and indoors
- Secure and sandbag doors
- Sandbag toilets and drains
- Tape windows
- Check your home and contents insurance policy – does it cover you for flooding and flash flooding? Does it include clean-up and debris removal?
- Check your car insurance policy – are you covered for an agreed value?

During flash flood emergency

- Stay calm
- Move to high ground with waterproof grab-bag for essential items – food, water, medication, mobile phone, radio
- Monitor emergency radio station for updates
- Let others know where you are or where you intend to go
- Do not drive through fast-moving water
- Beware spiders and snakes
- Beware electrical wires.

Helping the authorities to help you

- The Bureau of Meteorology has a network of storm spotters to give on-ground reports of dangerous weather including flash flooding, large hail, damaging winds and tornadoes. Storm spotters are given training and a phone number to report dangerous weather events directly to Bureau forecasters. To become a storm spotter, complete an application form available on the Bureau's website.

- To report dangerous weather, phone the Queensland Bureau of Meteorology forecasters on (07) 3239 8700.

Emergency phone numbers

- Emergency (Life threatening) 000
- State Emergency Service ____________________
- Local police station ____________________
- Queensland Fire and Rescue ____________________
- Local rural fire brigade ____________________
- Local ambulance station ____________________
- Local Bureau of Meteorology ____________________
- Local ABC radio ____________________

Appendix 2

Why report on trauma?

Many readers of the first edition of *The Torrent* have asked me how I managed to cope with hearing and writing so many traumatic stories. Other readers have asked what I learned from being so close to the people who experienced such an extraordinary disaster that affected eight communities in a fairly small geographic area.

For me, the reality of human existence includes the deepest sorrows and the greatest joys of life. One informs and validates the other. I am always inspired by the resilience of people to endure physical, emotional, economic and other challenges in their lives. I am willing to listen and to care about people who are experiencing tragedy or loss, however I recognise that I also need to limit my exposure. I do this by not dwelling on or feeling responsible for social or political problems that are beyond my ability to repair. Whenever I can, I report on positive, inspiring personal or group achievements or social developments. I also do not pursue negative or traumatic stories. In this way I limit my exposure to trauma by dealing with people who come to me and situations that are relevant to my fields of expertise as a reporter.

There is a common myth that traumatised people do not want to speak to the media. I have found to the contrary, that a very high percentage of traumatised people are willing to speak to the media. In my reporting and research to write the first edition of this book, 120 of the 125 people I approached for interviews were willing to speak about their experiences. This surprised me because so many of the flood survivors had lost so much – family, friends, homes, possessions – sometimes all four at once. I was cautious about how to proceed and willing to adapt how I had worked in the past because I could not imagine the burden of grief the people were carrying. After conducting the first few interviews and transcribing them I discovered that my questions had sometimes interrupted the person as they gave their account of the disaster. I also found that the interviewees were not easily able to pick up the thread of their narrative once they were interrupted.

I resolved in subsequent interviews to just listen to the whole narrative from each person before asking any questions. Before each interview I reminded each person that they did not have to answer any questions that they did not want to answer. During these narratives – that lasted in some cases for about one and a half hours – I listened and maintained eye contact, not breaking my attention even to write down emerging questions. When I transcribed these interviews I found the survivors had been able to order their thoughts and to express them in a coherent order. They were also able to moderate their emotions because they could jump over parts of the story that were traumatic to them. Once the narrative was completed, we both had a brief break. When the interview was resumed, I asked the questions I had stored up in my mind. I took the interviewee to various points in their story and asked if they could give any more detail about what happened next or what they had been thinking or feeling at the time. I found the interviewees were then able to give information about these moments that they had previously skipped over. They were able to recall events and articulate their emotional reactions to what had happened in quite extraordinary and compelling detail.

The question of why so many of the flood survivors were willing to speak to a reporter despite their traumatic ordeal became the subject of my Master's Degree research. In 2001, I asked the 33 people who had almost lost their lives in the floods why they had agreed to speak to a reporter. Interestingly, none of the interviewees were influenced by attributes of the reporter. They did not agree to speak because they thought I was friendly, because they knew of my work or simply because I was there. On the contrary, they all had personal reasons for engaging with the media. After most of the interviews, the interviewee hugged me or took both of my hands, thanked me for listening and solemnly told me to tell their story and to keep telling it, until all the necessary changes are made to keep other communities as safe as possible from similar tragedies in future.

When I collated the reasons for speaking to a reporter, they were all different but the reasons could be grouped into five categories. Some people gave more than one reason. The largest number – ten of the people interviewed – said they participated in an interview for their personal recovery. Nine people said they agreed to be interviewed because they wanted the public to know what happened. Six interviewees said they spoke because lessons needed to be learned from the disaster. Four people said their motivation was a sense of duty to make sure warning systems and disaster responses are improved in future. So that even though they were distressed by speaking about their ordeal, they did so to put their experience on the public record. Two people said they spoke because of the financial disinterest of reporters – the journalist just wanted to listen to the story and the survivor did not have to pay a psychologist to be heard. Two of the interviewees agreed to speak because enough time had elapsed and they felt able to speak. The outcomes of the research were distilled into two journal articles: one documenting why disaster survivors speak to reporters and one about how reporters can harness the power of real and virtual networks to improve their reporting of natural disasters.

Almost everyone I approached for a follow-up interview in 2016 agreed to participate. The accounts of the flood survivors illustrate the three cycles of trauma described by psychologist Elana Newman.

Traumatised people experience three opposite pairs of forces during the recovery process. These are approach and avoidance; resilience and vulnerability; and fragmentation and integration. For example, a person may at first need to leave the location of a disaster and to avoid experiences that remind them of it, such as being in water or rain. Over time, however, they feel a desperate need to find out very detailed information about what happened. The person may vacillate between these two extremes frequently or over longer periods of time. Secondly, the same survivor may feel resilient because they survived. Later, however, they may experience a sensation that they had a very near miss and experience feelings of fear and anxiety. Thirdly, the survivor may feel like the traumatic experience was a nightmare from which they will surely wake up and discover it was not real. Over following days, weeks, months and years they will gradually integrate the traumatic experience and the consequences of it as something that they experienced and which is part of their own life. Each of the three cycles move at different frequencies and to different amplitudes, so that a person who may feel desperate to find out information about what happened may at the same time feel vulnerable and as if the traumatic event is not connected to their life and is a fragment of memory that is not real. Interestingly, the 2016 interviewees identified strongly with the three different cycles and the different frequencies of moving from one extreme to another and back again.

For example, they saw themselves moving from avoiding memories, avoiding triggers such as rain or thunder storms and avoiding information or media coverage at some times, to experiencing a desperate need for information, a desperate need for details of times and places, details of what other people were doing during the flood, the state of knowledge of emergency services about their plight and why no-one came to save them.

Many of the flood survivors have experienced or still experience post-traumatic stress disorder. PTSD is defined in the current *Diagnostic and Statistical Manual* (DSM5) as a condition caused by exposure to actual or threatened death or serious injury of a person or witnessing a traumatic event such as the death or serious injury of a close family member or close friend. It is unsurprising that in some communities, the sudden deadly force of the torrent resulted in diagnoses of PTSD. The condition significantly affects a person's social interactions, capacity to work and other important areas of functioning. In addition, several of the interviewees experienced a re-triggering of older traumas in their lives. Feelings of being overwhelmed or helpless during the flood, for example, may have re-awakened feelings of being overwhelmed or powerless to escape danger. For this reason, some of the flood victims found it far more difficult to recover from the flood because they needed to simultaneously address their unresolved traumas from earlier in their lives as well.

Although trauma can have negative outcomes, I have also observed that some people who experience trauma seem to become emotionally stronger or to grow in some aspect of their character as a result. The survivor may be able to recall a distressing event but the memory no longer carries emotions of vulnerability or fear. They find consolation or make an energetic response that precipitates them to help others who have experienced a similar difficulty. The phenomenon of post-traumatic *growth* is only relatively recently being documented in the psychology literature. Post-traumatic growth results in improved relationships, a greater appreciation for life or a greater sense of personal agency despite the trauma. It does not negate the memory or the fact of the trauma but rises above it in a constructive way. Research has shown that post-traumatic growth usually emerges in circumstances where a victim of a trauma has personal support structures such as a home, a job, access to health care and a sense of confidence in the future, so that despite a traumatic event, they are able to recover relatively quickly. In the aftermath of trauma, people who have personal support and public validation and a relatively swift response that is appropriate are best equipped to experience post-traumatic growth.

Notes

~

The eyewitness accounts in this book have been taken from interviews the author conducted with survivors and rescuers from January to October 2011 and May to June 2016.

Most of the interviews were recorded in broadcast quality audio and have been submitted, with the permission of the interviewees, to the State Library of Queensland.

Details of some eyewitness accounts have been sourced from police statements provided to the Queensland Floods Commission of Inquiry, or from media sources.

Introduction to the second edition

The unprecedented nature of the flood in Grantham led to several hydrology studies being carried out Macintosh, John, 'Expert hydrology report 10 January 2011 flood – circumstances and contributing factors', Queensland Government, 11 August 2015, http://www.granthaminquiry.qld.gov.au/publications/hydrology-report.aspx

My radio documentary The day that changed Grantham, *aired on ABC Radio National* Gearing, Amanda, 2011, 'The day that changed Grantham', ABC Radio National, broadcast 9 and 15 October, 2011. It consists of 492 digital files including the recorded interviews, photographs, videos, as well as hand-drawn maps and speech notes. The Amanda Gearing Collection, 2014, State Library of Queensland, http://hdl.handle.net/10462/eadarc/8251;

Pappas, Zenovia , 'New Acquisition: Amanda Gearing Queensland Flood Collection 2011-12', SL Blogs, 20 May 2014, http://blogs.slq.qld.gov.au/jol/2014/05/20/new-acquisition-amanda-gearing-queensland-flood-collection-2011-.

From drought to flood

The pattern continued intensifying, becoming one of the strongest La Niña systems on record 'Variation of sea-surface temperature from average, June and December 2010', The State of Queensland (Department of Environment and Resource Management), 2011. www.longpaddock.qld.gov.au/seasonalclimateoutlook/seasurfacetemperature/index. (Viewed 24 July 2011.)

Record high monthly sea surface temperatures were set during 2010 Australian Government Bureau of Meteorology, 'Annual Australian Climate Statement 2010', 5 January 2011.

many locations received more than four times the normal monthly rainfall Australian Government Bureau of Meteorology, 'Report to Queensland Floods Commission of Inquiry: provided in response to a request for information from the Queensland Floods Commission received by the Bureau of Meteorology on 4 March 2011', March 2011, p. 12.

For two days during Exercise Orko, evacuation plans were rehearsed 'Exercise Orko', Exhibit 168, Floods Commission of Inquiry, 28 April 2011.

Queensland Premier Anna Bligh launched a public appeal to help victims of the floods AAP, 'Premier Anna Bligh launches Queensland Flood Appeal', *The Courier-Mail*, 29 December 2010.

At the briefings he predicted several hundred millimetres of rain James Thomas Davidson, statement of witness, Queensland Floods Commission of Inquiry, 4 April 2011, p. 10–11.

A severe weather warning was issued at 11 am Australian Government Bureau of Meteorology, 'Report to Queensland Floods Commission of Inquiry, March 2011, p. 41.

It continued moving south-west at 30 kilometres per hour Phillip Jordan, 'Hydrological advice to Commission of Inquiry regarding 2010/11 Queensland Floods: Toowoomba and Lockyer Valley flash flood events of 10 and 11 January 2011', 12 April 2011, p. 17.

With the city of Ipswich and the state capital under threat, their priority was flood forecasting Australian Government Bureau of Meteorology, 'Report to Queensland Floods Commission of Inquiry', March 2011, p. 44.

'. . . do you think BOM [the Bureau of Meteorology] is on the case . . .' Neil Pennell, *Weatherzone* forum, http://forum.weatherzone.com.au/ubbthreads.php/topics/925065/Re_SE_QLD_NE_NSW_FLOOD_DISASTE#Post925065. (Viewed 29 July 2011.)

'It has absolutely bucketed down in the last 30 minutes in Toowoomba' 'Adam Ant', *Weatherzone* forum, http://forum.weatherzone.com.au/ubbthreads.php/topics/928166/1/SE_QLD_Flood_Crisis_January_20. (Viewed 29 July 2011.)

Spring Bluff

More than 1,500 workers blasted tunnels Don Talbot, *Spring Bluff: a history of steam and flowers*, D Talbot, Toowoomba, 1998, p. 12.

Craig Ritchie keeps rainfall records in his diary There is no automatic rain gauge at Spring Bluff that transmits rainfall information to the Bureau of Meteorology.

A Queensland Rail stream gauge at Spring Bluff ICA Hydrology Panel, 'Flooding in the Brisbane River Catchment: January 2011, Vol. 4. Flooding in the Lockyer Valley Regional Council LGA', Insurance Council of Australia, 20 February 2011, p. 45. http://insurance.elders.com.au/assets/downloads/Ipswich_Volume_3_Part_1.pdf

A rain gauge at Holmes siding recorded 93 millimetres ibid, p. ii.

Sarah heard her mother Sandy in the background shouting Sarah Norman's account of the flood is sourced from her police statement: Sarah Norman, Queensland Police Service, statement of witness, 13 January 2011. Presented to the Queensland Floods Commission of Inquiry, April 2011.

Murphys Creek

In nearby Watts Road, Selwyn and Catherine Schefe lived with their daughter Katie, six David Murray, 'Loved ones gone in a brutal flash', *The Sunday Mail*, 16 January 2011. http://www.couriermail.com.au/ipad/loved-ones-gone-in-a-brutal-flash/story-fn6ck51p-1225988489802. (Viewed 27 June 2011.)

Toowoomba

A Toowoomba Regional Council rain gauge at Mount Lofty registered daily rainfall of 138 millimetres ICA Hydrology Panel, 'Flooding in the Brisbane River Catchment: January 2011, Vol. 4. Flooding in the Lockyer Valley Regional Council LGA', Insurance Council of Australia, 20 February 2011, p. 37.

She waited for 28 rings The conversations recorded in the triple zero calls from Donna and Jordan Rice are sourced from the Queensland Floods Commission of Inquiry, 20 April 2011.

At the same time, Toowoomba businessman Chris Skehan was driving Chris Skehan's account is sourced from his witness statement, made to the Queensland Police Service on 25 January 2011.

Three fire trucks were dispatched to the scene Rosanne Barrett, 'Jordan Rice's emergency operator "exemplary"', *Australian*, 12 May 2011.

Withcott

Gatton Creek is barely visible in the town and has no creek gauge James Thomas Davidson, statement of witness, Queensland Floods Commission of Inquiry, 4 April 2011, p. 4.

at about 1 pm, the rain became intense Withcott recorded 180 millimetres in the 24 hours to 9 am on 11 January. Australian Government Bureau of Meteorology, 'Report to Queensland Floods Commission of Inquiry', March 2011, p. 47.

Helidon

Neil asked on the online forum who should be told to get the message out Neil Pennell, letter to the Queensland Floods Commission of Inquiry, 2 March 2011.

Weather forum member Dave was also anxious 'Dave –Wx', WeatherZone forum, http://forum.weatherzone.com.au/ubbthreads.php/topics/928166/1/SE_QLD_Flood_Crisis_January_20. (Viewed 29 July 2011.)

Lockyer Creek gauge shot past the major flood level of eight metres James Thomas Davidson, statement of witness, Queensland Floods Commission of Inquiry, 4 April 2011, p. 4.

The flow gauge measured 3,000 cubic metres of water per second ICA Hydrology Panel, 'Flooding in the Brisbane River Catchment: January 2011, Vol. 4. Flooding in the Lockyer Valley Regional Council LGA', Insurance Council of Australia, 20 February 2011, p. 53.

'It's not hard to imagine what the response would've been' Neil Pennell, letter to the Queensland Floods Commission of Inquiry, 2 March 2011.

Grantham

there was no creek gauge there to warn of flooding in Grantham James Thomas Davidson, statement of witness, Queensland Floods Commission of Inquiry, 4 April 2011, p. 4.

Danny and group officer Stuart Damrow . . . asked police for a compulsory evacuation of the town Amos Aikman, 'Lives lost in flood response "shambles" say emergency crews', *Australian*, 29 January 2011, p. 12.

'[It's] concerning for the Gatton-Grantham area right now with that very large storm/rain area moving towards it Anthony Cornelius, *Weatherzone* forum, 10 January 2011.

With the roads open again, electrician Matthew Keep left his home in Railway Street The accounts of the flood by Matthew and Stacy Keep and their children Madison and Jacob are partially sourced from Michael Usher, 'Torn Apart', *60 Minutes*, Channel 9, 11 February 2011.

Graph of Lockyer Creek Gauge at Helidon for 7–12 January 2011 Australian Government Bureau of Meteorology, 11 January 2011.

Once there, he went out again to check on his mother's house beside Sandy Creek. The water was over the bridge Stacy Keep, 2011 Statement to QPS, 15 January 2011, http://www.granthaminquiry.qld.gov.au/public-hearings/listing.aspx?prefix=Exhibits/Exhibits%20201-250/216%20Keep%20Stacey%20statement%202011/

At about 3.30 pm retired timber cutters Kenly and Fran Arndt were at their house in Gatton Helidon Road when they received a panicked phone call Frances Arndt, Evidence to the Grantham Floods Commission of Inquiry, 2015, Gatton, Queensland.

Kym was across the creek on higher land near the piggery and could see fast-moving water coming from the west Frances Arndt, Evidence to the Grantham Floods Commission of Inquiry, 2015, Gatton, Queensland.

The record 1974 flood only came to the floorboards of the hotel Lance Richardson, statement of witness, 30 January 2011, Queensland Floods Commission of Inquiry, April 2011.

The aftermath

The only higher recorded flood was the great flood of 1893 Australian Government Bureau of Meteorology, 'Report to Queensland Floods Commission of Inquiry', March 2011, p. 43.

The Bureau of Meteorology predicted the biggest floods since 1974 would reach Brisbane in two days Jim Davidson, ABC radio, 11 January 2011.

Jordan Rice, who had died in Toowoomba, was honoured as a hero Amanda Gearing and Natasha Bita, 'Take my brother first: heroic final act saves sibling', *Australian*, 13 January 2011, p. 1.

Frightening stories emerged of people being saved by mere seconds Amanda Gearing and Hedley Thomas, 'The seconds that separated life and death', *Australian*, 12 January 2011, p. 1.

This time, the body of a victim was found Natasha Bita, 'Mud and debris slowly give up the dead', *Australian*, 17 January 2011, p, 1.

Stories of sacrifice and heroism emerged Amanda Gearing, 'Women who cheated death thank their saviours', *Australian*, 17 January 2011, p. 4.

In the Coral Sea, Cyclone Yasi was forming and heading for the north Queensland coast Satellite and Radar Timelapse: Tropical Cyclone Yasi http://www.theweatherchaser.com/videos/201101-tropical-cyclone-yasi (Viewed 10 October 2011.)

'*It was a second chance and I'm so thankful,*' Jared Owens, 'Farewell after tragedies of flood and fire', *Australian*, 11 August 2011, p. 6.

Rebuilding

The WMO has developed an international flash flood warning system World Meteorological Organisation, 'Global approach to address flash floods', in MeteoWorld, 2007, p 1. http://www.hrc-lab.org/publicbenefit/downloads/wmo-flashflood.pdf. (Viewed 13 March 2011.)

Controversy

From Dr Maroulis's observation of the remains of the quarry wall, he was able to say that the structures were not part of the natural landscape but were layered deposits of soil Interviews with Dr Jerry Maroulis, 2011 and 2014.

the need for a separate inquiry into the unprecedented severity and deadly nature of the flood in Grantham became obvious Queensland Floods Commission of Inquiry, *Final Report*, Queensland Government, 16 March 2012, http://www.floodcommission.qld.gov.au/publications/final-report/

and the coronial inquest findings were released in June 2012 Barnes, Michael, *Inquest into the deaths caused by the south-east Queensland floods of January 2011*, Office of the State Coroner, 5 June 2012, http://www.courts.qld.gov.au/__data/assets/pdf_file/0019/152362/cif-seq-floods-20120605.pdf

More than half of the people who died in Toowoomba and the Lockyer Valley had perished in one town where none of the many triple zero calls from those in peril could be responded to, except by helicopter Sofronoff, Walter, *Grantham Floods Commission of Inquiry Final Report*, Queensland Government, 7 October 2015, http://www.granthaminquiry.qld.gov.au/assets/grantham-floods-report-october-2015.pdf

Media coverage of the findings focused on the exoneration of the quarry from being implicated in the ferocity of the flood and in the deaths in Grantham Wilson, Courtney, 'Grantham floods inquiry: Quarry played 'insignificant' role in disaster, commission rules', ABC News Online, 8 October 2015, http://www.abc.net.au/news/2015-10-08/grantham-floods-final-report-commission-inquiry-handover/6835088

Five years on

The coronial inquest confirmed that the bodies of Steven Matthews, 56, and his wife Sandra, 46, had been located 2.1 kilometres and 2.3 kilometres downstream from their house Barnes, Michael, *Inquest into the deaths caused by the south-east Queensland floods of January 2011*, Office of the State Coroner, 5 June 2012, http://www.courts.qld.gov.au/__data/assets/pdf_file/0019/152362/cif-seq-floods-20120605.pdf

Stormwater drainage systems were upgraded to cope with a one-in-100-year storm event by widening the creek channels and increasing the capacity of underground drains CMC Group, 'West Creek Channel and Goggs St Project', http://cmc.net.au/project/west-creek-channel-and-goggs-street/; Davies, Adam, 'Toowoomba's drains to get $4.59m flood-proof overhaul', *The Chronicle*, 27 August 2013, http://www.thechronicle.com.au/news/toowoomba-state-government-flood-proofing-money/1997667/

A flood warning system for Toowoomba including automatic and manual river gauges was installed to enable authorities to monitor fast rises in East and West Creeks and to close roads and warn residents and businesses of flood threats via email and SMS messages Toowoomba Region, 'Flood Early Warning System – Toowoomba and Oakey', Queensland Government, http://www.tr.qld.gov.au/community-business/community-safety/be-prepared-for-emergencies/9656-fews

Downstream of the city, a warning system was installed to notify Oakey residents of flooding in Gowrie Creek Toowoomba Region, 'Flood Early Warning System – Toowoomba and Oakey', Queensland Government, http://www.tr.qld.gov.au/community-business/community-safety/be-prepared-for-emergencies/9656-fews

John set up the Jordan Rice Foundation to honour his son's name Jordan Rice Foundation, http://www.jordanricefoundation.com/

In April 2011, the Toowoomba RSL presented Jordan posthumously with the Spirit of

ANZAC Award in recognition of his self-sacrifice Jordan Rice Foundation, 'About Jordan', http://www.jordanricefoundation.com/About-Jordan.html

Appendix 1: Flash flood precautions

Emergency Management Queensland provides information on flood preparedness Emergency Management Queensland. http://www.emergency.qld.gov.au/emq/css/flood.asp. (Viewed 13 August 2011.)

Know how to monitor the Bureau of Meteorology website radar Australian Weather Watch Radar Network, Bureau of Meteorology. http://www.bom.gov.au/weather/radar/

rainfall and creek gauges Queensland flood warning river height stations: flood classifications. http://www.bom.gov.au/hydro/flood/qld/networks/section4.shtml. (Viewed 14 August 2011.)

To become a storm spotter, complete an application form available on the Bureau's website Storm Spotter Network application form can be accessed at: http://www.bom.gov.au/storm_spotters/National_Storm_Spotter_Application_Form.pdf.

Appendix 2: Why report on trauma?

When I collated the reasons for speaking to a reporter, they were all different but the reasons could be grouped into five categories Gearing, Amanda, 'Lessons from media reporting of natural disasters: A case study of the 2011 flash floods in Toowoomba and the Lockyer Valley' MA Research, School of Journalism, Queensland University of Technology, 2012.

The outcomes of the research were distilled into two journal articles: one documenting why disaster survivors speak to reporters Gearing, Amanda, 'Why disaster survivors speak to reporters', *Australian Journalism Review*, 35 (12), 2013, pp. 71–81.

and one about how reporters can harness the power of real and virtual networks to improve their reporting of natural disasters Gearing, Amanda, 'Harnessing the power of real and virtual networks during disasters', *National Emergency Response*, Journal of the Australian Institute of Emergency Services, Vol 26 Winter, pp. 8–11.

Interestingly, the 2016 interviewees identified strongly with the three different cycles and the different frequencies of moving from one extreme to another and back again Newman, Elana and Summer Nelson, 'Reporting on resilience and recovery in the face of disaster and crime: research and training implications', *Australian Journalism Review*, 34 (1), 2012, pp. 17–32.

PTSD is defined in the current Diagnostic and Statistical Manual *(DSM5) as a condition caused by exposure to actual or threatened death or serious injury of a person or witnessing a traumatic event such as the death or serious injury of a close family member or close friend* American Psychiatric Association, *Diagnostic and statistical manual of mental disorders*, (5th ed.), 2013, Washington, DC: Author, Fact sheet: http://www.dsm5.org/Documents/PTSD%20Fact%20Sheet.pdf

Post-traumatic growth results in improved relationships, a greater appreciation for life or a greater sense of personal agency despite the trauma Tedeschi, Richard G. and Calhoun, Lawrence, 'Post-traumatic growth: A new perspective on psychotraumatology', *Psychiatric Times*, 21 (4), 2004.

Acknowledgements

My grateful thanks go first to the many survivors, rescuers, emergency service personnel and others who were willing to speak to me about their sometimes terrifying experiences during the flood. Without them this book would not have been possible and the lessons taught could not have been recorded.

Thank you to:
Roy and Judy Abraham, Rod Alford, Gavin Anderson, Helen Besley, Norrie Blume, Ben and Anthea Burton, Lynette Campbell, Nathan Chadwick, Dave Crighton, Len Cullen, Ray and Val Cullen, Stuart Damrow, Steve Eastaugh, Matthew Eddison, Erin Edwards, Angela Emmerson, Rick Emmerson, Tim Fittkau, Scott Frame, Elizabeth Fraser, Garth French, Tom and Sandra Friend, Nelly Gitsham, Katherine Godley, Michael Hare, Norm Head, Ian Hegarty, Nathan Hickmott, Ian and Monica Hoddinott, Nicole Hore, Thelma Hughes, Rezwanul Huq, Jason Iacono, Wayne Iacono, Julie Johnson, Simon Johnstone, Dr Phillip Jordan, Matthew Keep, Mark Kempton, Gilbert Kilah, Frank King, John King, Johnathon Klaassen, Kevin Lees, Brad and Natasha Long, Rick Luchich, John and

Kathy Mahon, Shirley Marshall, Matt Kendall, Shauna Mayes, Peter McCarron, Russell McDuff, Warren McErlean, Danny McGuire, Inspector Stephen McInerney, Tony McIntosh, Terri-Ann McLachlan, Brad Mills, Susan Mouflih, Michael Munchow, Andrew Neil, Jeff Neumann, Susan Patterson, Neil Pennell, Paul Pepi, Geoff Purton, Angelika Pohl, Sharyn Powlesland, Shayne Richardson, Craig Ritchie, Rachelle Rogers, John Ryan, Hugh Sedger, Ruth Sedger, Neil Simpson, Chris Skehan, Jonathan and Annaka Sippel, Gary Smith, Treg Smith, Peter Souter, Eddie Spark, Hahns Spierling, Ilsa Spierling, Klaus Spierling, Lisa Spierling, Ean Stewart, Gayle Teal, Kendall Thompson, Mark Turner, Sue Turner, Greg Twidale, John Tyson, Peter and Marie Van Straten, Marty Warburton, Lloyd and Jean Warr, Peter Werder, Robert Wilkin, Brian Willmett, Kelly Wilson, Michael Woodham, Gavin and Kelly Zischke.

Thank you also to my supervisor, Dr Angela Romano of the Queensland University of Technology, for her constant support and wise counsel through my Master of Arts (Research) program. I am grateful for the generous financial support of the Adrian Scott Rural Journalism Scholarship awarded by the Creative Industries Faculty at QUT. It was humbling to be awarded this scholarship, which honours retired veteran ABC rural reporter Adrian Scott.

Finding a publisher is notoriously difficult for first-time authors. I am deeply grateful to University of Queensland Press publisher John Hunter who immediately warmed to my proposed book, asked for a chapter and said 'yes'. He then gave me a tight deadline to deliver a manuscript so that the book could be published in time for the first anniversary of the disaster. John's trust that I could deliver the manuscript was greater than my own. However, very generous cooperation from everyone, including my wonderful editor Lorelei Vashti and illustrator Gillian Scott, made it possible.

To my friends and colleagues who gave me useful comments and suggestions as the book took shape, thank you for your interest and encouragement.

The writing of this revised edition in 2016 and the additional chapters was made possible by the generosity of flood survivors and rescuers who were willing to speak about how they have recovered or are enduring ongoing trauma since the flood. This material breaks new ground in helping our society to understand the complexity of individual, family and community recovery. It also raises awareness of the medical and support services that are required for communities that experience severe disasters.

Those interviewed in 2016 were: Rod Alford, Fran Arndt, Helen Besley, Matthew Eddison, Angela Emmerson, Bess Fraser, Sandra Friend, Norm Head, Ian Hoddinott, Frank King, Kris Larkin, Brad Long, Kathy Mahon, Brad Mills, Sue Patterson, Neil Pennell, Angie Pohl, Sharon Powlesland, Neil Simpson, Peter Souter, Lisa Spierling, Marie Van Straten, Gayle Teal, Kendall Thompson, Mark Turner, Greg Twidale, Marty Warburton and Kelly Zischke. Additional material is sourced from evidence and statements to the QFCI, the inquest and the Grantham Floods Commission of Inquiry.

The scientific questions raised by this flood event have challenged meteorologists, hydrologists and other experts. The event may not be truly understood for a long time, until the frequency of severe events becomes clearer. I am grateful to various academics and specialists for contributing their expertise.

It has been a pleasure to work with UQP publisher Alexandra Payne, who commissioned the revised edition, and editor Cathy Vallance. I am grateful for the generous assistance of Sydney UTS journalism student Kayleen Bell for transcribing many of the 2016 interviews.

And finally to my husband Phillip, who has given me invaluable practical support, please accept my heartfelt thanks.